OS X®
Mountain Lion Server

FOR

DUMMIES®

OS X® Mountain Lion Server
FOR DUMMIES®

by John Rizzo

WILEY

John Wiley & Sons, Inc.

OS X® Mountain Lion Server For Dummies®

Published by
John Wiley & Sons, Inc.
111 River Street
Hoboken, NJ 07030-5774

www.wiley.com

Copyright © 2012 by John Wiley & Sons, Inc., Hoboken, New Jersey

Published by John Wiley & Sons, Inc., Hoboken, New Jersey

Published simultaneously in Canada

For general information on our other products and services, please contact our Customer Care Department within the U.S. at 877-762-2974, outside the U.S. at 317-572-3993, or fax 317-572-4002.

For technical support, please visit www.wiley.com/techsupport.

Wiley publishes in a variety of print and electronic formats and by print-on-demand. Some material included with standard print versions of this book may not be included in e-books or in print-on-demand. If this book refers to media such as a CD or DVD that is not included in the version you purchased, you may download this material at http://booksupport.wiley.com. For more information about Wiley products, visit www.wiley.com.

Library of Congress Control Number: 2012947904

ISBN 978-1-118-40829-2 (pbk); ISBN 978-1-118-41781-2 (ebk); ISBN 978-1-118-43165-8 (ebk); ISBN 978-1-118-42202-1 (ebk)

Manufactured in the United States of America

10 9 8 7 6 5 4 3 2 1

WILEY

About the Author

John Rizzo has been writing about computers for 25 years. His work has appeared in *Macworld, Infoworld, CNET, PC Magazine, eWeek,* the *San Francisco Chronicle,* and other publications.

John is the author of over a dozen books, including *Lion Server For Dummies, Snow Leopard Server For Dummies, Mac Mini Hacks & Mods For Dummies* (all by John Wiley & Sons), *Moving to Windows Vista* (PeachPit), and *Mac Annoyances* (O'Reilly). He's also written several books on Mac-and-Windows cross-platform networking and other topics on Mac and Windows hardware and software.

John publishes the website MacWindows.com, which, since 1997, has been the web's largest news and information resource devoted to helping Mac users get along in a Windows world.

John is also a member of the Board of Trustees at the San Francisco Community College District, where he promotes the use of technology to improve student learning.

Author's Acknowledgments

The ink was barely dry on my copy of *Lion Server For Dummies* when Apple announced Mountain Lion. In *Lion Server For Dummies,* I said that I would never write another book. People took me seriously. A reviewer at Amazon said that my pledge was the best part of *Lion Server.* I suspect that this is not the case, but I'm not completely unbiased on this subject.

In the past, the time between Apple revisions of its operating system was just long enough to make me forget how much work it is to write one of these books. But *Lion Server For Dummies* wasn't even six months old when Apple announced Mountain Lion. Naturally, I was hesitant to take on the new project. I pointed out the Amazon review to my publisher. The publisher then offered to pay me, so I put aside the humiliation of deceiving my readers and relented.

So I'd like to thank Kyle Looper, who kept my phone number despite all the trouble I caused him during the last book, and Susan Pink, a great editor who knows her stuff. Kyle made some great suggestions for this book, which I used in almost every chapter. Susan read every word of this book and suggested some better ones in a different order that usually made more sense. To her credit, she repeatedly asked me what the meaning of "it" is, which I learned is not the same as Bill Clinton asking in 1998 what the meaning of "is" is.

Now, I'm through with pledges. With *Mountain Lion Server For Dummies* under my belt, I've written a proposal for my 15th book, *Writing a Dummies Book For Dummies*. The publisher hasn't yet responded, but I'm hopeful.

Publisher's Acknowledgments

We're proud of this book; please send us your comments at http://dummies.custhelp.com. For other comments, please contact our Customer Care Department within the U.S. at 877-762-2974, outside the U.S. at 317-572-3993, or fax 317-572-4002.

Some of the people who helped bring this book to market include the following:

Acquisitions and Editorial

Project Editor: Susan Pink

Senior Acquisitions Editor: Kyle Looper

Copy Editor: Susan Pink

Technical Editor: Dennis Cohen

Editorial Manager: Jodi Jensen

Editorial Assistant: Leslie Saxman

Sr. Editorial Assistant: Cherie Case

Cover Photo: background: © iStockphoto.com/ teekid; screen insets: © iStockphoto.com/ Matt Kaminski

Cartoons: Rich Tennant (www.the5thwave.com)

Composition Services

Project Coordinator: Katherine Crocker

Layout and Graphics: Joyce Haughey, Christin Swinford

Proofreaders: Melissa Cossell, Jessica Kramer, Lauren Mandelbaum, Bonnie Mikkelson

Indexer: Estalita Slivoskey

Publishing and Editorial for Technology Dummies

Richard Swadley, Vice President and Executive Group Publisher

Andy Cummings, Vice President and Publisher

Mary Bednarek, Executive Acquisitions Director

Mary C. Corder, Editorial Director

Publishing for Consumer Dummies

Kathleen Nebenhaus, Vice President and Executive Publisher

Composition Services

Debbie Stailey, Director of Composition Services

Contents at a Glance

Table of Contents

Introduction

· ·

*Y*ou're about to become a magician. Soon you'll be providing your users with the illusion that they have direct access to the world of communication and information. The reality is that servers — ubiquitous, imperceptible, and indefatigable — provide every connection, communication, and bit of information that the computer user sees.

But only if you make it so. You're going to set up Apple's Mountain Lion Server for your users, configure the wonderful services it offers, and keep it running. This book will help you do it.

About This Book

OS X Mountain Lion Server For Dummies takes you through the steps required to get your users doing amazing and productive things. I provide step-by-step procedures to accomplish specific tasks, such as configuring an e-mail server and setting up user accounts. In some instances, I also describe how to set up your users' Macs or Windows PCs to work with the server.

This book introduces you to the tools that Apple provides with the server and the best ways to use them. I take you through many of the options and network configurations available in Mountain Lion Server and describe the best practices you should adopt.

I also describe the new features in Mountain Lion Server that you'll want to know about (trust me on this). And I've peppered the chapters with plenty of tips and tricks that will help you become proficient.

I'm a fan of the English language, so I favor it over the technobabble found in much of computing. Where the acronyms are unavoidable, I provide explanations. You will not, however, find the word *empower* in this book. A writer can be pushed only so far.

Conventions Used in This Book

Flip through this book, and you'll find different uses of type to point out different things. Here's what I do:

- ✔ In the step-by-step directions, the actions you perform are in bold type, **like this.** The description of what happens after the action is in normal type.

- ✔ To point out a web address, the book uses a monofont that looks like this: `www.apple.com`. You see the same font in the rare instances when I show you something that you need to type in a command line (in the Mac's Terminal application), such as `fsck -fy`, and for text that a command line returns to you in response. The book uses monofont to indicate folders. For example, to indicate the Utilities folder, which is inside the Applications folder, the path is used, `/Applications/Utilities`.

- ✔ In rare cases when you need to use a menu at the top of the screen, this book uses a convention that looks like this: File⇨Get Info, which means you need to choose Get Info from the File menu. I don't use this convention for menus that aren't at the top of the screen, such as pop-up menus.

What You're Not to Read

If you're going to read this book, you don't need to read the entire thing or to read it in any particular order. The book is organized in a logical manner from beginning to end, but it's not a narrative. Rather, it's *modular.* You need to read only the portion that applies to a specific project or technique.

If you already have Mountain Lion Server installed, you can skip Part I. And you don't have to read Part VI to accomplish any server project. Consider it the chocolate center of a Good Humor bar.

A lot of the chapters are arranged from general to specific. For example, Chapter 7 gets you up and running with file sharing. If you want to get into the nitty-gritty of advanced tweaking of user permissions, read Chapter 8. If you're a Windows administrator with experience with Active Directory, you can skip Chapter 5 on network directories and go right to Chapter 6, which deals specifically with Macs and Microsoft networks.

I think you'll enjoy the text next to the Technical Stuff icons, but you can skip them if you want I won't be insulted (well, not much).

Foolish Assumptions

Unlike some other computer books, you won't find a lot of filler here — no dissertations that have no bearing on the task at hand. I assume that you bought this book to accomplish specific tasks, using Mountain Lion Server.

You also won't find lectures on what's in the Print dialog box or how to search for a file because I assume that you're already a computer user. But I don't assume that you're an Apple-Certified System Administrator. I explain the alphabet soup of acronyms that you find in some of the Server's technospeak.

Don't worry if you're new to the Mac. I explain any Apple-specific knowledge that you need. Experienced Mac users can skip bits of Mac-specific material. Similarly, you don't need any experience with Windows if you want to support Windows clients with your Mac server. I show you what you need to know.

I don't make any assumptions about what hardware you're running. I provide some guidance as to what Mac is right for you in Chapter 2.

How This Book Is Organized

OS X Mountain Lion Server For Dummies is organized in six parts, each with several related chapters. The parts are arranged in the order in which you might go about using the server. But you don't have to read the book sequentially, as each part can stand alone as a sort of minibook on a topic. You don't even have to read all the sections in any particular chapter. You can use the table of contents and the index to find the information you need and quickly get your answer.

I do recommend taking a glance, at least, at Part I. You find some information about installing Mountain Lion Server that you won't find in Apple's documentation.

Part 1: Getting Mountain Lion Server Up and Running

I start Part I with a description of Mountain Lion Server — what it comes with, what you can do with it, and what you need to get it running. If you need advice on which Mac model to use as your server and what should be in it, look in this part. I also describe some hardware needs in the server and on the network. If you haven't already installed Mountain Lion Server, read the step-by-step directions in Part I.

Part II: Creating and Maintaining User Accounts and Directories

For networks with more than a handful of users, setting up user directories can help automate security and simplify maintenance. Part II describes what you can do with a directory, including setting up user authentication and connecting your server to a bigger network.

Part II also covers the options you have for directory services, including Open Directory, which comes with Mountain Lion Server. I devote Chapter 6 to the issue of using Mountain Lion Server to connect your Macs to Microsoft Active Directory, which is common on Windows networks.

Part III: Serving Up Files and Printers

Part III covers the meat and potatoes of servers: sharing files and printers with multiple users. File and print sharing were the first tasks for servers when personal computers came on the scene in the 1980s. Sharing is still the most common task, though other services are often wrapped around it. This part also describes limiting access to certain folders by using permissions.

Part IV: Facilitating User Collaboration

Part IV is one of the longer parts of this book. Mountain Lion Server offers an array of services that help users work with each other. Part IV covers e-mail, calendar sharing, meeting scheduling, and the sharing of contacts, as well as web-based services, from your basic website to wikis and blogs.

I describe how to set up these services and point out some of the more interesting and perhaps less obvious things you can do with them.

Part V: Managing Clients

Client computers — the Macs and PCs on the network — can be a chore to maintain all by yourself. Fortunately, you can use your server to automate some of this work for you. You can even manage the notebook computers that float in and out of the building. Part V describes how to use the tools for configuring and managing clients.

Viruses, data spies, identity thieves, and other threats are all commonplace in the electronic world that computers live in. Chapter 18 describes how to keep out the nasties and how to enable users to access the server remotely without letting in the malware. I also describe how to get Mountain Lion to alert you to problems that may indicate an ailing server.

Part VI: The Part of Tens

In Part VI, I show you ten nifty things you can add to Mountain Lion Server that can make it even more useful, or at least more interesting. I also deliver ten quick tips for doing even more with Mountain Lion Server.

Icons Used in This Book

To make this book easier to use, five icons appear to the left of the text. These icons are here to help you find information as you flip through the pages. Think of them as signposts, each pointing to a different way to think about what's being said.

Tips are the best bits of the description that make the job easiest or better. They aren't always the only way to get something done, but they do point out the best way to accomplish a task. Sometimes you can reuse a tip for other tasks.

When you see the Remember icon, I'm flagging something that you don't want to forget to do, unless you want to mess up what you're doing.

The Warning icon highlights lurking danger. With this icon, I'm telling you to pay attention to what you're doing or to what you shouldn't do.

This icon marks a general interesting fact that's a technical explanation of what's going on or why you need to do something. I didn't want to turn this book into an engineering textbook, so I kept the tech stuff short.

Readers who have extensive backgrounds with Windows but who may be new to Macs can be on the lookout for this icon, which points out terminology or features that PC users may find unfamiliar.

Where to Go from Here

Where you start is up to you — begin with Chapter 1, dive right into file servers in Chapter 7, or check out the tips in Chapter 19. The section "How This Book Is Organized," earlier in this Introduction, can guide you. Use this book as a reference (a *For Dummies* technical encyclopedia) or read it from start to finish for the complete picture. I wrote this book so that you can find all sorts of useful information however you choose to approach it.

Occasionally, we have updates to our technology books. If this book does have technical updates, they will be posted at

dummies.com/go/osxmountainlionserverfdupdates

Part I
Getting Mountain Lion Server Up and Running

The 5th Wave   By Rich Tennant

"We should have this fixed in Mountain Lion Server."

In this part . . .

Mountain Lion Server is an amazingly versatile and scalable solution, serving a small workgroup or acting as part of an integrated network of thousands of users. Unsurprisingly, the process of getting it up and running can involve vastly different software and hardware configurations.

The chapters in this part describe the many different services available to your users and the hardware the server runs on, from the little Mac mini to the beefy Mac Pro, and how to choose the best Mac model for your use of the server.

Mountain Lion Server offers several possibilities of installation, depending on your use. This part shows you how to get ready for your installation and how to install it in different scenarios.

In addition, Chapter 3 shows you how to get Mountain Lion Server up and running quickly in a common simple setup, from installation through setting up the basic services. Chapter 4 goes into more detail with different installation options.

Chapter 1

Mountain Lion Server: An Overview

In This Chapter

▶ Answering the burning question: Why do I need a server?

▶ Discovering what you can do with Mountain Lion Server

▶ Setting up and managing with the Server application

*F*or $20, you could buy a pair of movie tickets, or a good pizza, or a week's worth of dry cleaning.

$20 could also buy you an array of services: file sharing, calendaring, contact management, web, e-mail, instant messaging, device management, and more. The $20 Mountain Lion Server is versatile enough to support Macs, Windows PCs, and iPad, iPhone, and iPod touch devices. It will work at home as well as in a network of hundreds of devices.

Mountain Lion Server is reliable, built on the solid foundation of Unix. At the same time, it has the ease of use of a Macintosh. Anyone can set it up, get it running, and manage it. Seriously technical professionals will find tools for the kind of configuration customization that they're accustomed to.

So should you spend the $20? This chapter gives you reasons why you should. And if you already gave up a pizza for Mountain Lion Server, this chapter will help you decide what to use it for.

You now manage Mountain Lion Server almost entirely with a single tool, the Server application, as described later in the chapter. First, however, take a tour of Mountain Lion Server.

Why You Need Mountain Lion Server

You've probably discovered that you can have a small network without a server. Macs and PCs can talk to each other. Computers can share files and printers, and you may be able to use a router to share an Internet connection.

But a server enables users to collaborate in ways that aren't possible without it. A server gives you control; it centralizes data, making it easier to manage. A server provides fast access to information and collaborative tools and provides network security. It enables you to manage the computers and iPhones and iPads that are connected to it. And a server is always there when users need it.

Why you need Mountain Lion Server at home

Home use is *not* Mountain Lion Server's primary purpose, but there is certainly enough in it that justifies dedicating a Mac as a server. Here are the most common home uses of Mountain Lion Server:

- **File sharing:** Sure, you can share files without a server, but centralized storage takes shared files off your Mac and safely stores them where everyone can always get at them. Don't want your kids to get into your tax returns? You can prevent certain people from accessing private files. Mountain Lion Server also shares files with iPad, iPhone, and iPod touch devices running Apple's Keynote, Numbers, or Pages — wirelessly. You can't do that without OS X Server. Another great file-sharing feature is the capability to quickly search the server with Spotlight, which is important if you have a lot of stored files.

- **Centralized management of Macs, iPhones, iPods, and iPod touches:** OS X Server's Profile Manager lets you keep control of all your devices from a central location. You can set users' passwords and settings for network access and install software on the client computers from the server. Make changes from the server, and the new settings are pushed out to the devices automatically.

- **Automatic backups to a central location:** You don't need to remember to back up info for safekeeping. The server does it for you, and lets you restore when needed — even when you're away. You can back up Windows too, but you'll have to add software to your server Mac.

- **Secure remote access to home Macs:** Need to access information at your house while you're away? Remote access through the built-in virtual private network is simple enough to use at home.

Setting up Mountain Lion Server is more automated than ever. For home use, a quick setup procedure is all you need. I describe this process in Chapter 3. For a small business or a group in an enterprise, you can do more with Mountain Lion Server, with a little more work.

Why you need Mountain Lion Server in business and education

All the great things described in the preceding section make even more sense in business or education. For a small network, Mountain Lion Server will serve your PCs and your Macs, too. On a large network, Mac OS X will peacefully coexist with Windows servers, serving your Macs like no Windows server can.

A friend may roll his eyes and tell you that a Linux server is the only logical choice. He'll tell you that Linux is inexpensive and reliable, and that many of the servers powering the Internet are running Linux. All true, but it takes an expert to configure and maintain a Linux server. And it still doesn't support Mac clients as well as Mountain Lion Server does.

Still not convinced? Well, you probably are because you're reading this book. But maybe your boss isn't convinced. Here are some reasons why your server should be Mountain Lion Server.

The price is right

Windows and Linux servers can scale up to some very large networks, which OS X Server isn't designed to do. But Windows servers cost more than Mountain Lion Server, and Linux costs you in terms of technical expertise.

Better service for Mac clients

Mountain Lion Server supports Mac clients better than any other server. For example, Mountain Lion Server offers services specifically for the Apple software on your users' Macs and iOS devices, including Contacts and Calendar (known as Address Book and iCal on older Macs). Mountain Lion Server turns these apps into groupware and works more smoothly for the user and the administrator than other servers and Mac clients. A server version of the Mac's Spotlight makes searching the server quick and easy.

But even for generic services, such as file sharing, OS X Server supports Mac clients better than do other servers. OS X Server supports any filename that the Mac supports, and it doesn't split files into two parts or leave small, empty files on the server, which are problems that can occur when Mac clients access Windows and Linux servers.

OS X Server is also the best way to manage the settings for groups of Macs. And for public Macs, such as school computer labs, OS X is the best way to automatically keep control of what's on the Macs, including settings and software.

Support and management of iPad and iPhone devices

In a business setting, management of iOS devices — proliferating numbers of iPads and iPhones on your network — can present challenges in several ways. The more such devices and the larger the network, the higher the security risk. Mountain Lion Server provides a simple way to configure and manage iOS devices, as well as Mac clients running Mac OS X 10.7 or later.

You can also use Mountain Lion Server to integrate devices into your network directory, as well as to define management policies for iOS devices (as you can for computers, users, and groups).

Mountain Lion Server can push configuration changes, calendar invitations, and events to the devices using Apple push notification service. And the Server optimizes wikis and blogs for viewing on iOS devices.

The Servers in Mountain Lion Server

Mountain Lion Server is not one server but more than two dozen servers and tools for managing Mac clients. Figure 1-1 lists the services available to you, as you see them in the Server utility. Other services not displayed in the figure are also available. Many of them can be turned on and off with a few mouse clicks.

Figure 1-1: Lion Server is actually a set of servers.

Services
- Calendar
- Contacts
- DNS
- File Sharing
- FTP
- Mail
- Messages
- NetInstall
- Open Directory
- Profile Manager
- Software Update
- Time Machine
- VPN
- Websites
- Wiki
- Xsan

Next is a quick look at what services you get, and what you can do with them. After this, we take a look at the management tools.

File server

The bread and butter of a server, the file server may be all that some people need from Mountain Lion Server. File servers provide folders that everyone on the network can see. You can also limit access so that some people can't get into certain folders. OS X Server provides file sharing via the Mac-native Apple Filing Protocol (AFP), which is Mac only, and Microsoft's Server Message Block (SMB), which Windows and Linux clients use. Mountain Lion Server also provides the WebDAV protocol for iPad devices and, optionally, for backing up Macs using Time Machine. You can also set up FTP, used for uploading and downloading big files over the Internet. If you're adept in the Unix command line, you have access to Network Files System (NFS) for Unix and Linux.

The file server also has a robust set of access controls, both the simpler Unix file permissions, as well as sophisticated access control lists used on Windows networks. The Mac's Spotlight search feature works with the access controls; Spotlight won't display a file in search results if the user doesn't have permission to see the file.

Directory services

OS X Server uses the standards-based Open Directory to store and manage user account info and other user data that all the services employ. You can connect the server to other directory services on the network, including Microsoft Active Directory. To keep the network secure, directory services authenticates clients that log in with the LDAP, Kerberos, and SASL standards.

Open Directory includes a feature called Locales, which lets you specify which replica directory server that a client computer will connect to based on a network location — a handy feature that keeps notebook computers connected to the directory no matter where they are.

Contacts Server

Contacts Server (formerly known as Address Book Server) enables users to share and synchronize both personal and group contacts with the Mac Contacts or Address Book application, and with the Contacts app on the iPhone, iPad, and iPod touch. It works also with a CardDAV-compatible client on Windows.

To the user, Contacts Server works like Apple's iCloud service. Changes in contacts appear automatically on all devices sharing the contacts. OS X Server does this through Apple push notification service. But by hosting the contacts on your local server rather than iCloud, you can integrate the contacts list with your local LDAP directory service, including Open Directory.

Calendar Server

With Calendar Server, users on the network can schedule events, book conference rooms, and view one another's calendars. People can send an invitation to a meeting that includes an agenda and accept the invitation. Contacts Server keeps track of who is inviting whom as well as what people are scheduling at any point in time. OS X Server can send e-mail invitations to people outside your group who don't have accounts on your network or Mac server.

OS X Server works with the calendar on OS X and on iPhone, iPad, and iPod touch devices, as well as with the older iCal application. Windows clients can add open source software supporting the CalDAV standard. And you can set up the server to provide access through a web browser.

As with Contacts Server, Calendar Server provides the user experience of Apple's iCloud service through the use of Apple push notification service. Changes to a shared calendar appear on all devices subscribing to the calendar.

Messages Server

Instant messaging isn't just for mobile phones. Users of Mac OS X, Windows, iPhones, and iPads can have a virtual meeting by using Messages instant messaging. Messages Server supports audio and video, as well as file transfers. Users can access persistent chat rooms, which are always there. The server also stores each user's account info so that a user can use the service from any computer. Messages Server replaces iChat Server, which is found in earlier versions of OS X Server.

Network services for Internet connections

You can use Mountain Lion Server as a stand-alone system in your organization or home. But Server also provides network services that enable it to interact with the Internet. You can get these services in other ways, such as in a wireless router or from other servers on a larger network, but OS X Server has them if you need them. These services are

- ✔ **Domain name service (DNS):** DNS translates a domain name, such as `mycomany.com`, from an IP address. DNS is required somewhere on the network for just about all network services that you share with the Internet, including web hosting, mail, and calendaring.

- ✔ **Firewall:** Mountain Lion comes with a firewall to protect your server from intruders. Chapter 18 describes Mountain Lion Server's firewall.

- ✔ **Virtual private network (VPN) service:** VPN is a secure method of enabling people to access your network and server through the Internet from home or on the road. The VPN service in Mac OS X Server supports several standard methods of access.

Mail Server

Mail Server provides standard e-mail service for Macs, PCs, and hand-held devices. Through integration with Apple push notification service, the server can notify iPhone and iPad devices when they have mail.

OS X Server enables users to search the content of files attached to e-mail stored on the server. This search works for Microsoft Office and iWork files, PDF files, and others.

As a full-featured e-mail server, Mail Server blocks spam and e-mail that contain viruses from reaching users' desktops and can make e-mail available from a web browser. You can read more about the e-mail server in Chapter 13.

Web hosting

You can use OS X Server to host one or more of your own websites fairly easily, with default settings that take care of a lot of what is required to get your content on the Internet. A single mouse click in the Websites pane of the Server app (shown in Figure 1-2) enables these settings. Mountain Lion Server supports virtual hosting of multiple sites, and lets you use multiple IP addresses and virtual domains, all without programming. The web server in Mountain Lion Server is a marked improvement over the one in the previous version, Lion Server.

Mountain Lion Server's web server is really a package of technology, starting with the Apache web server, the most popular web server on the Internet. The web server also includes the powerful PostgreSQL database engine. A Perl plug-in is loaded with the web server, enabling you to use Common Gateway Interface (CGI) scripts for creating dynamic web pages and for functions, such as taking data that a user enters in a web-based form and moving it to the database. PHP for dynamic content is also included. For security, SSL is provided.

You don't need to be a programmer to take advantage of these features because a lot of this technology sits under the hood working with your content. Mountain Lion Server has the infrastructure needed to make WordPress or Druple run, should you need to add them.

Wiki Server

Built on OS X Server's under-the-hood web technology is Wiki Server. This feature provides an automatically created, full-featured *wiki,* which is a type of website that users can edit from their web browser. (This is the *wiki* in *Wikipedia.*) You can use a wiki as a group collaboration tool for projects or brainstorming. Users can edit text, add hyperlinks to web pages, upload photos and documents to share, and then review the history of the changes that have been made and revert to earlier versions. Wikis automatically update to tell readers what changes other users have made.

Wiki Server also integrates blogging software. Blogs in your organization are great for posting status updates and reports. Like blogs on the Internet, the Mountain Lion Server blog feature has a space at the bottom for users to post comments.

Wiki Server sites look great on an iPad in Safari. The site automatically creates a special view on an iPad to make it easier to use. Each wiki appears as a stack of documents that you tap to enter. From Apple's Pages, Numbers, and Keynotes apps, iPad users can create content and upload and download files attached to a wiki.

Profile Manager for iOS and OS X

Mobile device management is reason enough for businesses and schools that have iOS devices to run Mountain Lion Server. Profile Manager is a web app for creating and distributing configuration files that can automatically set up iOS devices, as well as Macs running OS X 10.7 and later. A profile can contain basic network settings and user accounts for mail, calendar, contacts, and other things.

Profile Manager also lets you place restrictions, such as rules for passwords and restrictions on what a user may access. For example, if you don't want your students downloading Angry Birds from the App Store, you can block App Store access on all your devices at once. You can distribute profiles to devices via e mail or have users download them from a self-service web page. You can also have the push notification service automatically deliver updates to configuration profiles on devices.

Software Update Server

Mac users can choose whether or not to update their software through the Mac's Software Update feature, but this can lead to different users running different versions of software in an organization. Software Update Server controls what versions of updates from Apple get installed on your Macs.

You can restrict what software updates are installed on client Macs, as well as when they get installed, so that you can test updates first. The client Macs get the updates from the server instead of downloading them individually.

Software Update Server lets you install an update to multiple Macs all at once, without having to go around to each Mac.

NetInstall

NetInstall lets you deploy Mac OS X and application upgrades on users' Macs, which prevents you from having to go to each Mac and install and configure software manually.

NetInstall also lets you restore, from the server, a customized OS X configuration to Macs that need it.

NetBoot

NetBoot is great for a group of Macs that are available to multiple users, such as in a school computer lab or a classroom. This service enables Mac clients to boot up from the serverrather than from their own hard drives. The NetBoot server can use a single disk image to boot multiple Macs. This process prevents the boot system from being altered or tampered with and makes sure that every system boots in exactly the same configuration. NetBoot also lets you update the system software of all the Macs at one time, simply by updating the disk image on the server.

Spotlight searching

For Mac users, Spotlight is an indispensable search feature that lets you find a file almost instantaneously. OS X Server does the same for files on the server without bogging down server performance by indexing the content of the files. Users get advanced search features, including Boolean logic and the use of quoted phrases, and stores search criteria in the form of Smart Folders.

Time Machine backup

OS X Server works with the Time Machine backup software in all Mac clients to have them automatically back up to the server. You can also use Time Machine to back up the server data to a backup hard drive. When disaster strikes, Time Machine will back up both clients and the server.

Management Tools in Mountain Lion Server

Flipping through this book, you see that I mostly describe two tools: the Server application and Workgroup Manager, which plays a smaller, more specialized role.

The Server app is included with Mountain Lion Server. You'll find it in the Applications folder, but you won't find Workgroup Manager. You have to go get it yourself from Apple at this location: http://support.apple.com/kb/DL1567.

Introducing the Server App

Previous versions of OS X Server gave you a folder full of stuff to administrate the server. With Mountain Lion Server, Apple centralized the administration of OS X Server in a single application, the Server app (shown in Figure 1-3). This is where you not only set up file sharing and manage devices but also install the server software itself.

Figure 1-3: The Server app gives you easy access to configuring services.

The Server app enables you turn services on and off and configure them. You can assign user passwords and manage mail, calendar, and messaging services. You can also turn on remote access via a virtual private network. The Time Machine icon in the Server app lets you set automated backups of server data.

Configuring services and accounts with the Server app

To start a service, click an icon under Services in the left sidebar. The pane at the right displays configuration options for that service, as shown in Figure 1-4. Click the big switch in the upper right to turn on the service. (It may take a few seconds for the service to start.)

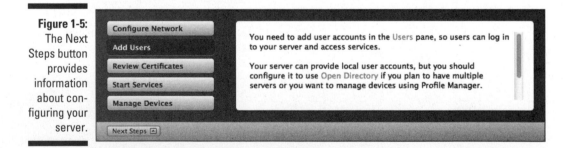

Figure 1-4:
The File
Sharing
pane of the
Server app.

You also use the Server app to create user and group accounts. (Workgroup Manager can also create user accounts and gives you more configuration options.) Click Users or Groups under Accounts in the sidebar. You can then enter user and group names and passwords.

The Server app includes built-in guidance to help you configure Mountain Lion Server. Click the Next Steps button in the lower left of the Server app to expand the bottom of the window. Several new buttons appear, as shown in Figure 1-5. Clicking one of the buttons displays information about your server's current setup and provides links to settings windows that will enable you to complete other tasks.

Figure 1-5:
The Next
Steps button
provides
information
about con-
figuring your
server.

| Configure Network |
| Add Users |
| Review Certificates |
| Start Services |
| Manage Devices |

You need to add user accounts in the Users pane, so users can log in to your server and access services.

Your server can provide local user accounts, but you should configure it to use Open Directory if you plan to have multiple servers or you want to manage devices using Profile Manager.

Next Steps

For example, in Figure 1-5, the Server app tells you that the users added are local user accounts, residing only on the server Mac and not in a network directory. Clicking the Open Directory link in the text takes you to a screen where you can start setting up Open Directory.

Monitoring your server and making general settings changes

The Server app provides several ways to view the status of your server. In the sidebar under Status are three items:

- **Alerts:** Here, you find alerts that Mountain Lion Server can send you. You're alerted to conditions of low disk space, e-mails that might contain a virus, expired SSL certificates, changes to network settings, and available software updates. You can also use this pane to designate an e-mail address where Mountain Lion Server can e-mail alerts to you.

- **Logs:** This item represents the log files for the various services, which track what's going on under the hood. Log files can be useful when troubleshooting.

- **Stats:** Stats provides live graphs of your server's processor usage, memory usage, and network traffic.

Under Hardware, you can click the name of your server to get access to four tabs of information and some settings as well:

- **Overview:** This tab (refer to Figure 1-3) provides information about the Mac model and hardware configuration, the version of OS X Server, and how long the server has been running.

- **Settings:** Here, you can change settings for remote login and administration, screen sharing, push notifications, and SSL certificates.

- **Network:** This tab displays (and lets you change) the Mac's computer name and the server's host name. It displays also the IP addresses of your network interfaces.

- **Storage:** This tab displays the amount of free space on any storage devices attached to the server. It also lets you change permissions for shared folders (see Chapter 8).

Workgroup Manager

Workgroup Manager is a more advanced tool for setting and managing user accounts than the Server app. You can use Workgroup Manager to control aspects of users' computers, doing some of the things that Profile Manager can do. But Profile Manager doesn't support Macs running operating systems earlier than OS X 10.7. You can use Workgroup Manager to manage your older Macs or all your Macs.

For example, you can require users to change passwords at regular intervals, create standardized preference settings for client Macs, or allow only certain applications to run. You can use Workgroup Manager also to configure certain security measures, such as blocking computers from seeing external hard drives or from burning CDs and DVDs. And you can create groups to manage settings for multiple sets of computers at once.

For more on Workgroup Manager, see Chapter 16.

Command-Line Administration

The Server app is really just a front end to a set of server software that lies below the service. Much to the chagrin of some Mac administrators, Apple has been simplifying the graphics front-end management tools of OS X Server to make OS X "the server for everyone."

But most of the less frequently used, more technical features and settings of previous versions are still in OS X Server. The only way to reach them, however, is through the Unix command line. If you're experienced in the Unix shell and networking, you can administer the entire OS X Server without ever having to launch the Server app.

Unix commands are accessible in the Terminal application, which comes with every version of Mac OS X. You can use one of the Unix shells that come with Terminal: bash (the default), sh, csh, tsh, and zsh. If you're managing one or more servers over a network, use ssh, or Secure Shell. Many of OS X Server's features can be managed with the serveradmin command-line tool.

But even if you aren't a Unix geek, you may come across a tip that can work around a problem by typing a couple lines of text. You occasionally find such tips throughout this book.

You can find more information about OS X Server's command-line tools at www.apple.com/osx/server/specs/ and www.apple.com/server/docs/Command_Line.pdf.

Chapter 2

Choosing Server Hardware

· ·

In This Chapter

▶ Dissecting hardware requirements

▶ Choosing the right RAM and hard drives

▶ Selecting the right Mac for your server

▶ Upgrading the Mac mini for use a server

▶ Reviewing other network hardware

· ·

*Y*ou've chosen the software — Mountain Lion Server. Now you need to pick a Mac to run it on. You can spend anywhere from under $1,000 to over $10,000 (with storage options), and no one Mac model is best for running Mountain Lion Server. It runs on everything from a Mac mini to the Mac Pro, with varying amounts of memory and hard drive space. Which one is for you?

This chapter takes you through criteria for choosing a Mac and a configuration that best meets your needs as a server. By matching your anticipated uses to the available hardware, you can avoid getting an underpowered Mac server or spending too much for more than you need. If you already have a Mac in mind for use as a server, this chapter helps you decide whether it will work for what you want to do with it. I also describe how to open up a Mac mini and upgrade to make it server-worthy.

If you already know what hardware configuration you need and you're ready to install now, skip to Chapter 3 or 4.

Criteria for Selecting Server Hardware

Before you think about processor speeds, do some planning to determine what you'll be doing with the server. Here are the two key issues: the number of users who will be accessing the server and what the users will do with the server. When you have both pieces of information, your hardware options become clearer.

Number of users

The effect of an increasing number of connected clients on server performance isn't linear. You may not notice slower service as the number of connected clients increases until you get to a tipping point, when performance suddenly slows to a crawl.

The Mac mini can handle a maximum of around 20 to 50 simultaneous client computers doing lightweight tasks. The more hardware-intensive services you run, the lower that number is. With up to ten or so users, the lower-end Macs can handle multiple tasks at once. If you add more users later, you can always add more lower-end Mac servers for other tasks. Current iMac models have faster processors and architecture than the minis, can hold more RAM, and can handle more clients.

The top-of-the-line Mac Pro can potentially handle hundreds of clients, again depending on what services you run. With the Mac Pro or an older Xserve, adding more higher-end storage or large amounts of RAM can help enlarge the client load that the server can handle. *Network capacity* (number of Ethernet cards and their speed) is also important in serving large numbers of clients.

Type of use

The number of users doesn't tell the whole story about what Mac to use to run Mountain Lion Server. Five users accessing a database program might require beefier server hardware than ten users accessing a server-based website.

In Chapter 1, I describe the services that come with Mountain Lion Server. The following paragraphs describe some typical uses listed in *approximate* order of how much demand they place on your server hardware.

Web servers: Lightweight server use

Web servers don't use a lot of hardware resources. The server often caches web pages and doesn't have to access the hard drive to load web pages. Web serving also doesn't take a lot of RAM or processing power. You can run a web server on any Mac that Mountain Lion Server runs on, and you can generally run it along with other services without affecting performance.

E-mail, DNS (domain name service), and Internet gateway functions are similarly lightweight services in terms of server hardware.

File servers: Light on processor, big in storage

File serving is generally not an intensive use of the server hardware and doesn't use a lot of processing power. File servers primarily need a lot of storage. You can choose among a wide range of Macs for use as file servers, as long as the Mac has enough hard drive space in one or multiple hard drives. Unless you have a lot of users, file servers can run alongside other services.

File servers also need frequent backups or high levels of redundancy to preserve the data.

The more users and the bigger the users' files, the more total storage you need. Frequent movement of a lot of very large files, such as video, may require a *storage area network (SAN),* which is storage connected directly to a network or *RAID (Redundant Array of Individual Disks)* systems.

Backing up users' Macs and PCs to the server with Time Machine or another server-based backup program is also a type of file sharing and a lightweight use of server processing power. Backing up multiple users at the same time can be a heavy use of network bandwidth and may slow down a wireless network, but a faster Mac server won't make a difference.

Database server: Moving lots of data

If you install a third-party database server, it can take more resources than file serving, especially if a lot of users are accessing the database. A database server can require more frequent use of the hard drive and processor than file servers, depending on the data being served and how often.

Directory services: Give it what it needs

Directory service, which is supplied by Open Directory in OS X Server, can be one of the most actively used services on the network, particularly a large network. Don't underpower a directory server, or you may slow the whole network.

Directory servers store information about users and groups, permissions, and configuration information for client computers; they authenticate clients and store information that determines which clients can access which files. Running directory services on a midsize to large network is equivalent to running multiple databases simultaneously. Fast storage is the most important directory services requirement for any size network. A lot of memory is necessary to keep up performance. For large networks, consider dedicating a server for directory services and using one or more other Macs for other services, such as mail.

However, directory service doesn't use a lot of CPU power. For smaller networks, running directory service along with other services should work fine.

Server-based home directories: Server stress

Mountain Lion Server can host the home folders of users, also called *mobile home folders.* In this case, each user stores all documents, settings, and preferences on the server. A Mac mini can handle a few dozen users accessing their server-based home directories, while a Mac Pro can handle several hundred.

NetBoot: Heavy-duty server stress

NetBoot probably places more demand on the server's hardware resources than any other service in Mac OS X Server. NetBoot is where client Macs boot from the server itself instead of from their local hard drives. Even for a small network, you need a fast Mac server with multiple processors and fast hard drive storage, and lots of it.

You'll also need fast networking. Wireless networking is too slow for NetBoot, which is why it supports only Ethernet connections. A server with multiple Ethernet interfaces can prevent slowdowns. Check your Ethernet switch: You'll want 100BaseT at a minimum; Gigabit Ethernet is better. Your network will slow to a crawl if you have an old 10BaseT switch and are using NetBoot.

With a lot of Mac clients, NetBoot may be too much for one server to handle, so the software supports load balancing on multiple Mac servers.

Hardware Requirements for Running Mountain Lion Server

You can install Mountain Lion on the following Mac models:

- ✔ iMac (mid-2007 or later)
- ✔ MacBook (13-inch Aluminum, 2008; 13-inch, early 2009 or later)
- ✔ MacBook Pro (13-inch, mid-2009 or later; 15-inch, 2.4/2.2 GHz; 17-inch, late 2007 or later)
- ✔ MacBook Air (late 2008 or later)
- ✔ Mac mini (early 2009 or later)
- ✔ Mac Pro (early 2008 or later)
- ✔ Xserve (early 2009)
- ✔ Any Mac introduced after the publication of this book, 2012 or later

Following are the minimum requirements for running Mountain Lion Server:

- ✔ **Computer:** A Mac. Although you can hack non-Apple hardware to run the Mac OS X operating system, doing so violates the user license agreement.

- ✔ **Processor:** A 64-bit Intel processor. The oldest 64-bit processor found in Macs that support Mountain Lion is a Core 2 Duo. Mountain Lion won't run on Macs with an Intel Core Solo or a Core Duo, which were the first generations of Intel processors that Apple used.

- ✔ **Graphics card:** Mountain Lion requires a graphics card that supports the OpenGL standard. This means that Mountain Lion won't run on some older Mac models that are compatible with Lion.

- ✔ **RAM:** 2GB RAM base.

- ✔ **Hard drive space:** 8GB of free hard drive space.

The processor is determined, for the most part, by the Mac model you use. Macs with a dual-core Intel Core 2 Duo are slower than Macs with a dual-core Intel Core i3. Quad-core processors, such as the Intel Core i7, are faster yet. The quad-core Intel Xeon processors offered in the Mac Pro are faster than the Core i7. (Core i5s come in dual-core and quad-core models.) The Mac Pro has the option for a six-core processor.

The gigahertz (GHz) rating is less important than processor model and number of cores. It has meaning only when you compare two processors of the same model and same number of cores. So a 3.2 GHz Intel Core i3 is faster than a 3.06 GHz Intel Core i3.

As a general rule, use more RAM in a computer than the minimum amount of RAM required by the operating system. Some Macs can hold several dozen gigabytes of memory, which is more than most people need. See the section "Putting enough RAM in your server," later in this chapter, for more information.

Selecting Processors for Your Mac Servers

To get a particular type of processor in a Mac, you have to select the Mac model. For any given model, Apple offers choices in clock speed. The Mac Pro provides the most options in processors at purchase time, giving you a choice of different processors and a choice of having a second processor.

Processors with multiple cores act as multiple processors. Two dual-core processors are equivalent to one quad-core processor, which is why processing power is sometimes described in terms of the number of cores rather than the number of processors.

You don't need a brand-new Mac for Mountain Lion Server. An older Mac is perfectly fine — as long as it has a 64-bit Intel processor. When in doubt, check the About This Mac window (see Figure 2-1), accessible from the Apple menu. This window also reveals how much memory you have in the machine.

Figure 2-1: The About This Mac window identifies the processor and amount of RAM.

For most Mac models, you can't upgrade a processor. You can upgrade a processor in Mac Pro, but doing so is difficult and voids the warranty. For a Mac Pro no longer under warranty, check out this website: www.everymac.com/systems/apple/mac_pro/faq/mac-pro-mid-2010-westmere-how-to-upgrade-processors.html. Here, you can find information for various releases of the Mac Pro from 2008 and earlier to more modern models.

Only the discontinued Xserve has an officially upgradeable processor. Apple still has directions at its website: Go to www.apple.com/support/manuals and search for *Xserve processor.* You find PDF documents for each Xserve revision, such as *Xserve (Early 2009) DIY Procedure for Processor (Manual).*

Mountain Lion won't run on an old PowerPC Mac, and you can't replace the PowerPC processor with an Intel processor. The architecture of the machines is just too different. Don't even try.

Putting Enough RAM in Your Server

RAM is important for speed in the OS X operating system, and this is particularly true for servers. Server applications can often run faster when you add RAM. More RAM also increases the number of simultaneous client connections that the server can handle without bogging down. On the other hand, filling a Mac Pro with the maximum 64GB of RAM will cost thousands of dollars (if you buy it from Apple), which is a big waste if the server isn't using it.

The minimum amount of RAM you should consider is 4GB. This amount should provide acceptable results for up to 200 users for light, occasional uses, or for a small network of fewer than 10 computers for file sharing. But keep in mind that the Server configuration of the Mac Pro starts at 8GB of RAM.

If you're not sure if your system has enough memory, you can check usage after you've been running the server in normal use for a few hours. You can use Activity Monitor (in the server's Utility folder) to keep an eye on RAM usage. At the bottom of the Activity Monitor window, click the System Memory tab (see Figure 2-2). Look at the Page Ins and Page Outs numbers. If the size of the page outs is more than 5 to 10 percent of the page ins, the operating system has to write information from RAM to disk because it doesn't have enough RAM, which translates to slower server performance. If that happens, adding RAM will increase performance.

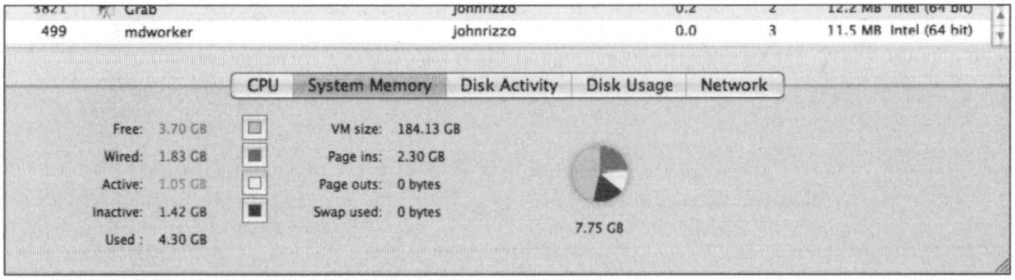

Figure 2-2: Activity Monitor displays the page ins and page outs.

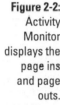

In Figure 2-2 the page outs are 0 bytes and the pie chart shows plenty of free RAM, which indicate that this server has plenty of RAM.

Another place you can check your system's memory usage is in the Server app, which is installed in the Applications folder when you install Mountain Lion Server. Click Stats in the sidebar on the left, and then select Memory Usage from the pop-up menu. A graph of memory usage over a time period that you designate appears, as shown in Figure 2-3. If the usage is maxing out a lot, adding more RAM may improve performance.

If your system does need a lot of RAM, it's cheaper to buy extra RAM and install it yourself rather than buy it from Apple when you order a new Mac. The price difference can be hundreds of dollars for an 8GB RAM module. To find the best prices, check out Ramseeker (www.ramseeker.com), which lets you compare prices from multiple vendors — like Orbitz does with airline tickets. Just select your Mac model from a pop-up menu, and Ramseeker gives you a list of vendors and prices.

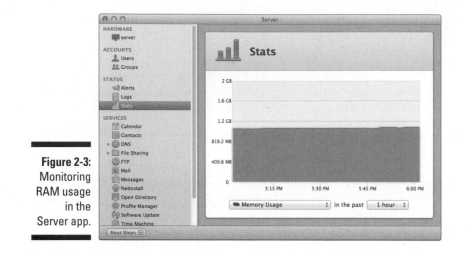

Figure 2-3:
Monitoring
RAM usage
in the
Server app.

Selecting Hard Drive Storage

Apple gives you some hard drive choices when you buy a Mac. The drives vary in capacity, and with some models, you have a choice of rotational speed. You can also replace the hard drive in an existing Mac with a bigger or faster drive.

You may also want to look at two other options for expanded capacity outside the Mac: NAS (network attached storage) and SAN (storage area network), which, despite the acronyms, aren't opposites. I discuss both later in this section.

Rotational speed

Rotational speed is a measure of hard drive speed in revolutions per minute (rpm), the speed at which the platters inside the drive spin. The faster the rotational speed, the faster the drive performance.

The lowest rotational speed you'll find in a Mac that supports Mountain Lion is 5,400 rpm, which Apple used in some Mac mini and MacBook models. A speed of 5,400 rpm isn't particularly speedy for a server, so consider replacing such a drive with the next level up, 7,200 rpm. This is the fastest drive you'll see in notebooks and many desktop computers, aside from a solid-state drive. 7,200 rpm is also the standard in the high-end Mac Pro.

Apple used to offer 15,000-rpm hard drives for the Mac Pro and Xserve. In some models, Apple now offers solid-state drives, which are faster than even 15,000-rpm hard drives. Solid-state drives have no moving parts, like USB flash drives. Solid-state drives are also significantly more expensive per gigabyte than hard drives.

Server-grade, or enterprise-class, drives

You'll sometimes see a drive labeled with the interchangeable terms *server-grade* or *enterprise-class.* Apple uses the first term for the drive in its Time Capsule network storage product.

The basic feature of a server-grade, or enterprise-class, hard drive is a high *mean time before failure (MTBF) rating,* which represents the average working life of a drive before it needs repair. The MTBF of some server-grade drives is 1 million hours, which is 114 years! Although not a lifetime guarantee, a high MTBF reduces the chances of hard drive failure during

the life of the computer. Manufacturers usually provide longer warranties for server-grade drives, and five-year warranties are common.

Server-grade, or enterprise-class, drives also feature high performance, which can include more cache, a high rotational speed (such as 15,000 rpm), and faster throughput with an SAS interface. A server-grade hard drive costs more than an ordinary drive. Unless your network constantly gives your drive a workout, you don't need to go out of your way to find a server-grade tag on a drive.

You can't replace a drive with a 15,000-rpm drive in lower-end Mac models because 15,000-rpm drives use a different, faster hardware interface — *serially attached SCSI (SAS)* — than slower drives. Drives of the past few years that are 7,200 rpm and slower use the Serial ATA interface. You can't plug an SAS drive into a Serial ATA connector. The Mac Pro and Xserve, however, include drive bays that accept either Serial ATA or SAS drives.

The size of a hard drive's cache is also an indication of drive performance: More is better but sometimes isn't noticeable.

Drive form factor

Internal hard drives come in two form factors: 2.5 inches and 3.5 inches (the size of the disc inside the drives). The 2.5-inch drives are traditionally used in notebook computers, but some servers use them as well. Most desktop computers, including iMacs, use the 3.5-inch drive. The oddball here is the Mac mini, a desktop computer that uses a 2.5-inch hard drive.

RAID storage

The Mac Pro, the server version of the Mac mini, and the discontinued Xserve contain multiple drive bays that give you the option to set up multiple drives to work together as a RAID (Redundant Array of Individual Disks) to increase performance, protect data, or both. You can also plug an external RAID box into a FireWire 800 or Thunderbolt port. Apple software supports four types of RAIDs:

✔ **RAID 0** isn't actually redundant, despite the name. RAID 0 uses a *striping* technique to make multiple hard drives work together as a single, fast, large hard drive. Data from a file is fragmented and written on multiple drives. When reading the file, the system can read the fragments from all the drives simultaneously, greatly increasing performance. RAID 0 also lets you create a very large single volume for storing giant files, such as video. If one of the drives in a RAID fails, all the data is lost. RAID 0 requires a minimum of two hard drives.

✔ **RAID 1** uses a *mirroring* technique to write the same data to two drives simultaneously. If one drive fails, the other drive still contains all the data. RAID 1 requires a minimum of two hard drives and is a good use in a Mac mini with two internal drives.

✔ **RAID 5** makes more efficient use of hard drive space than RAID 1 and has better performance. The drawback to RAID 5 is that it requires a minimum of three hard drives.

✔ **RAID 0+1** (also known as RAID 10) first creates a *RAID 0 striped array* — a very large volume from two hard drives — giving you the fast performance. RAID 0+1 then mirrors the first array with a second striped pair, giving you the redundancy. The drawback to RAID 0+1 is that it requires at least four hard drives.

NAS and SAN

Network attached storage (NAS) is a stand-alone storage device that plugs directly into the network through Ethernet or wireless (802.11 Wi-Fi). You should definitely use Ethernet for connecting a NAS device to a server. Multiple servers or computers can access a NAS device directly. Apple's Time Capsule is an example of a NAS unit, although other NAS devices with multiple drive bays can be more flexible for use with a server. NAS units are often used for backup.

Whereas a NAS device can be a low-end home, office, or small to medium business device, a *storage area network* (SAN) is a high-performance, high-cost investment used as primary server storage in large networks. A SAN can be a subnetwork of hard drives connected with a high-speed Fibre Channel switch. Multiple servers can access a SAN, centralizing storage on the network.

Apple offers Xsan software ($999, `www.apple.com/xsan`) that enables multiple desktop and server computers to directly access and share RAID storage. Xsan can handle up to 2 petabytes, which is 2 thousand terabytes, or 2 million gigabytes. The calendar server that comes with Mountain Lion Server is optimized to work with Xsan so that multiple calendar servers can access the same SAN storage. This server *clustering* enables Mountain Lion's calendar to serve thousands of users. Mountain Lion Server's mail server is similarly optimized for Xsan.

If you want to bone up on SANs, try *Storage Area Networks For Dummies,* 2nd Edition, by Christopher Poelker and Alex Nikitin (John Wiley & Sons, Inc.).

Choosing the Right Mac for Your Server

There are four types of Macs to consider using as a server: Mac mini, iMac, Mac Pro, and the discontinued Xserve. Additionally, a MacBook Pro running a server in a virtual machine can work as a testing platform. Each Mac is good for some type of network, and no size fits all. The specifications for Mac models change every year, so it's a good idea to check the Apple website from the Tech Specs link on each Mac's web page.

You don't need a brand-new Mac, though. A server is a good use for an older Mac, provided it has enough power for what you plan to do with it and meets the minimum requirements.

You also don't need a display monitor connected to the server. After you install Mountain Lion Server, you can run the server *headless,* using the Mountain Lion Server administration tools on another Mac on the network.

Mac mini as a server

While I was writing the first version of this book, *Snow Leopard Server For Dummies,* an internal reviewer scoffed at the idea of using a mini as a server platform, saying that it "makes no sense." I was undaunted. Several months after the book's publication, Apple came out with a special server version of the Mac mini.

I would like to believe that Apple read the book and thought, "What a great idea!" For years, however, many people have been using Mac minis as servers. They're inexpensive, fit in small spaces, and are very quiet. You can use a single Mac mini for a small group of Macs for basic services or as a general-purpose web server. You also can use multiple Mac minis to serve larger networks. A commenter at the Apple Discussions forum once claimed that his company's data center held 500 Mac minis.

In the server version of the Mac mini, Apple replaces the optical DVD drive with a second hard drive, and both drives are of the faster 7200-rpm type. You can install software remotely from another Mac, or use the MacBook Air SuperDrive, a USB optical drive.

TIP

Not all Mac minis are alike. Starting with the mid-2010 model, also called *unibody,* the mini became a much better server than earlier models. First, it includes an SD card slot for flash RAM from which you can quickly boot the Mac in case of an emergency. Second, it includes a removable panel for easy access to the RAM slots. And it eliminates the power brick of older models by incorporating the power supply inside the unit. (Figure 2-4 shows a modern mini.)

Figure 2-4:
The mid-2011 Mac mini is quiet and unobtrusive and is available with two hard drives.

Photo courtesy of Apple.

Best uses

For a network or workgroup of about 5 to 15 client computers, a single Mac mini can handle file sharing, e-mail, web services, calendar service, DNS (domain name service), and Open Directory with Kerberos authentication. For any one of these services, a recent mini model is good for 200 users, assuming access to appropriate storage.

TIP

DNS usually works better on a server with two physical Ethernet ports. You can add a second Ethernet port to the mini by buying the $29 Apple USB Ethernet Adapter. It's made for the MacBook Air but works fine with a Mac mini. Keep in mind that the adapter is slower than a built-in Ethernet port. But for something like DNS, speed shouldn't matter.

You can always spread a server load over several Mac minis, as long as you don't tax the hardware. You also probably don't want to host more than a few dozen user home directories.

Pros

Using Mac minis to run Mountain Lion Server has several advantages:

✔ **Inexpensive:** You can buy three or four for the price of a basic Mac Pro. The cost is low enough that it might be worth springing for a new mini rather than using an older and slower Mac. If you find your network is outgrowing your Mac mini, you can add more minis for a small investment.

✔ **Small:** At just 1.4 inches high, a stack of many minis is still smaller than a toaster. You can easily mount a Mac mini on a wall or under a desk with brackets made for that purpose. You can even rack-mount Mac minis as you would other server hardware. The MX4 V2 Rack Tray (see Figure 2-5) from Macessity ($60, www.macessity.com) holds four Mac minis and fits into a standard equipment rack.

✔ **Quiet and energy efficient:** Mac minis are very quiet and can coexist nicely in a school library or office. They don't use a lot of power or generate a lot of heat, so you won't need to use a lot of energy for cooling.

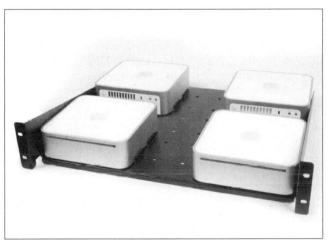

Figure 2-5:
This tray holds four Mac minis in a standard network equipment rack.

Cons

Using Mac minis to run OS X Server has disadvantages as well:

✔ **Slower processor:** The Mac mini processor is slower than that of the iMac or Mac Pro, which limits its uses.

✔ **One Ethernet port:** The Apple USB Ethernet Adapter fixes this issue, though it is slower. If multiple fast Ethernet ports are a necessity, get a Mac Pro.

✔ **Inconvenient drive replacement:** Although the newer minis make adding RAM easy, replacing a drive is still a little complicated. The best choice is to buy the server version of the mini, which has two preinstalled internal hard drives.

Upgrading Mac mini RAM and hard drive, 2010 model and later

Contrary to popular belief, the Mac mini *is* upgradeable. After you get into the box, you can increase the RAM and replace the drive with a bigger, faster drive.

Upgrading RAM in the newer Mac minis is easy. Here's how:

1. **Place the Mac mini upside down on a towel.**

2. **Rotate the circular panel counterclockwise a few degrees and remove it.**

   The two RAM slots are now visible.

3. **To remove a RAM module, press the tabs on either side of the module away from the center and firmly pull the module out.**

   To add a RAM module to an empty slot, insert the module.

4. **When you're finished, replace the circular panel.**

Replacing the hard drive is more tedious, and reassembling can be a bit tricky and more difficult than in older models. After you dig out the hard drive, peel away the vinyl blanket covering the hard drive. (Retain the vinyl blanket — you'll need to replace it on the new drive.) Two temperature sensors are also glued to the hard drive.

If you still want to proceed with drive replacement, you can find a number of websites with illustrated directions. The best YouTube video of the procedure that I've seen is at www.youtube.com/watch?v=wZy0wPniqqo.

Upgrading older Mac mini hard drive and RAM, pre-2010 models

Replacing an older Mac mini's 5,400-rpm drive with a 7,200-rpm drive not only gives you faster performance but also can triple the amount of storage. Be aware that when you do this job, the Mac mini runs hotter and the internal fan runs more frequently.

Although the pre-2010 Mac minis are officially not user-serviceable, you can open them to upgrade RAM and the hard drive. Replacing the hard drive on an older mini is actually easier than in the new models. You need a 1-inch-wide putty knife; it's helpful to bevel one side of the putty knife with some sandpaper first. Then follow these steps:

1. **Place the Mac mini upside down on a towel.**

2. **Position the knife blade where the outer casing meets the inner plastic housing and then press down firmly until the putty knife slips in about half an inch.**

3. **Push the handle of the putty knife outward and down to release the internal plastic tabs, working your way around the unit until the base is free from the cover.**

   The hard drive is located at the bottom of the internal plastic frame that also holds the DVD drive and the fan.

4. **Remove the frame by removing three small screws that hold it to the base.**

5. **Unplug the small cable for the fan.**

6. **Pull the base straight up, unplugging an interconnect board in the frame from a connector in the base.**

7. **With the frame removed, turn the mini upside down.**

   You find the hard drive attached with four screws.

8. **Upgrade the RAM.**

   You find two RAM slots on the base, connected to the motherboard.

Replacing an older (pre-2010) Mac mini DVD drive with a second hard drive

A DVD drive doesn't get a lot of use in a server, but a second internal hard drive would come in handy and would be much faster than an external FireWire drive.

The optical drive is parallel ATA (also known as IDE), but most drives sold today are Serial ATA (SATA). Make sure that you buy an IDE drive, which is not as high capacity as SATA.

 Tom's Hardware (www.tomshardware.com) is a good resource for locating hard drives. Look for drives that are internal, 2.5-inch, and 7,200-rpm, and have an IDE interface.

Removing the DVD drive is easier than replacing the hard drive:

1. **Remove the Mac mini's cover, as I describe in the preceding section.**

   You don't need to remove the internal frame because the DVD drive is right at the top, held in place by four screws, two on each side.

2. **Remove the four screws holding the DVD drive in place; then remove the two screws that hold the DVD drive to a daughter card that it plugs into.**

   Plug the new IDE hard drive into the daughter card.

iMac as a server

Running Mountain Lion Server on iMac isn't as common as on Mac mini. Sleek and beautiful, the all-in-one iMac sits in between the Mac mini and Mac Pro in terms of power and price. But the iMac's bright, clear display and attractive form are wasted when it's used as a server.

Best uses

A server is a good use of an older iMac (Intel-based) that you might have sitting around. Maybe you're replacing a user's older iMac with the latest and greatest iMac or MacBook. You might buy a new iMac for a server in some situations, such as when you can make use of the display or have some multimedia use in mind.

As a server, the iMac handles the networks that the Mac mini can (which I describe in the previous section), plus more — larger networks, more services, and possibly more internal storage. Exactly how much more depends on the iMac. Apple offers iMacs in a wide range of processor and storage options. The highest-end iMacs rival Mac Pros in terms of speed. In fact, new top-shelf iMacs are faster than the Mac Pros of a few years ago.

Pros

Should you decide to use iMac as a server, you'll enjoy these upsides:

- **Speed:** The performance is surprisingly fast. At any given time, Apple puts faster processors in the iMac than in the Mac mini. The iMac was the first Mac to get a quad-core processor (in 2009) — even before the Mac Pro. Higher-end newer iMacs can be faster and have more storage than Mac Pros that are a few years old.

- **Built-in display:** A built-in display is useful if the server is sitting in your office or out in the open, and you want to use it to administer and monitor the server instead of using another Mac.

- **Configuration:** The base configuration has bigger, faster hard drives than the Mac mini. (iMacs use 3.5-inch drives.)

- **Upgradeable RAM:** You can easily upgrade the RAM by removing two screws that hold a plate on the bottom.

- **Cost:** An iMac can cost thousands less than a Mac Pro, though both series have models with wide price ranges. Usually, the top-end iMac is about $500 less than the low-end Mac Pro.

Cons

These downsides can plague you if you use the iMac as a server:

- ✔ **Difficult hard drive upgrade:** Except for RAM, the iMac is really not upgradeable, even less so than the Mac mini. Although you can remove the mini's top in a minute when you know how, it's very difficult to disassemble an iMac to replace the hard drive. Reassembling it is also difficult. You can find directions if you Google *iMac take apart,* but I don't recommend it.

  If you're buying an iMac for the purpose of using it as a server, consider ordering the largest drive Apple offers.

- ✔ **Lack of expansion:** If you need multiple drive bays or expansion slots for multiple Ethernet cards, you'll need a Mac Pro. (Like the Mac mini, the newer iMacs include an SD card slot, however.)

- ✔ **Lack of second Ethernet port:** As with the Mac mini, you can add an inexpensive (and slower) USB Ethernet port.

Mac Pro as a server

The Apple power workstation includes features designed for use as a high-powered server. Up to 12 processing cores, expansion slots, multiple internal drives, and 2 built-in independent Ethernet connections make the Mac Pro (see Figure 2-6) well suited for running Mountain Lion Server in demanding network situations. Even older models make great servers.

As with the Mac mini, Apple offers a server version of the Mac Pro. The server version is similar to the entry-level Mac Pro configuration but with an extra hard drive, more memory, and Mountain Lion Server preinstalled.

Best uses

A Mac Pro can support file serving for hundreds of active users. For example, Mac Pro can work as the file server for an entire school and run third-party server software at the same time. The Mac Pro also works for running directory services and connecting a network of Macs to a Microsoft Active Directory network. If you're using a server only for web, e-mail, DNS, and light file-sharing tasks, the Mac Pro may be more than you need.

Figure 2-6:
A Mac
Pro tower
makes a
powerful
server.

Photo courtesy of Apple.

Pros

The Mac Pro leaves the Mac mini and the iMac in the dust as far as performance goes. The high points:

- ✓ **Up to 12 processing cores and a fast system architecture:** Note that 12 is more than most servers would need.

- ✓ **Four internal hard drive bays, one more than old Xserve:** With the optional RAID card, you can use these in a RAID system.

- ✓ **Easily accessible drives that can be replaced without futzing with cables:** Just open the side door and slide them in or out.

- ✓ **Room for lots of memory:** Eight RAM slots are available for up to 64GB.

- ✓ **Two Gigabit Ethernet ports:** This feature is designed for using the Mac Pro as a server. You can use one port to connect to the local network and another port to connect to the Internet. This configuration enables you to use the Mac server as a gateway, such as for network address translation (NAT) running the firewall or a virtual private network server. You can also use the two ports together, for twice the bandwidth.

  ✔ **Three extra expansion slots:** For more Ethernet ports, add Ethernet cards.

Cons

The Mac Pro as a server also has its low points:

  ✔ **Can be noisy:** For quiet, go with a Mac mini or iMac.

  ✔ **Costs more than the Mac mini or iMac:** But you also get more server power.

Xserve as a server

Although Apple discontinued the Xserve in January 2011, many units are still in use. A survey by the Enterprise Desktop Alliance showed that 65 percent of respondents planned to continue using Xserves for two or more years or until they stop functioning — which could be a while, considering the Xserve's industrial-strength design and easily replaceable parts.

If you've never seen an Xserve before, you wouldn't know that it's a Mac. The flat, horizontal body, shown in Figure 2-7, was designed to be mounted in a standard 19-inch equipment rack and to be run headless, though you can plug in a graphics card.

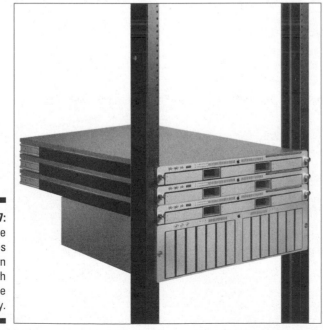

Figure 2-7:
Three
Xserves
mounted in
a rack with
a storage
array.

Photo courtesy of Apple.

Fans of the Xserve like its support of high-powered add-ons, such as internal RAIDs, with multiple, big, high-speed hard drives, including serially attached SCSI (SAS) drives, and eight RAM slots. The Mac Pro has all this, but the Xserve also has features to keep it running in mission-critical situations.

When it was last updated in 2009, the Xserve was similarly powered to the Mac Pro. Today's Mac Pros have surpassed the Xserve, but the latter is generally good for the same uses as the Mac Pro, running multiple services for hundreds of users. The Xserve is better suited than the Mac Pro to a growing network because you can easily upgrade the processors.

The Xserve is also built for mission-critical situations. If you absolutely can't afford to have any server downtime due to hardware failure, the Xserve is better than the Mac Pro. You may never have to shut down an Xserve. It comes with the option of a redundant power supply: If one power supply fails, the other takes over. Simply pull out a power supply and replace it — without shutting down the Xserve. (Replacement power supplies are still available at `www.welovemacs.com`, or you can Google *xserve power supply.*)

The Xserve also features hot-swappable hard drives: If a drive fails, you can pull out of Xserve without shutting it down or opening it.

The Xserve is the only Mac with official user-upgradeable processors. To get upgrading instructions, go to `http://support.apple.com/manuals` and search for *Xserve processor.* Manuals for the different Xserve models appear in the results.

These features are all reasons why many owners don't easily give up their Xserves.

Considering Other Network Hardware

This section provides some information for those readers who are thinking of building a network from scratch.

Power backup for your server

All networks should have an *uninterruptible power supply (UPS)* for the server. A UPS is an external box that keeps the server running in the event of a power failure in the building, giving you a chance to shut down the server in an orderly fashion. Simply shutting off the power in the middle of operations can damage the data on the server, and power surges related to the power failure can damage the server hardware.

A basic UPS contains a backup battery and a surge protector. The server's power cable plugs into the UPS and runs off battery power when the building power goes out.

More sophisticated UPS units include *automatic voltage regulation (AVR)*. AVR guarantees a constant level of power to the server in the event of fluctuations in delivered power, including short drops in power levels, or dips or surges that might occur before a total power outage.

One parameter to look at is the electrical load capacity, measured in volt-amperes (VA). For a Mac mini or iMac, 350VA should do it. For a Mac Pro or Xserve, you can start at about 800VA. Extra drives and expansion cards draw more power and require a higher load capacity.

At the lower end, UPS boxes start at about $100 for a single outlet without AVR and can cost several hundred dollars for multiple outlets. The manufacturer will tell you how long the battery will run the computer, depending on the load capacity: typically an hour or two at these price points, up to eight hours for units costing over $1,000.

A highly respected supplier of solid UPS systems is APC (www.apcc.com), which offers a range of home, office, and enterprise-class products. Tripp Lite (www.tripplite.com) and Belkin (www.belkin.com) are also known for quality UPS systems.

Data backup for your server

Although you can use your server to back up your client Macs, you should also have your server data automatically backed up. For a smaller network, you can use a network attached storage (NAS) device, such as Apple's Time Capsule, along with backup software, such as Apple's Time Machine or Dantz's Retrospect. In larger networks, back up your Mac server to tape or a SAN system with Windows-based software such as Bakbone's Bakbone system or Symantec's Backup Exec. NAS and SAN are described earlier in this chapter.

Ethernet switches and cables

In today's wireless world, you still need some wires for your network infrastructure. Even if all your users' computers are wireless, the server should have an Ethernet interface to the Internet connection for a more reliable and faster connection.

If you're going to go wired to your client computers, you'll need an Ethernet switched hub (or an Ethernet switch), which is a box to which everything on a wired network plugs into.

The uncommon *plain* (unswitched) Ethernet hubs aren't as fast as Ethernet switched hubs. If the device is stand-alone, make sure that it's a switch.

You can often find Ethernet switches built into other devices, such as wireless access points, Internet routers, DSL or cable modems, firewalls, and virtual private network gateways. Apple's AirPort Extreme and Time Capsule have Gigabit Ethernet switches in them.

Ethernet speeds

Ethernet switches come in different performance levels. You want one that supports *gigabit Ethernet* (or *1000BASE-T,* a gigabit-per-second maximum), which is the top bandwidth supported in all Mac models and many PCs. Gigabit Ethernet switches are sometimes referred to as *10/100/1000 switches* because they're backward-compatible with older, slower 100 megabits per second (Mbps) and 10 Mbps Ethernet hardware. If a switch is 10/100, it's only 100 Mbps — one-tenth the bandwidth of Gigabit Ethernet.

Even faster are *10 Gigabit Ethernet* switches. You can take advantage of a 10 Gigabit switch with a 10 Gigabit Ethernet card installed in a Mac Pro.

Ethernet ports

Ethernet switches have anywhere from 4 to 24 ports (see Figure 2-8, which shows an 8-port Gigabit switch). You can also connect (daisy-chain) switches together if you outgrow your current switch.

Figure 2-8: An 8-port Gigabit Ethernet switch.

You need one of your switch's ports for your Internet connection (or for a connection to a bigger network). You need another port to plug in the server, another one for a networked printer (if it has an Ethernet port), and another port to plug in to a wireless access point if you're providing Wi-Fi connection to your network. The rest of the ports are for your client computers. Some switches also have USB ports to share a USB printer.

If you're using the server as an Internet gateway, the Internet connection would plug directly into the server, and the server's second Ethernet port would connect to the switch.

Cables

Ethernet cable comes in several grades. At minimum, you want Category 5e (commonly known as *Cat 5e*) cable for Gigabit Ethernet. Cat 5e cables can be used to a maximum length of about 100 meters from the switch to the computer, though interference can shorten this.

A higher grade of Ethernet cable — Cat 6 — is more immune to noise and might be considered a minimum grade for reliable use on a gigabit network. Cat 6 can also handle 10 Gigabit Ethernet (10GBASE-T), which some network devices support.

For big networks, you can connect a server to a Gigabit Ethernet switch with optical cable known as 1000Base-SX Ethernet. For this, you need a switch with an optical port and a Mac Pro or Xserve with a 1000Base-SX Ethernet card in it. Optical Ethernet offers higher performance and longer distribution due to the near-total absence of electromagnetic interference.

Wireless equipment

With your server safely connected to the Internet through Ethernet, you can let your client computers and even printers go wireless. Apple's AirPort Extreme and Time Capsule are wireless access points that contain small built-in Ethernet switches. Each supports up to 50 wireless client computers. Time Capsule also contains a hard drive. The clients on a small network can back up to the Time Capsule by using the Time Capsule software that comes with Mac OS X 10.5 and later.

You don't need Apple's wireless hardware, however, because plenty of available options work. If you get a third-party wireless access point, make sure that it supports the 802.11a/b/g/n standard. (The letters signify different revisions to the wireless 802.11 standard; *g* is faster than *a* and *b,* and *n* is the fastest.) All Macs built today, as well as many PCs, support 802.11n. Older Macs and PCs may support only 802.11g or 802.11b.

Chapter 3

The Quick and Easy Installation and Setup

*T*he chapter is designed to help you get up and running in a hurry. It provides the simplest installation scenario, assumes that you've done your planning, and takes you through creating user accounts and starting a few services, soup to nuts. Think of this chapter as a condensed version of *Mountain Lion Server For Dummies.*

The quick and easy installation described here assumes that you are updating OS X 10.6.8 or 10.7 to Mountain Lion, or that you already have the user version of Mountain Lion installed. For a clean install, or for various other installation scenarios, see Chapter 4.

Installing the Software

Installing Mountain Lion Server involves installing the base operating system and then adding the server bits.

Upgrading the base OS to Mountain Lion

This section describes upgrading Snow Leopard (10.6.8) or Lion to Mountain Lion. If you already have Mountain Lion installed on your Mac, skip this section and go to the next.

If you aren't doing a clean install, you are installing from a Recovery Partition or from a Recovery Drive. In this case, you will see additional steps than those presented here. A clean install is described in Chapter 4.

You start by going to the App Store and purchasing Mountain Lion and downloading it to your hard drive. When the download finishes, the installer will launch. At this point, quitting the installer lets you copy it to a DVD or other drive for reuse. By doing this, you won't have to download it again should you have to reinstall OS X.

To upgrade your Mac's OS X to Mountain Lion, follow these steps:

1. **Launch the installer (called Install OS X Mountain Lion) to launch the OS X Mountain Lion screen shown in Figure 3-1. Click Continue.**

Figure 3-1:
Starting
Mountain
Lion.

2. **Agree to the license agreement, select a drive on which to install the OS, and then click Install.**

   Time for a coffee break. Software installation commences and you see a progress bar. When installation is complete, the installer restarts to a Welcome screen.

3. **Click Continue.**

4. **On the Apple ID screen, type an Apple ID and password and then click Continue.**

It's best to use an Apple ID for your organization, not the one you use to buy music on iTunes. If you don't have an Apple ID for your organization, click the Create a Free Apple ID button in the lower left and follow the instructions. Or you can skip the Apple ID page altogether by clicking Skip.

5. **In the Terms and Conditions window, click Agree.**

6. **In the Set Up iCloud window, make sure that the Set up iCloud on This Mac check box is not selected and then click Continue.**

7. **In the Thank You window, click Start Using Your Mac.**

The Mountain Lion desktop appears.

The pre-server-install check

Now that you've installed Mountain Lion, you should do the following before you install the server components:

- **Check for the latest updates to Mountain Lion.** Go to the Apple menu, select Software Update, and install any updates found.

- **Decide whether or not you are serving to the Internet.** If you want to host a website, an e-mail server, or another service that Internet users will access, make sure that you own a domain name. (You can purchase one from an Internet registry such as Network Solutions or Godaddy.com.)

- **Check that you have a static IP address set for the Mac.** A static IP address is less important for home use but is recommended for other situations. Open System Preferences from the Apple menu and select Network. Click the main network interface. In the Configure IPv4 menu, select Manually.

- **Turn off Sleep.** Servers shouldn't sleep. Choose System Preferences➪ Energy Saver and then set Computer Sleep to Never. You can set Display Sleep to some finite time.

Downloading and installing server components

With Mountain Lion installed and the items in the preceding section taken care of, you can now proceed to downloading, installing, and configuring the server components. The configuration part is highly automated. The most important thing you do here is decide on a host name. Follow these steps to install and configure the server components:

1. **From the Dock, launch App Store.**

2. **In the search field, search for OS X Server. When you find it, purchase it to begin the download.**

3. **When the download is complete, go to the Applications folder and launch the Server application.**

   What launches is called Server, but is actually the Server Setup Assistant, as shown in Figure 3-2.

Figure 3-2:
The Server
Setup
Assistant.

4. **In the Set Up Your Server window, click Continue.**

   Alternatively, click the Getting Started button to bring up a Help file.

5. **Agree to the license agreement and then type your Mac's administrator password. Click Continue.**

6. **In the Apple Push Notifications window, type an Apple ID and password and then click Continue.**

   The ID you enter should be an Apple ID used for your organization, not your personal Apple ID that you use for iTunes.

   Clicking Continue signs you up for the Apple push notification service and a push notification certificate is created for your server. Apple push notification service is used for Profile Manager and other services for Macs and iOS devices.

If your Mac doesn't have a previous version of OS X Server installed or cannot find any DNS information, the Host screen (shown in Figure 3-3) appears. It is important to get the information here right the first time because this information can be difficult to change later.

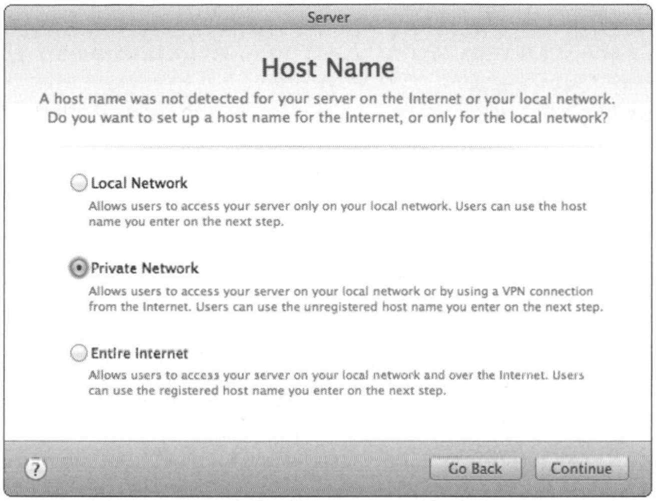

Figure 3-3:
The Host
Name
window.

7. **Select one of the three radio buttons in the Host Name window and then click Continue.**

   Choose Private Network if you are *not* serving to the Internet (such as web or e-mail). Choose Entire Internet if you have a registered Internet host name (`www.example.com`) for this server and intend to provide services to Internet users.

   The other choice, Local Network, is almost the same as Private Network, but less flexible. The Private Network selection gives you the option to remotely access the network from the Internet by using a secure virtual private network (VPN) connection, should you choose to, but doesn't require you to turn on VPN.

8. **In the Computer Name field of the Connecting to Your Mac window, change the entry from the default personal name (such as "Bob's Mac") to something more recognizable as a server (such as "Mac Server").**

   Mac and PC users will use this computer name to connect to the server for file sharing and screen sharing, if enabled. Mac users on the network will see this name in the Finder sidebar.

9. **In the Host Name field, shown in Figure 3-4, type a host name that reflects the choice you made in Step 7 or have previously configured.**

   If the Mac has a previous version of OS X Server on it, the Server Setup Assistant may locate your server's host name from a DNS server.

   When the Server Setup Assistant does not find a DNS server with information for your server on the network or the Internet, it will set up DNS services on your server based on the information you entered in the Host Name and Connecting to Your Mac windows. If you decide to change the host name later, you will also have to edit the DNS records on the Mac. Getting this information right at this point will save you a lot of trouble later.

Server

Connecting to Your Mac

Users will connect to your server by using the server's name or address.

Computer Name: | Server Mac |

Enter a name that users will see in Finder or when connecting over a network.

Host Name: | server.acmecrumpets.private |

Network Address: 192.168.206... on Ethernet | Edit... |

(?)   Go Back   Continue

Figure 3-4:
The Connecting to Your Mac screen.

---

10. **(Optional) Click the Edit button to change the server's IP address or assign a static address; click Apply when done.**

11. **Check your settings in the Connecting to Your Mac window and then click Continue.**

    The Configuring Services window appears, displaying progress messages that tell you what the Server Setup Assistant is doing. Here it tests the settings you provided, setting up DNS if needed, obtains an Apple push notification certificate, and performs other tasks.

12. **In the Congratulations window, click the Finish button.**

    The Server app launches, shown in Figure 3-5, and opens to the Overview tab of the Server pane. At the bottom of the window is an area called Next Steps, which describes some of the things you can do next.

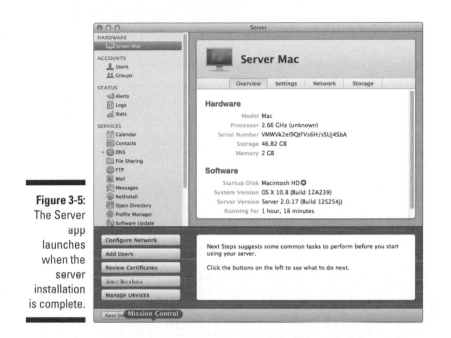

Figure 3-5:
The Server app launches when the server installation is complete.

Configuring Services and Accounts

After you install the server software and the Mac reboots, you can create group accounts and turn on services with the Server app.

The Next Steps area, shown in Figure 3-5, is a good place to start. (If you don't see this area, click the Next Steps button to expand the window.) It provides suggestions based on your configuration and what the Server Setup Assistant did. The links in the Next Steps text take you to the help system or to different panes in the Server app.

The buttons in the Next Steps area are arranged in the order in which you should proceed with configuring your server. For instance, you should check your network DNS settings before doing anything else, and you should decide whether you want local or network user accounts before setting up services.

Checking network settings

If you need to change or correct the basic settings of your server — the host name or IP address — do so now, before you set up anything else. Click the Configure Network button in the Next Steps area, as shown in Figure 3-6. You see your Mac's host name and IP address, and find out whether the server is visible to the Internet or just to your local network.

Figure 3-6:
The Configure Network button of Next Steps tells you the host name and IP address.

You can change your IP address in the Network pane of System Preferences. To change your host name, do the following:

1. **At the top of the Server app's sidebar, click your server's computer name.**

2. **Click the Network tab.**

3. **Click the Edit button next to your current host name (see Figure 3-7).**

   A Change Host Name assistant appears and presents some of the same choices you had when clicking through the Server Setup Assistant.

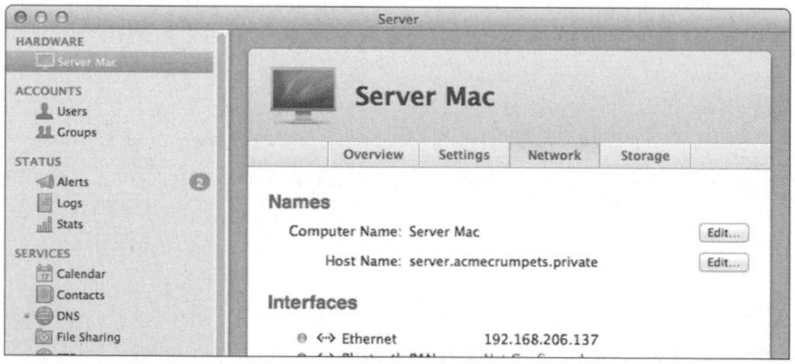

Figure 3-7:
The Network tab of the server pane in the Server app.

4. **Choose whether you want a host name for use on the Internet or only for your local (or private) network, and then click Continue.**

   If your host name is not serving the Internet, the Host Name for Private Network choice is better than Host Name for Local Network. The former gives you the option of logging in remotely over a virtual private network.

5. **In the Connect to Your Mac dialog, edit your host name.**

   You can also change the Ethernet address here. (For more on about Ethernet addresses, see Chapter 4.)

6. **Click Continue, and follow the directions in the rest of the dialogs.**

Whenever you change the host name or IP address, you'll need to change the DNS settings on servers to reflect the new IP address or host name (assuming that you've already set up DNS). If you're hosting DNS on your Mac, the Change Host Name Assistant will make the required DNS changes.

You should also check whether you actually need DNS running on the Mac. If the Server Setup Assistant did not find a DNS server containing your server's information, it created DNS records and turned on DNS service. But if you typed the wrong host name when setting up the Mac and are now correcting it (or are planning to host DNS elsewhere), you don't need DNS running on your Mac and can easily turn off Mountain Lion Server's DNS service. Select DNS from the Server app's sidebar and click the big switch to the Off position.

Chapter 4 has more on DNS and also describes other things to consider about your network, such as routers and wireless devices.

Considering Open Directory

When you are sure that your network settings are okay, it's time to consider where you will store your user accounts. Click the Add Users button of the Next Steps area, to see whether your server is hosting local user accounts or if Open Directory is enabled, as shown in Figure 3-8.

Figure 3-8:
The Add Users pane of Next Steps tells you if you are running Open Directory.

A *directory* is a list of user accounts. A *local directory* is stored on a single Mac; a *network directory* is available to multiple servers. The network directory that comes with OS X Server is called Open Directory. You need to run Open Directory if you have other servers on the network or if you want to use the Profile Manager feature (described in Chapter 16). Network directories have other advantages as well, as described in Chapter 5.

For a home or small-office network, running OS X Server with local user accounts works just fine, and you don't need to use Open Directory. But if you ever want to use Profile Manager, you will have to create all the user accounts again after you start Open Directory.

If you want to turn on Open Directory (also known as creating an Open Directory master), select Open Directory in the sidebar and click the big switch to the On position. This launches a setup assistant, which asks you if you want to create a new Open Directory domain or join an existing one. If this is your only Mac server, you want to create a new domain.

There is much more to say about network directories. In addition to running Open Directory, OS X Server can bind to network directories hosted on other servers. See Chapters 4 and 5 for more on these topics.

Creating users and groups

After you decide whether or not you're going to use Open Directory, you can start adding user and group accounts to the server. Here's how:

1. **In the sidebar of the Server app, click Users.**

2. **Click the Add (+) button to display the New User dialog shown in Figure 3-9.**

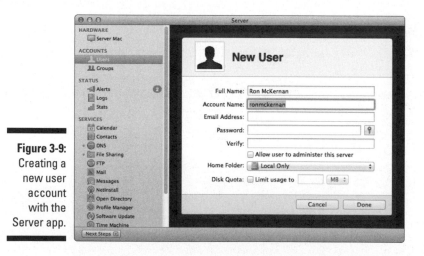

Figure 3-9: Creating a new user account with the Server app.

3. **Type a user's name and then press the Tab key to automatically gener-ate a short name in the Account Name field.**

   A *short name* is the account name used by the system. By default, the short name is the first and last names of the user, without a space and all lowercase.

4. **Type a password for the user.**

5. **(Optional) Type the user's e-mail address.**

6. **(Optional) Select Allow User to Administer This Server to grant administrator privileges to this user.**

7. **Click the Done button.**

You can also create group accounts, which contain a list of users. You can assign access to certain services to groups rather than to individual users. For instance, if you want only the people in your art department to have access to a shared folder, create a group called Art Department and add those individuals to the group.

To create a group, select Groups from the sidebar of the Server app and then click the Add (+) button. Give a name to the group and click Done. Now click User in the sidebar, double-click a user account, type the name of the group in the Groups field, and click Done. Do this for each user you want to add.

Turning on file sharing

If you click the Start Services button in the Next Steps area, it will tell you which services you have running. At this point in our example, only DNS is running. Now you can start turning on user services, such as file sharing.

Setting up file sharing falls into three basics tasks: Turn on the service, identify a folder to share, and give users permission to read or write. A shared folder is called a *share point*. You can quickly set up file sharing, using the default settings. Follow these steps:

1. **In the Server app's sidebar, select File Sharing and then select the Share Points tab, which is shown in Figure 3-10.**

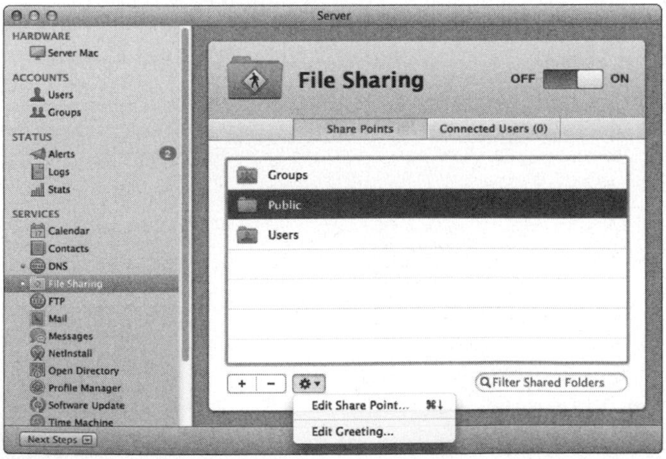

Figure 3-10: Creating share points in the File Sharing pane.

2. **Click the big switch to the On position.**

3. **Double-click one of the folders listed in the pane (Groups, Public, or Users) or navigate to another folder to share by clicking the Add (+) button.**

   A pane displays settings for the folder, as shown in Figure 3-11.

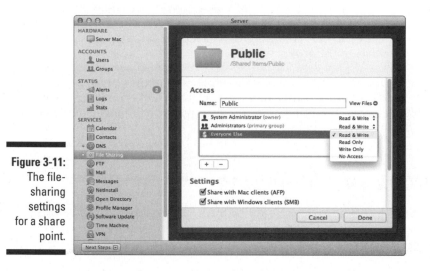

Figure 3-11:
The file-sharing settings for a share point.

4. **Use the field in the middle of the pane to set access permissions for the folder.**

   To enable everyone on the network to both read and write to the folder, click the double arrows next to Everyone Else and choose Read and Write.

   To give a group or user access to the folder, click the Add (+) button and type a group or user name. Then assign the group or user an access permission from the double arrow menu at the right. The options are Read & Write, Read Only, Write Only, or No Access. (Write Only access means the user or group can drop files into the folder but can't open it.)

5. **When you are finished, click the Done button.**

See Chapter 7 for more information about file sharing. Chapter 8 describes the many different options for limiting access with permissions, including the use of access control lists (ACLs).

Backing up Macs to the server

Thumbing through this book, you see lots of services that you have the option of setting up for your users. But I have one service that you should consider part of the quick-and-easy setup described in this chapter: Time Machine back-ups of your client Macs to the server. Time Machine is the backup software that comes with all Macs. Windows PCs can also back up to the server, but you need to purchase software for those Windows machines (some are described in Chapter 19.). You can also back up the server data itself.

You can back up to any drive attached to the server Mac, such as the boot drive, a second internal drive or partition, or an external drive. Use the boot drive only if it is a very large drive and you have a small network, such as at home or in a small office.

First, you must enable file sharing, which is described in the preceding section. Then you enable the Time Machine backup in the Server app as follows:

1. **In the sidebar, select Time Machine**

2. **Click the big switch to the On position.**

   A dialog appears.

3. **Select a hard drive to use for backup and then click Use for Backup.**

Now, on a user's Mac, go to the Apple menu, select System Preferences, and click the Time Machine icon. The window in Figure 3-12 appears. Click the big switch to the On position to bring up a list of drives. Select the drive on the Mac server from the list and click the Use Disk button.

Figure 3-12:
The Time Machine pane of System Preferences.

Oddly enough, you use this same method to back up the *server's* data to the backup drive you designated in Step 3. This time, open System Preferences on the server Mac and use the Time Machine pane there to select the server backup drive.

Finally, you can use Mountain Lion Server's Profile Manager to push these settings and many others to your client Macs. This process is described in Chapter 16.

Chapter 4

Advanced Installation and Setup

C hapter 3 shows you a simple scenario for getting Mountain Lion Server up and running quickly. In this chapter, I delve deeper into server installation and setup, as well as server upgrades. This chapter looks more carefully at preparation, which is important in more-complex installations. You also find more-detailed information about the server and networks.

This chapter looks at the three phases of creating a functional server: things to do to get ready, the actual installation process and its options and variations, and the initial setup tasks that you perform afterward.

A Road Map to Installation and Setup

A little planning and knowledge of options and pitfalls go a long way to a smooth installation of Mountain Lion Server. This chapter is organized along the main decision points and tasks for installing and setting up Mountain Lion Server:

1. **Collect data about the server Mac and your network.**

2. **Decide whether you want a new installation on an erased disk drive (commonly known as a *clean install*) or an upgrade.**

3. **Decide the role of the server in your network.**

   Your choices include local user accounts or shared network accounts; working alone or with other servers. A stand-alone server could have access to the Internet by remote secure access (VPN) only or could be visible to the Internet.

4. **Run the installer and, if necessary, download the server components after installing the client.**

5. **After installation, perform basic postinstallation configuration tasks, such as create a shared directory, add users, or further configure DNS.**

6. **Check DNS and Open Directory, if necessary.**

The rest of this chapter looks at the details of this road map. I start with the common point of departure for all installation and configuration routes: collecting network information.

Collecting Info Before You Install

It's a good idea to gather some information about your server Mac and your network before you start installation and configuration. By having the info in front of you, you may speed up your setup time and you'll have a record of how you set up the server. And the process of gathering the information will help you understand the type of setup you need. This section describes information you may collect and explains some of the terms that the installer software uses.

Hardware ID numbers

Two hardware identification numbers are useful to record if your network contains multiple servers: the MAC address and the serial number. If you're using remote management software for multiple clients and servers, this information may help you configure that software.

The *MAC address* doesn't refer to the Macintosh; it's the acronym for *Media Access Control.* The MAC address is a unique hardware identifier that specifies each Ethernet port or wireless network card. In general, if a Mac has two Ethernet ports, it will have two MAC addresses. (The exception is Xserve, which has a built-in Ethernet port that has *two* MAC addresses — one used by the server's processor and the other used by Xserve's special Lights Out Management processor.) The MAC address is a series of two-digit characters separated by colons, like this: 00:23:32:b5:d0: 43. Apple also refers to the MAC address as the *Ethernet ID*.

The *serial number* is a unique number that identifies every Mac. A Mac can have only one serial number. All Macs list the serial number somewhere on the outside case. Many Macs also include the MAC address/Ethernet ID. The Mac Pro's serial number is written on the back side on a label located under the video ports, for example. Xserve has a pullout tab in the middle of the rear panel.

If you can't get to the serial number because the Mac is in a difficult-to-reach location, try this old OS X trick, which been around for many years (although even some diehard Mac fans don't know about it): Choose Apple menu⇨About This Mac. Click the OS X version number twice, and it changes to the hardware serial number, as shown in Figure 4-1.

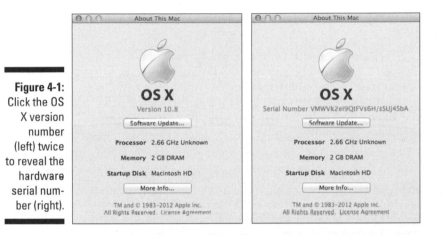

Figure 4-1: Click the OS X version number (left) twice to reveal the hardware serial number (right).

To get the MAC address/Ethernet ID in Mac OS X 10.6 and earlier, click the More Info button to launch System Profiler. Remember that each Ethernet port and AirPort card has a MAC address, so be sure that you identify the Ethernet ports that you'll use for your network. Click Network in the left pane, and the MAC address will be listed under Ethernet in the right column.

Network ID numbers

During the installation and setup process, you may be asked for variety of numbers that identify your network and the server's role in it. You may need the following information for each network port you'll use, though some of these numbers may be supplied automatically if your server is connected to the network during installation:

✔ **IP address:** If you're upgrading a Snow Leopard or later client to Mountain Lion Server, set the IP address before starting the installation. Every network port (including wireless) on a computer on the network has an IP address that identifies it to other computers. For client computers, the IP address is usually set automatically via DHCP (Dynamic Host Configuration Protocol). But servers need an IP address that never changes in order for the network to find them, so it's best to manually assign an IP address to the server, called *static* IP addressing. On a Mac, you set the IP address in the Network pane of System Preferences.

The IP address is four numbers separated by periods, such as `169.254.13.3`. Each number can be from 0 through 255. See the "Rules for IP addressing" sidebar for more details on selecting IP addresses.

✔ **Subnet mask:** This number appears in the form of four numbers, which are often 255 or 0, separated by periods, such as `255.255.0.0`. Use a different subnet mask for each Ethernet port. The computers connected to a server's Ethernet port are on a subnet. The subnet mask limits the size of the subnet. The subnet mask can also be set automatically via DHCP.

✔ **Router:** You may need the IP address of the hardware that moves data between local subnetworks and the Internet, such as an AirPort base station. The router might also have a DHCP server that automatically assigns IP addresses to your computers. If you're setting up services that will be visible to the Internet, you may need to configure port forwarding on the router.

If you have your Mac connected to the network during installation, the installer software may detect the router and provide its IP address.

✔ **DNS servers:** Before setting up your Mac server, you need to know if you have domain name services (DNS) servers on your network or provided by your Internet service provider or domain name registrar. Otherwise, you can disrupt your server and parts of the rest of the network. You may need to record the IP addresses of DNS servers, and you should record any domain names used. The domain name comes in the form of `mycompany.com` or `myserver.mycompany.com`. The DNS server translates domain names to IP addresses. If you configure this manually, you'll obtain the IP address of the DNS from your Internet service provider. This setting is one of the more important ones for getting your server to work properly.

✔ **Computer name:** The installation procedure will create a computer name, which you can change. This is a uniquely Macintosh network name that identifies Macs to other Macs, as well as Windows running Bonjour for Windows. On Mac clients, this name will appear in the Finder sidebars and in various dialogs. You can also set the computer name in the Sharing pane of System Preferences.

A Mac computer name can be 63 characters or less. Use any roman characters except for the equal sign (=), the colon (:), and the at sign (@). Spaces are okay. Users find it helpful if the name has some significance, such as *Computer Lab Server*. A computer name translates into a *local network name,* such as `computer-lab-server.local`. The local network name is used only on the local subnet, in addition to a DNS name of the server. (The Mac computer name is not used in DNS settings.)

Rules for IP addressing

When you set an IP address manually (known as *static* addressing), you need to follow some rules. An IP address takes the form of four numbers from 0 through 255, separated by periods, such as 169.254.13.3.

The total IP address range is 000.000.000.000 through 255.255.255.255, but within that are some ranges that are used for specific purposes, such as public and private IP addresses. A *public* IP address is one that the entire Internet can see. Every computer on the planet that the Internet can directly see has a unique public IP address. Usually, your Internet service provider provides a public IP address, either manually or automatically.

A *private* IP address is one that the Internet can't see because the computer is connected to the Internet through an Internet gateway or router. The Internet sees only the IP address of the gateway. The computers on this type of local network use private IP addresses from one of several private address ranges. You might give your server a private IP address if another server or hardware box is acting as the Internet gateway. (You can also have a private IP address assigned automatically through DHCP.)

There are several private address ranges. One range starts with 169.254:169.254.0.0–169.254.254.255. **Note:** For this range, the last number can be 255, but the number before it can only go as high as 254. The other two private ranges are 10.0.0.1 through 10.255.255.254 and 192.168.0.1 through 192.168.0.254.

If you manually configure the IP addresses of your Mac for a local network, you can use IP addresses from any of these ranges as long as all the Macs on the network are in the same range. They also need the same subnet mask, and *no* two computers on your *subnet* can have the same IP address. A *subnet* consists of all the computers connected to one Ethernet port on the server.

Planning Installation Scenarios: Clean Install, Update, and Server Migration

You can install OS X Server in several ways, depending on whether you want a fresh start or want to keep data or settings from a previous version of OS X Server:

✔ **Perform a clean install.** This is where you install a fresh copy of the operating system on a freshly formatted, blank hard drive. Conventional wisdom is that a clean install gets rid of the flotsam and jetsam of old configuration files and settings that accumulate over the years and slow things down.

With a clean install, you start the Mac with one drive while erasing and installing on a second drive. The most convenient way to do this is to create a *recovery drive* on a USB flash drive by using Apple's

Recovery Disk Assistant. I describe this process later in the chapter, in "Performing a Clean Install of the Base OS with a Recovery Disk."

✔ **Upgrade from a previously installed OS X client.** This is the quick and easy option described in Chapter 3. You upgrade Mac OS X 10.6.8 or later to the latest version of Mountain Lion, and then install the server components.

✔ **Upgrade from a previous version of OS X Server.** In this scenario, you have things you want to preserve: user data, an Open Directory database, or websites. But because OS X Server changes with each major new version, the older the version of OS X Server, the less successful the upgrade.

✔ **Migrate from a previous version of the server.** As with the server upgrade scenario, you want to retain accumulated user data but you also want a clean install. Use Apple's Migration Assistant to move an older server version to a clean install. This scenario can be trickier than a simple server upgrade but gives you the spring-cleaning features of a clean install.

Before I get into the particulars of installation, however, here is a section on how to erase a drive.

Erasing, Partitioning, and Creating a RAID by Using Disk Utility

If you're planning to erase a hard drive for a clean install or a migration, you can use Apple's Disk Utility either before the installation process or during it. Disk Utility gives you three formatting options:

✔ Use a simple erase.

✔ Divide a drive into multiple partitions.

✔ Use multiple drives together in a software RAID (redundant array of independent disks).

You can use Apple's Disk Utility to do this formatting at the beginning of the installation process while your system is booted from a recovery drive.

Erasing or partitioning a drive

Erasing a drive in Disk Utility is similar to partitioning. Both destroy any existing data on the drive. Erasing a volume simply wipes the data off it. *Partitioning* a hard drive divides it into multiple volumes. Each volume appears as a separate hard drive to the user. You can use one partition as the startup disk containing OS X Server (the operating system and services) and use another, larger partition to store the user data. If something goes wrong with the user data volume, the server can keep functioning — or at least it won't have to be re-created. This scheme also prevents the boot partition from running out of disk space because of growing user data.

Having multiple drives gives you better system performance than multiple partitions. But if have a 500GB or larger startup disk and plan on storing user data elsewhere, you'll have a lot of wasted space if you don't partition.

One essential thing to remember about partitioning: You must use the default GUID Partition Table, not the Apple Partition Table. If you use the latter, you won't be able to boot from the drive.

You also need to choose a format. For a startup disk, you can use two formats:

- ✔ **Mac OS Extended (Journaled):** Most people use this standard format.
- ✔ **Mac OS Extended (Case-sensitive, Journaled):** Some people who are hosting static websites use this format because it improves performance, with a better mapping between URLs and files.

For drives that you won't use as startup disks, you can use the nonjournaled versions of these two formats, though there isn't a compelling reason to do so.

To partition a drive, either before or during installation, do the following:

1. **Launch Disk Utility (either from a recovery drive or from `/Applications/Utilities`).**

2. **Click the hard drive you want to partition in the left pane.**

   The drive is the leftmost item; a partition on the drive is indented.

3. **Click the Partition tab, which is shown in Figure 4-2.**

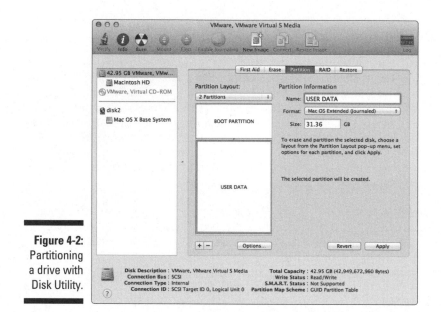

Figure 4-2:
Partitioning
a drive with
Disk Utility.

4. **In the Volume Scheme pop-up menu, choose the number of partitions you want to create.**

   The space below the pop-up menu has a number of boxes representing the partition sizes.

5. **Drag the bar that separates the boxes to resize them to the partition size (in gigabytes) that you want for each.**

6. **Click a box to select it and then type a name for it in the Name field for each partition.**

   Figure 4-2 shows that I've used the names Boot Partition and User Data.

7. **In the Format pop-up menu, make sure that Mac OS Extended (Journaled) is selected.**

8. **At the bottom of the window, check that GUID Partition Table is selected for Partition Map Scheme.**

   If not, click the Options button and select GUID Partition Table.

9. **Click Apply.**

Erasing is simpler. Select the drive or volume from the column on the left and click the Erase tab. Choose a format from the Format pop-up menu and then click the Erase button.

Creating a software RAID

For Macs with multiple hard drives, Disk Utility can set up multiple drives to work together as a software RAID to increase performance, protect data, or both. Software RAID takes some of the computer's processing power, and it isn't as secure as a hardware RAID controller system. For example, a system crash could affect a software RAID but would not affect a hardware RAID. However, a software RAID is far less expensive than a hardware RAID and does provide the benefits of data redundancy. You can also use external FireWire drives in a RAID set.

Here's how to create a software RAID:

1. **Launch Disk Utility.**

2. **Select one of your drives and then click the RAID tab.**

3. **Drag and drop drives from the left pane to the RAID pane.**

   Use drives — *not* volumes — from the left pane. Partitions/volumes are listed under the drive name and are indented.

4. **Type a name for the RAID set.**

5. **In the Format pop-up menu, make sure that Mac OS Extended (Journaled) is selected.**

6. **From the RAID Type pop-up menu, choose Mirrored, Striped, or Concatenated:**

   - *Mirrored (or RAID 1)* writes the same data to two drives simultaneously. If one drive fails, the other drive still contains all the data.

   - *Striped (or RAID 0)* makes multiple hard drives of the same size work together as a single, fast, large hard drive. Data from a file is fragmented and written on multiple drives. When accessing the file, the system reads the fragments from all the drives simultaneously. If one of the drives in a RAID 0 fails, all the data is lost.

   - *Concatenated* combines multiple hard drives into one without the speed benefits of striping, but you can combine drives of different sizes. Concatenating gets really interesting when used with another RAID. For example, concatenate two FireWire drives that add up to the capacity of the internal drive and then mirror the internal drive with the concatenated FireWire drives. You can also use it to create a RAID 1+0. For example, if you have four drives, concatenate a 2-drive mirror array with a 2-drive striped array. This gives you the performance of striping with the redundancy of mirroring.

7. **Click the Create button.**

   Disk Utility can take several hours to create the software RAID set.

The Mountain Lion installer won't create a recovery partition on a RAID set.

Performing a Clean Install of the Base OS with a Recovery Disk

The easiest way to do a clean install of the Base Mountain Lion OS is to create a recovery disk on a USB flash drive. (Any USB drive will work, as long at it is 1GB or larger.) You then boot from the recovery disk to erase the destination drive and install Mountain Lion on it. The recovery disk doesn't include the entire operating system but has just enough to boot the Mac and download the rest.

Creating a recovery disk

You create a bootable recovery disk, using Apple's Recovery Disk Assistant (a free download at http://support.apple.com). Here's how:

1. **Plug a 1GB or larger USB flash drive into your server Mac's USB port.**

2. **Download and launch Recovery Disk Assistant.**

3. **Agree to the license agreement.**

4. **Select a USB drive and click Continue, as shown in Figure 4-3.**

5. **Type your password when prompted and then click OK.**

   Recovery Disk Assistant creates the recovery boot disk on your flash drive.

The next section describes doing a clean install by using the USB recovery disk.

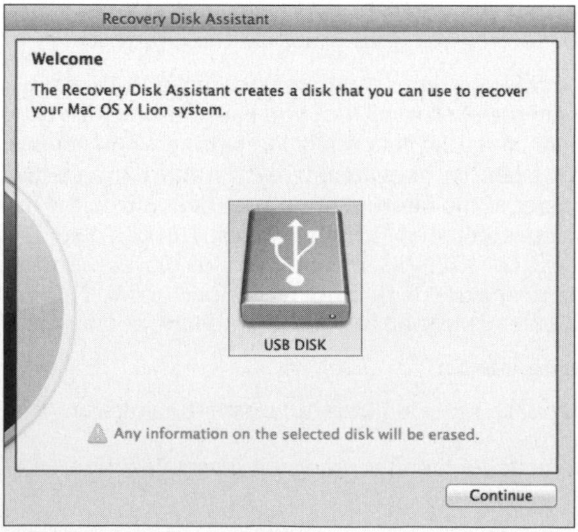

Figure 4-3: Creating a recovery disk with the Recovery Disk Assistant.

Performing a clean install of the base OS

You can do a clean install, using the recovery disk you created in the preceding section. Make sure that the Mac is connected to the Internet (Ethernet preferred), because the recovery disk will download the Mountain Lion operating system. In addition to booting from the USB flash drive, a clean install has a few more steps than that upgrade install described in Chapter 3.

1. **Insert the USB recovery disk. Hold down the Option key while restarting, select the recovery disk, and then reboot.**

   The OS X Utilities window (shown in Figure 4-4) is displayed when the Mac boots up.

Figure 4-4:
OS X
Utilities
appears
when
booting from
a recovery
disk.

2. **Double-click the Disk Utility icon.**

3. **Select the hard drive you want to format, and perform one of the set of steps described in the "Erasing, Partitioning, and Creating a RAID by Using Disk Utility" section, earlier in the chapter.**

4. **Quit Disk Utility to return to the OS X Utilities window shown in Figure 4-4.**

5. **Select Reinstall OS X and click Continue.**

6. **Click Continue in the OS X Mountain Lion screen.**

7. **Agree to the license agreement, select a drive on which to install the OS, and then click Install.**

Time for a coffee break. The assistant will download the OS, enabling you to purchase it if necessary. When installation is complete, the installer displays *Installation Successful* and restarts. A Welcome screen appears after restart.

8. **Click through the Welcome and Keyboard screens.**

   The Transfer Information to This Mac screen is displayed, as shown in Figure 4-5.

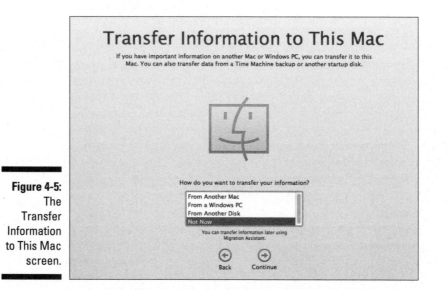

9. **Choose an option and then click Continue.**

   Choose Not Now if you're simply installing the software. If you're importing settings, data, or applications, choose From Another Mac, From Another Disk, or From a PC, depending on which is applicable. You'll then be instructed to select items to move to the Mac.

10. **In the Enable Location Services window, make sure that you *deselect* the Enable Location Services for This Mac check box. Click Continue.**

    This option is a nice feature for notebooks, but it's not a good idea to enable people to find the physical location of a server.

11. **In the Apple ID screen, type an Apple ID and password and then click Continue.**

    It's best to use an Apple ID for your organization, not the one you use to buy music on iTunes. If you don't have an Apple ID for your organization, click the Create a Free Apple ID button in the lower left and follow the instructions. Or you can skip the Apple ID page altogether by clicking Skip.

12. **In the Terms and Conditions window, click Agree.**

13. In the Set up iCloud window, make sure that the Set Up iCloud on This Mac check box is not selected and then click Continue.

14. In the Create Your Computer Account window, type a name and password for what will be the administrator account (see Figure 4-6).

This account is the administrator for the Mac, the main user.

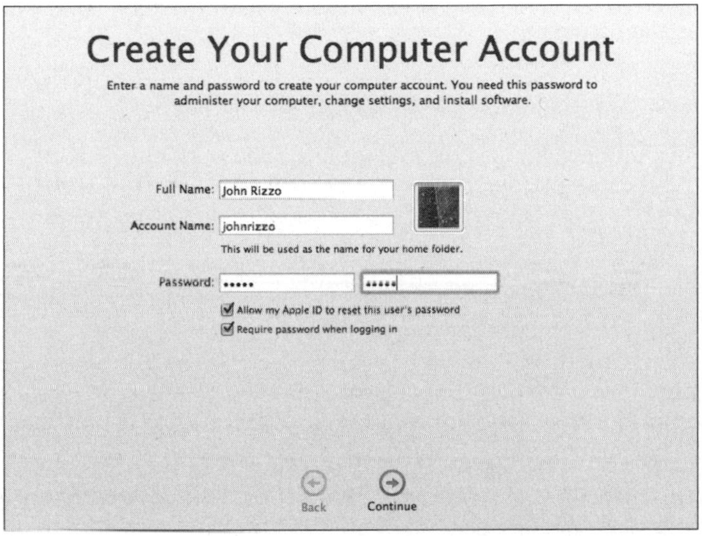

Create Your Computer Account

Enter a name and password to create your computer account. You need this password to administer your computer, change settings, and install software.

Full Name: John Rizzo

Account Name: johnrizzo

This will be used as the name for your home folder.

Password: ••••• •••••

☑ Allow my Apple ID to reset this user's password
☑ Require password when logging in

Back   Continue

Figure 4-6:
Creating the administrator account.

15. Click through the Time Zone and Register windows. In the Thank You window, click Start Using Your Mac.

You can now download, install, and configure the server components, a process described in the next section.

Downloading and installing the server components

With Mountain Lion installed, you can now proceed to downloading, installing, and configuring the server components. The configuration part is highly automated. The most important thing you do here is decide on a host name.

Follow these steps to install and configure the server components:

1. Launch the App Store from the Dock.

2. In the search field, search for OS X Server. Then purchase OS X Server to begin the download.

Quit the App Store application when the download is complete.

3. **Go to the Applications folder and launch the Server application.**

   What launches is called Server but is actually Server Setup Assistant.

4. **In the Set Up Your Server window, click Continue.**

   Or to display a help file, click the Getting Started button.

5. **Agree to the license agreement and then type your Mac's administrator password.**

6. **In the Apple Push Notifications window, type an Apple ID and password and then click Continue.**

   This action signs you up for Apple's push notification service and has Apple create a push notification certificate for your server. Push notification service is used for Profile Manager and other services for Macs and iOS devices.

   The ID you enter should be an Apple ID used for your organization, not your personal Apple ID that you use for iTunes.

   If your Mac doesn't have a previous version of OS X Server installed, or cannot find any DNS information, the Host Name window appears. It is important to get the information here right the first time, as this information can be difficult to change later.

7. **In the Host Name window, choose one of the following options and then click Continue.**

   Choose Private Network if you are _not_ serving to the Internet (such as web or e-mail).

   Choose Entire Internet if you have a registered Internet host name (www.example.com) for this server and intend to provide services to Internet users.

   The other choice, Local Network, is almost the same as Private Network, but less flexible. The Private Network selection gives you the option to remotely access the network from the Internet by using a secure virtual private network (VPN) connection, should you choose to, but doesn't require you to turn VPN on.

8. **In the Computer Name field of the Connecting to Your Mac window, change the entry from the default personal name (such as "Bob's Mac") to something more recognizable as a server (such as "Mac Server").**

   Mac and PC users will use this computer name to connect to the server for file sharing and screen sharing, if enabled. Mac users on the network will see this name in the Finder sidebar.

9. **In the Host Name field, type a host name that reflects the choice you made in Step 7.**

If the Mac contains a previous version of OS X Server, Server Setup Assistant may locate your server's host name from a DNS server.

WARNING!

If Server Setup Assistant does not find a DNS server with information for your server on the network or the Internet, it will set up DNS services on your server based on the information you entered in the Host Name and Connecting to Your Mac windows. If you decide to change the host name later, you will also have to edit the DNS records on the Mac. Getting this information right at this point will save you a lot of trouble later.

10. **(Optional) To change the server's IP address or assign a static address, click the Edit button. Click Apply when done.**

11. **In the Connecting to Your Mac window, recheck your settings and then click Continue.**

    The Configuring Services window appears, displaying progress messages that tell you what Server Setup Assistant is doing. Here, it tests the settings you provided, sets up DNS if needed, obtains an Apple push notification certificate, as well as other things.

12. **In the Congratulations window, click the Finish button.**

    The Server app launches and opens to the Overview tab of the Server pane.

Upgrading Older Servers

When you upgrade an older server to Mountain Lion Server, you first install the Mountain Lion client on top of the old OS, and then you download and install the server components, as described in the preceding section. Upgrading requires Mac OS X Server 10.6.8 or later.

Upgrading from Lion Server (10.7) is a smoother process and retains more data than upgrading from Snow Leopard Server. The next few sections describe what you can expect.

What's not moved from Snow Leopard Server

Mountain Lion Server doesn't include several services and features that were part of Mac OS X Server 10.6. When you migrate or upgrade from version 10.6, the settings and data for these items will not be moved to Mountain Lion Server:

- ✔ Print service
- ✔ Windows Primary Domain Controller (PDC) or Backup Domain Controller (BDC)

- ✔ Wiki data
- ✔ Wiki-based mailing list and archives
- ✔ Apache Tomcat and Apache Axis web services
- ✔ Mobile Access
- ✔ QuickTime Streaming Server (QTSS)
- ✔ NetBoot images that were created with versions of Mac OS X Server before version 10.5

The MySQL database is also not included in Mountain Lion Server; Apple replaced with PostgreSQL in OS X Server 10.7. However, the upgrade and migration processes will move MySQL and its data to Mountain Lion Server — but you will lose the graphical user interface to manage MySQL. You'll need to use the command line in the Terminal utility to manage MySQL.

Note also that an upgrade procedure will delete launch daemons located at /System/Library/LaunchDaemons. The update replaces them with newer Mountain Lion Server versions. This shouldn't be an issue unless your server includes customized launch daemons.

You can't use any of the administration tools from previous versions of Mac OS X Server. You need to use the version of the Server application that comes with Mountain Lion Server as well as Workgroup Manager 10.8, available as a separate download at http://support.apple.com/kb/DL1567.

Migrating or upgrading mail

When performing an upgrade, you need to have any partitions or drives that contain the mail data and database connected and mounted to ensure the automatic installation of your mail service in Mountain Lion Server. If these items aren't available during the upgrade to Mountain Lion, you'll have to move them manually, using the command line. You'll also need to manually migrate mail data that is installed on an Xsan volume.

You can find details of a manual migration of mail in Apple's manual *Mountain Lion Server Upgrading and Migrating*.

Recovering Podcast Producer data

With Mountain Lion Server, Apple dropped Podcast Producer. If you're upgrading your server, the Mountain Lion Server installer preserves the old Podcast library data.

If you upgraded from Mac OS X Server v10.6.8, you'll find the date here: `Library/PodcastProducer/Shared/`.

If you upgraded from Lion Server 10.7.x, the old Podcast library data is here: `Library/Server/Previous/Library/Server/PodcastLibrary/`.

DNS in Mountain Lion Server

After installing your server, you need to consider DNS service.

Domain name service (DNS) is the system that *resolves* IP addresses to domain names. For example, when you type `dummies.com` in a web browser, the DNS system tells your browser the IP address of the server hosting the site at John Wiley & Sons, Inc., allowing your computer to send a request to that host. Without DNS, you'd have to type the IP address of the Dummies website in your browser. DNS is not just for the web, though. It's used for most types of server communications on the Internet and on your local network.

DNS can run on your server Mac or on another computer on your local network, or can be provided by a network domain registrar or other Internet service.

If the Server Setup Assistant did not find another DNS server with your server's host name and IP address, it turned on DNS service in the Server app's DNS pane, as shown in Figure 4-7. The DNS pane in the Server app is a new feature in Mountain Lion.

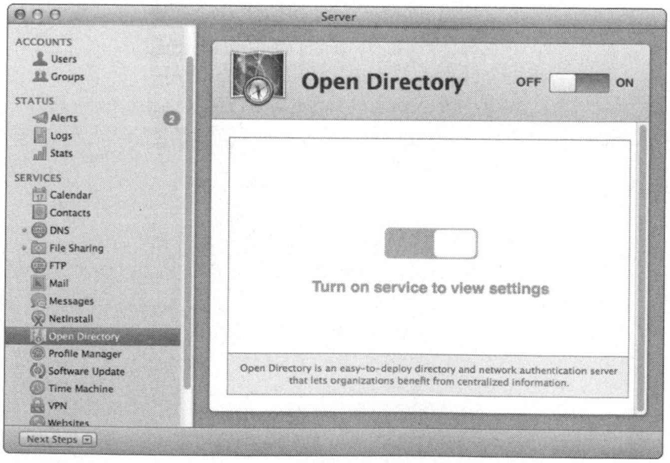

Figure 4-7:
The DNS pane in the Server app.

The default view here is a simple one. To see all DNS zones and records, choose Show All Records from the Action (gear) menu, as shown in Figure 4-8. This figure shows the records created by Server Setup Assistant.

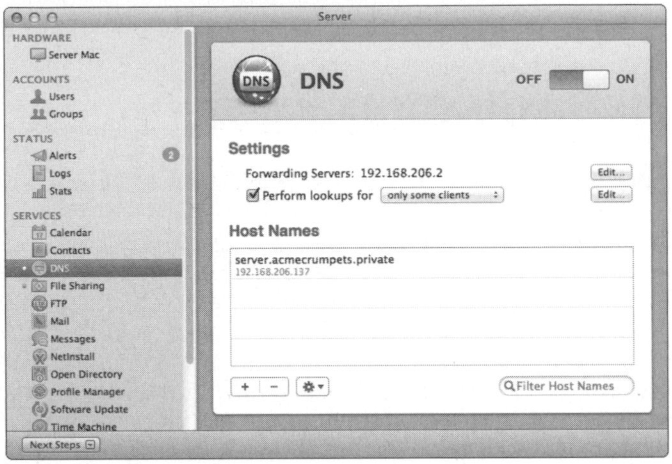

Figure 4-8:
The Show
All Records
view of the
DNS pane.

The DNS pane in the Server app is a feature that is new to Mountain Lion. But even with the simple interface, DNS is still a complicated subject, with many variables and settings for different situations. I could write an entire book about DNS service, but I fortunately don't have to because Blair Rampling and David Dalan already wrote *DNS For Dummies* (John Wiley & Sons, Inc.). Their book focuses on Windows and Unix servers but provides the theory and terminology about the DNS system that is common to all servers.

If your server is part of a bigger network that already has DNS servers, check with your network administrators before making changes to DNS on Mountain Lion Server. Otherwise, you may inadvertently cause problems throughout the network. Similarly, if your Internet service provider supplies your DNS service, check with them before making changes.

Understanding DNS concepts: Zones and records

When you configured Mountain Lion Server, the Server Setup Assistant may have created a *master zone with reverse lookup* and a machine record for your primary DNS name. A *DNS zone* is an organization entity that contains different types of records that relate to a domain. You could have a zone that contained IP addresses for servers in the `acmehigh.edu` domain, such as `www.acmehigh.edu` and `mailserver.acmehigh.edu`.

A master (primary) zone contains all the records for the zone, and it is the Internet's authority on that domain. A secondary, or slave, zone contains copies of master zone information that is stored on another server.

A DNS zone can contain several types of records. Here are the most common:

- **Machine record, also called Address (A):** This basic record holds the IP address for a domain name for a server or service.

- **Canonical name (CNAME), also called an alias:** You can use CNAMEs to resolve multiple domain names to one IP address (such as `www.abc.com`, `ourserver.abc.com`, and `mail183.abc.com`). For example, you might have a DNS zone with a CNAME record and an A record, as follows:

  ```
  www.abc.com.  CNAME  ourserver.abc.com.

  ourserver.abc.com.  A      192.168.10.20
  ```

  In this case, when there is a lookup for `www.abc.com`, the IP address `192.168.10.20` is returned. (Note that a dot is always used in domain names in DNS records.)

- **Mail exchange (MX) record:** This record identifies a computer as a mail server. Server Setup Assistant does not create MX records during installation/configuration.

- **Service (SRV) record:** This record identifies services that are hosted by one or more servers. It maps requests for the service to an IP address.

The Server app automatically creates a reverse lookup zone when you create a master zone. A *reverse lookup zone* supplies a corresponding domain name when another computer presents an IP address.

Using the Server app to configure DNS zones and records

To add a DNS zone or a record, click the Add (+) button and select the type of record to add, as shown in Figure 4-9. In the dialog that appears, enter a host name for the service. Throughout this book, I describe adding particular DNS records required for different services.

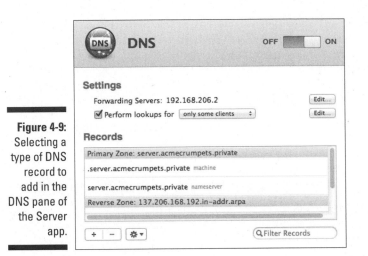

Figure 4-9:
Selecting a
type of DNS
record to
add in the
DNS pane of
the Server
app.

To check that DNS is properly configured, open Terminal (in /Applications/ Utilities) to access the command line and type **NSLOOKUP *hostname***. If configured properly, the DNS server reports the IP address of the server. To check the reverse, type **NSLOOKUP ipaddress**. If configured correctly, the DNS server reports the host name for your Mac OS X server. If either of these fails, DNS is not properly configured for your server.

Keeping Control of Mountain Lion Server Updates

The Mac's Software Update application automatically checks for updates that Apple recommends you run after you install Mountain Lion Server. Checking for updates is reasonable and security updates are important, but I don't recommend installing any update on your brand-new Mountain Lion Server installation without doing some homework. Apple creates updates to fix problems or make improvements, but despite Apple's best intentions, system updates can also break functionality or cause conflicts with third-party software. You may want to skip an update if it's known to cause problems that would affect what you do with the server. You also need to wait for third-party software developers to catch up and release an update that is compatible with Apple's latest update.

So instead of blindly installing Apple updates, here's your homework assignment:

 ✔ Research what others are seeing.

 ✔ Configure Software Update properly.

> ✔ Download and test the update on another Mac or in a virtual machine, using a product such as Parallels Desktop (www.parallels.com) or VMware Fusion (www.vmware.com).

Researching the update

Check up on what other people are experiencing with the update. Then if you decide to install the update, test it first.

You can check websites that cover Apple software updates to see what other users are experiencing with the most recent update. If a lot of people are reporting the same problems with third-party networking or server software, you may want to delay the upgrade. Are people reporting that the update fixes any problems that you're seeing? Don't take Apple's word for it.

The following three websites report problems with Mac updates:

✔ www.macwindows.com: My website, MacWindows, running since 1997, focuses on problems and solutions with Macs and PCs working together. When a new version of OS X Server or a client is released, I report problems or bugs that people experience.

✔ www.macintouch.com: Macintouch from Ric Ford specializes in all things Macintosh.

✔ www.apple.com/discussions: In the Apple Discussion forums, click the link for Mac OS X Server 10.8 and check for problem reports.

One report of a problem doesn't usually indicate a widespread issue, but if you see the same problem reported on multiple websites, beware. This is true for all your client Macs and Windows PCs. Don't install upgrades for them without researching first and testing the upgrade on one machine before rolling it out on all your clients.

When you do update, first perform a full backup of the server boot drive. If something breaks, you want to be able to get back to the last stable version as soon as possible.

Configuring Software Update properly

On every Mac, Software Update is available in the Apple menu. Its preference window, however, is accessible in System Preferences by clicking the Software Update icon. As one of the final touches on your Mountain Lion Server installation, open this preferences pane and edit the settings. The default settings aren't exactly dangerous, but they are more appropriate for a client computer than for a server.

By default, Software Update is set to check for updates weekly and to download them. Don't worry, it doesn't install, download, and update. Instead, it displays a dialog asking you if you want to install the update. To prevent this, in the Software Update Preferences window, make sure that the Download Important Updates Automatically check box is deselected.

You might also want to deselect the Check for Updates check box so that the server isn't regularly checking for updates by itself. Best practice is to use the Check Now button to manually check for updates or simply launch Software Update. You might set up a repeating calendar reminder in Calendar to remind you to check once a month or so.

If you want to update your server to a version later than what you have but earlier than the latest, you can. Apple offers older updates at its website, which you can download with a web browser. You can find updates at www.apple.com/support/downloads.

Downloading and testing updates

Test an upgrade on a spare Mac or in a virtual machine before you roll it out on your server. This means downloading the upgrade on your test machine or virtual machine, *not* on your server.

Here's how to safely download an update:

1. **Choose Apple menu⬥Software Update.**

   Software Update automatically checks for new updates, including updates to the operating system (a Mac OS X 10.8.x update), updates to components (such as Java), or security updates.

   Security updates are important, but they have also been known to cause compatibility issues.

   Software Update tells you whether it found anything.

2. **If Software Update did find something, click the Show Details button to display the updates.**

   Never install an update without knowing what it is, even on a test machine.

   Software Update shows you a list of the updates it found.

3. **Select the check boxes next to the updates that you want to install.**

4. **Click the Install button.**

You can now test the update. Try replicating the kinds of things your users do. Make sure that you test on Mac, Windows, and Linux and iOS clients.

Changing Ethernet Addressing

After your initial setup, you may need to change the IP addresses of your Ethernet port(s) or change the addressing scheme from automatic (DHCP) to manual (static). You can do either task in System Preferences:

1. **Open System Preferences from the Dock or the Apple menu and then click the Network icon.**

   The Network window appears. On the left, you see a list of network ports, including AirPort.

2. **Click the Ethernet port you want to configure.**

3. **Click the Configure pop-up menu and choose DHCP, Manual, or another type of addressing you'll use.**

4. **In the appropriate fields, type the IP addressing and domain name information.**

5. **Click Apply.**

After you change an IP address, you may have to update other settings, such as DNS.

Part II
Creating and Maintaining User Accounts and Directories

The 5th Wave   By Rich Tennant

"A centralized security management system sounds fine, but then what would we do with all the dogs?"

In this part . . .

Users are the reason for servers. Keeping track of users is the reason for much that's in Mountain Lion Server. This part focuses on maintaining shared network directories that enable multiple users and servers to communicate and enable network administrators to keep track of it all. I describe *user authentication,* the process in which a user connects to the computer with a name and password.

Directory services enable you to manage not only user accounts but the computers themselves. Here, I describe how OS X Server's Open Directory can centrally store information about the users and the computers in a single place, and in a secure manner. A shared directory also separates the user from a specific computer so that a user can log in from any computer and access his or her home directory.

On large networks, you may need to access other directory servers hosted on Windows servers. That's no problem for Mountain Lion Server and Active Directory, as you discover in this part.

Chapter 5

Controlling Access with Directories and Open Directory

S hared network directories have features that a local directory does not. For instance, a directory service such as Open Directory or Microsoft's Active Directory can offer users *single sign-on,* using Kerberos authentication. With this feature, users need to log in to the directory only once to gain access to multiple services and resources. They don't have to log in to different network resources individually.

This chapter describes the concepts of directory services and how they apply to Mountain Lion Server. You also find out how to create an Open Directory master and replica on Mountain Lion Server.

Defining Directories

When your entire network infrastructure consists of a computer on a desk in your living room, management of your user accounts and preferences is simple and straightforward. Your account and data are stored in one physical location. Add a second computer and maybe a laptop for travel, and you now have two or three sets of user accounts, passwords, and data.

Now multiply the computers by tens, hundreds, or thousands, and you see how managing users and data becomes beyond cumbersome in a large network. The solution is to create network directory services to aid managing many computer systems and users. A *network directory* is a shared list of users, accounts, and other resources that reside on the network. From a single location, you can manage a directory of all this information for hundreds of users. A directory can reside in one server computer or can be handled by dozens of servers on a large network.

Directory services also handle the job of *authenticating* users, which confirms the identity of users logging in from a client computer. Directory services handles authentication for other services, such as e-mail or file sharing, or to the entire network, or for the entire network at once — known as *single sign-on.*

Mountain Lion Server can host a directory for your network of Mac, Windows, and Linux computers. It can also make use of a directory residing on other servers. And it can help integrate your Mac users into a Windows-based Active Directory network. Mountain Lion Server supports two directory brands: It can host the open source Open Directory and connect to Microsoft Active Directory (see Chapter 6).

Network directories contain a hierarchical list of data that describes user accounts, attributes, and preferences, and can contain information about network resources. The data in a directory may be separated into containers associated with different physical locations, departments, or other conditions.

The structure of a directory's database — the specific types of data it stores and how it's stored — is called a *schema.* Strictly speaking, the directory consists of the schema and the data. *Directory services* are a collection of software that forms the framework for sharing information among servers and clients and which provide authentication.

Local and shared directories and domains

Both client computers and servers store account data and information about the computer in a local database on each system. These databases of user information can't be distributed among multiple computers. Even if you create a network directory, each computer will still have a local database with one or more user accounts in it.

Mountain Lion Server can store the network user accounts in its local directory. You know that they're in the local directory because you see these users in System Preferences (as well as in the Server app). A local directory may work for a small network of users with a single server and few network services. But if you had multiple servers, you'd have to set up accounts on every server machine on the network, and users would find themselves using different passwords for different file servers. You also can't use Profile Manager if you don't have a shared network directory.

With a shared directory, multiple servers share the account data, and users can log in to multiple file servers by using the same account and password. Users that are *bound,* or connected, with a directory can access any of the services that reside on servers that are also bound to the same directory. The use of shared directories goes much further, allowing administrators to manage clients and set password policies. It also enables servers to host home folders for computer users. A server-based home folder means that a user can log in to any computer on the network and have access to her data and settings.

Local and shared directories are also sometimes referred to as local and shared *domains.* In this context, a domain doesn't refer to a registered Internet domain but is used in the sense of *spheres of influence.* A local domain has an effect on only one computer. A shared domain covers a certain area of a network of computers.

Don't get confused if you see directory domains that end in `.com` or `.net`, like Internet domains. The reason for the use of these endings has to do with directory services' heavy reliance on DNS (domain name server, described in Chapter 2), which you see if you set up a directory in Chapter 6.

Account types in a directory

In network directories, accounts come in many flavors, not just the user account:

- ✔ **Users:** This type of account is usually an individual but not necessarily unique to a single person. Several individuals who manage a server may have access to an administrator account, for example. User accounts are the most common types you encounter and manage in a directory.

- ✔ **Groups:** You can combine one or more individual user accounts to form a group account. Members of a group account get access to the same shared data or resources, such as files in a folder.

- ✔ **Computers or machines:** Specific computer systems identified in a directory are computer or machine accounts.

- ✔ **Computer or machine groups:** As with users, directories can combine several computer accounts into a group. You can easily manage multiple computers with a group.

When you're ready to create a directory, the differences and benefits of various accounts become more evident.

With the Server app, you can create and manage only user and group accounts. Workgroup Manager also lets you create and manage computer accounts and computer groups. Chapter 16 describes using both of these tools to create and manage the four account types.

Authenticating with LDAP and Kerberos

Directory services also provide the authentication that allows users to access other services. The common authentication backbones of many prevalent directories are Lightweight Directory Access Protocol (LDAP) and Kerberos. These two technologies are built into Apple Open Directory and Microsoft Active Directory. The descriptions here just scratch the surface of LDAP and Kerberos; for more information on each technology, see www.openldap.org and http://web.mit.edu/kerberos.

Although directory services facilitate user authentication through passwords, the passwords are not usually stored in directories because anyone with access to the directory can usually browse its information. In OS X Server, passwords can be stored either in the Open Directory Password Server database or in a Kerberos realm, which is a kind of holding place. When authenticating, Open Directory checks with the Kerberos realm first.

In OS X Server, Open Directory never even reads the passwords. Each account password is stored as encrypted value called a *shadow hash* for each user. When the user submits a password for authentication, Open Directory runs it through the hash and compares the values of the hashes. If they match, the user is authenticated. Open Directory doesn't read the actual password.

LDAP

In most modern network directories, LDAP defines how clients communicate with the directory over TCP/IP networks. Computers use LDAP to read and edit information in LDAP-compatible directories. (LDIF, the LDAP Data Interchange Format, defines how data is stored in the LDAP database.)

The LDAP search base tells the client where to start looking within the directory for data — usually account information.

LDAP also has a role to play with the Password Server database, mentioned in the preceding section. When you authenticate against a shared directory in OS X Server, you're telling LDAP who you are, but Password Server checks your password to verify your identity. Kerberos authentication does not use Password Server.

Authentication proves who you are with your username and password credentials. *Authorization* is what you can do after authentication, such as accessing file sharing or viewing your e-mail inbox. Kerberos is an authentication protocol. LDAP can be used for both authentication and authorization.

Open Directory is compatible with LDAP directories, including Active Directory and eDirectory.

Kerberos and single sign-on

If a user needs to connect to many unique services, he or she could send a username and password to each service, opening a path for an evildoer to intercept and crack your password. The more secure alternative is to use Kerberos *single sign-on* authentication, in which the user enters a password once and gets access to all services. With Kerberos enabled, the password is never transmitted over the network. Instead, a ticketing system issues encrypted tokens called *tickets* and authenticates you once (usually from the OS X login screen); subsequent tickets allow access to other shared services.

Think of Kerberos as spending the day visiting a popular amusement park. The first thing you do when you arrive at the park is buy a pass. This pass is your Kerberos ticket granting ticket (TGT), issued by Kerberos Key Distribution Center (KDC) when you log in to OS X on a shared directory. At the park, you pay the entry fee and access the grounds all day. Users log in once and get access to the entire park.

The pass doesn't automatically mean that you can jump on any ride or that you get hot dogs and popcorn. You still need to queue for each ride and pay for your snacks. In Kerberos, your TGT is presented when accessing a service, such as file sharing or e-mail. The KDC creates a new service ticket that your client uses to authenticate to the service. But the user isn't presented with a login screen after that first login.

When the park closes, your pass is not good for the next day. In Kerberos, when you log out, the TGT and service tickets are destroyed. TGTs are good for a set period of time only: ten hours after the login to OS X Server. (This time period limits damage if someone manages to figure out how to break in to the ticket system.) And the Kerberos tickets are stored in RAM, not the hard drive.

OS X Server is easy to set up as a KDC; when you set it up as an Open Directory master, a KDC is set up automatically. Open Directory can also make use of another KDC running on another server, such as an Active Directory domain controller. In OS X, you can view, create, and destroy TGTs by using the Ticket Viewer application, shown in Figure 5-1, found in /System/Library/CoreServices.

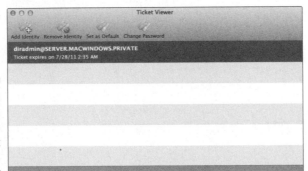

Figure 5-1: Kerberos tickets in Ticket Viewer.

TIP

View TGTs and service tickets for the current user by typing klist in Terminal and pressing Return. Here's an example of what you might see:

```
client:~ lianabare$ klist
Default principal: lianabare@MASTER.EXAMPLE.COM
Valid Starting Expires Service Principal
06/30/11 14:24:40 06/30/11 00:24:40 krbtgt/MASTER.EXAMPLE.COM@MASTER.EXAMPLE.COM
 renew until 06/30/11 14:24:34
06/30/11 14:24:41 06/30/11 00:24:40 afpserver/fileserver.example.com@MASTER.
            EXAMPLE.COM
 renew until 06/30/11 14:24:34
06/30/11 14:24:59 06/30/11 00:24:40 http/ical.example.com@MASTER.EXAMPLE.COM
 renew until 06/30/11 14:24:34
06/30/11 14:26:27 06/30/11 00:24:40 xmpp/ichat.example.com@MASTER.EXAMPLE.COM
 renew until 06/30/11 14:24:34
```

If you've created a network directory (instead of a local one), you've created an Open Directory master, Mountain Lion Server's shared storehouse for network user and resource information. If you haven't created an Open Directory master, you can easily create a directory using the Server app, or Workgroup Manager, or both. You don't have to host your own directory: Mountain Lion Server can connect to other directory servers and use their information.

Determining Whether You're Running a Local or Network Directory

Before you decide on anything about Open Directory, you need to determine what Mountain Lion Server is using to store user accounts. Depending on the choices you made when you installed Mountain Lion Server, you may not be using a network directory at all. Even if you've been adding user accounts, you still may not have a network directory configured: The Server app lets you add dozens of user accounts, keeping you blissfully unaware that you're creating *local* accounts that are not shared on the network. If that occurs, it means a lot of retyping after you do create a shared Open Directory master.

Here are a few ways to find out if your directory is local and you're not running Open Directory:

- ✓ **The Server App will tell you.** Expand Next Steps at the bottom of the Server app and click the Manage Users button. Next Steps lets you know whether your user accounts are local.

- ✓ **Look in System Preferences in the Dock.** Click the Users & Groups icon. If the user accounts you've added are all listed here, you've created local accounts on the Mac, not in a shared network directory.

If you upgraded to Mountain Lion Server from Snow Leopard Server or Lion Server running as an Open Directory master (or replica), your updated server is also configured as an Open Directory master (or replica).

Not everyone needs to run a shared network directory. You can get away with local accounts if you're running Mountain Lion Server at home or in a small workgroup and don't need services that require a network directory, such as Profile Manager. You can provide file sharing just fine by using just local accounts on Mountain Lion Server, for example.

Planning for an Open Directory Deployment

You might be tempted to jump right in with the instructions you find later in this chapter (in the "Creating an Open Directory master or replica with the Server app" section) and create a shared domain. Don't give in to temptation just yet.

First, write something. Your plan is best implemented when it exists in a format that you document and reference. Collaboration is also key when you and your colleagues are simultaneously working toward implementing a shared directory.

Documentation can also save your hide if the worst happens, and you're forced to rebuild your directory. And don't forget that you might not be the only administrator of the directory — especially if you finally win the lottery and forget all about your love of OS X Servers. The next administrator benefits from your documentation, too.

Open Directory relies upon other services to run properly. Domain name service and time synchronization are critical to a healthy and happy directory.

Factors to consider for your plan

Whether you use a detailed Gantt chart, a whiteboard, or just a quick sketch on a napkin, start your Open Directory deployment with a plan. Here are some considerations to ponder prior to your deployment:

- **How many servers do you need?** For a small domain of ten or so users, you could have just one server, but consider a second for larger networks. A minimum of two Open Directory servers provides you with redundancy and failover — the capability to switch automatically to a second server in the event something goes wrong with the first.

   Two Open Directory servers can take you quite far. Apple states that Open Directory's technical limitations are

   - *LDAP records:* 200,000

   - *Simultaneous client connections:* 1,000

   Each client may open multiple connections to an Open Directory server during the initial login and when requesting additional authentication. However, a two-server Open Directory deployment handily manages several hundred clients in a local network.

- **Are you accounting for physical security?** The directory servers in your shared domain contain sensitive information, such as user passwords and permissions. Treat your Open Directory servers with the same care and caution as any of the other important data on your network.

- **Who will have responsibility for domain maintenance and backups?** When you specify an administrator to primarily manage your domain, you likely reduce mistakes and complications that result from ill-timed software updates and improperly made backups.

Master, replica, and relay servers

Mac servers can play different roles in Open Directory: master, replica, or relay. Another role a Mac server can have is to simply connect, or *bind,* to a directory. When planning your network, think about which role you'll use.

Open Directory masters

An *Open Directory master* is the primary Open Directory server on the network. If you have a single OS X Server Mac that is hosting a shared list of users and groups, it is an Open Directory master.

A master contains a read/write LDAP-compatible database and hosts the Kerberos Key Distribution Center (KDC) and the Open Directory Password Server database. The Open Directory master is the only server that can make changes to the LDAP-compatible database. An Open Directory master is analogous to the Primary Domain Controller of Windows-based shared directory systems.

Open Directory replicas

After creating the Open Directory master, you can add one or more Open Directory *replicas,* which are mirror servers that create a distributed directory environment with redundancy and client failover. Each Open Directory replica has a read-only copy of the LDAP directory, the Password Server database, and the Kerberos KDC that are synchronized periodically with the master and each of the other replicas. If you want to make changes to accounts in a domain, you must make them on the master server. However, password database changes, such as a user changing his or her password, are allowed while connected to any Open Directory server in the domain. (Passwords aren't stored in the LDAP database.) Background synchronization among all the Open Directory servers updates the changed data across the domain.

Open Directory relays

You can deploy Open Directory servers in a topology sometimes referred to as a *tree* or a *nested approach.* Each Open Directory master can have up to 32 replica servers. Additionally, each of these replica servers can have up to 32 replicas. Thus, a theoretical limit of 1,057 Open Directory servers exists for a single domain:

> 1 master + 32 replicas + (32×32) nested replicas

When an Open Directory replica has its own replicas, that server is an *Open Directory relay.* A relay with additional replicas might be useful in a widely distributed network of client systems.

Open Directory replicas, including relays, that connect directly to the master are *first-tier replicas.* Replicas that connect to a relay are *second-tier replicas.*

A good example of the use of an Open Directory relay is a school system with multiple school buildings spread out in a city or a county. You'd install Open Directory relay and additional replicas in each school, while the Open Directory master remains safely installed at the school system's data center, which creates a closer, faster connection to the Open Directory domain for clients in each building.

Server connected to a directory but not hosting one

You don't need Open Directory running on every server. Another Open Directory role is to bind to an Open Directory domain instead of hosting one. You avoid the overhead of running directory services on your server, and users still get access to domain resources. You might use this option if your server is running user services, such as file sharing, e-mail, or Mountain Lion Server's wiki collaborative environment. Your services can also make use of Kerberos authentication from the bound server. To connect a server to a directory, you bind it to the domain and add it to the Kerberos realm.

Mountain Lion Server can bind to an Open Directory Master running on Mac OS X Server 10.6 Snow Leopard. In order to have Snow Leopard Server authenticate your Mountain Lion Server's users — particularly users of the wiki and podcast services — Snow Leopard Server must be running version 10.6.8 or later. A deployment of Mountain Lion and Snow Leopard Open Directory servers can't include older Mac OS X Server releases (Tiger 10.4 or Leopard 10.5, for example).

Additionally, when installing software updates on Mountain Lion Server, such as Mac OS X Server 10.8.1, 10.8.2, and so on, start with your replica servers and finish by updating on the master.

An OS X Server that doesn't host or bind to a shared directory is a *stand-alone server.* This type of server has only a local database of user and group accounts, as in any OS X system, and results from selecting a host name for a local network (`hostname.local`) in the server assistant's setup.

Regardless of the OS X Server Open Directory role, it always has a local database of at least one user. It's important not to confuse the local accounts, which can't be shared with other servers and clients with the accounts in the Open Directory domain. In Chapter 16, you see cues in Workgroup Manager that help differentiate which database of accounts you're working with.

After you configure an Open Directory domain, other servers and client systems utilize binding to connect and access the shared directory for authentication and authorization. Clients connect to the fastest responding Open Directory server, based on *ping response times* — the time required for a small packet of data to travel and return to the sender. If the master or any replica server fails, clients connect automatically to another Open Directory server in the domain without interruption to the user.

Prerequisites

Before running Open Directory, you need to properly configure two aspects of your network: domain name service (DNS) and time synchronization for Kerberos.

Checking for proper DNS setup

If, during initial setup, you configured Server Setup Assistant so that it created an Open Directory master for you, it should have also set up DNS. If you didn't do this configuration during initial setup or have a DNS server running on another server, you'll need to ensure that DNS is configured to support Open Directory.

Properly configured DNS is critical to the configuration and normal operation of an Open Directory domain. All Open Directory servers need static IP addresses, a zone with the host domain name, and two types of records: a fully qualified DNS address (A) and pointer (PTR) records. Verify the server's DNS records prior to promoting an OS X Server to either master or replica status.

In an A record, also called a *machine record,* the system's host name is resolved to an IP address. That is, when another computer requests the IP address for a given domain name, the machine record supplies it. A pointer (PTR) record, also known as a *reverse lookup,* resolves a domain name for any given IP address. *Reverse resolution* inquires about an IP address and returns the host name.

By default, the domain's LDAP search policy and Kerberos realm are the same as the fully qualified host name of the Open Directory master and are generated when a server's role is changed to master. Without correct DNS records, promotion to an Open Directory master or replica will likely fail or create only a partially functional domain.

If you don't mind typing a one-line command in the Terminal utility, you can easily verify that DNS forward and reverse lookup are configured correctly. Type this, exactly:

```
sudo changeip -checkhostname
```

If forward and reverse DNS are working correctly, you see this, but with your server information:

```
Primary address = 192.168.1.69
Current HostName = ourserver.macwindowsco.com
DNS HostName = ourserver.macwindowsco.com
The names match. There is nothing to change.
dirserv:success = "success"
```

Synchronizing time for Kerberos reliability

If you plan on using Kerberos as part of your Open Directory deployment (and why wouldn't you?), time synchronization is critical. *Time skew,* or the difference in time between the KDC and clients requesting Kerberos tickets, can be no more than five minutes. Time zones and daylight saving time aren't considered in factoring the time skew as long as the relative time between systems is the same.

In other words, if you have a client in pacific time and a KDC in eastern time, they both need to be set correctly for their respective time zones. Manually changing the time to match the local time but not changing the time zone causes a time difference of several hours — much more than five minutes. Open Directory compares time based on Universal Decimal Time (UDT).

It's best to set your OS X Server and client systems to use a time synchronization server running the Network Time Protocol (NTP) to avoid problems with Kerberos and single sign-on for users. The Server Setup Assistant configured NTP during initial setup, but you can change it. Apple provides several publicly accessible NTP servers via the Internet, or you can run your own time server in Mountain Lion Server on a local network.

A public Internet connection isn't required, but public NTP servers often connect to trusted sources of accurate time data, such as an atomic clock. If you don't use a public server, manually adjust the time of your private time server in the Date & Time pane of System Preferences.

Enabling time server synchronization

You can use System Preferences to either add or change the NTP server to automatically have the system adjust the clock. These steps set a time server on both OS X clients and OS X Server. Here's the procedure for System Preferences:

1. **Choose Apple menu⇨System Preferences and then click the Date & Time icon.**

2. **In the Date & Time tab, select the Set Date & Time Automatically check box.**

3. **From the pop-up menu to the right of the check box, choose an Apple public time server or enter another time server in this field.**

   If you're not using Apple's time servers, enter the host name or IP address of another time server (like those found at support.ntp.org) or a private time server on your local network.

4. **When you're done, quit System Preferences.**

Configuring Open Directory

You can do several Open Directory tasks with the Server app, depending on how you configured your server during initial installation and setup, including importing users and groups from another Open Directory server or Active Directory server and creating an Open Directory master.

The Server app is also good for adding or removing users and groups and for other user account management tasks.

Creating an Open Directory master or replica with the Server app

Open the Server app from the Dock or the Applications folder. If prompted, enter the username and password for the local administrator. To set up an Open Directory master (a shared directory domain), follow these steps:

1. **In the sidebar of the Server app, select Open Directory.**

   The Open Directory pane appears, as shown in Figure 5-2.

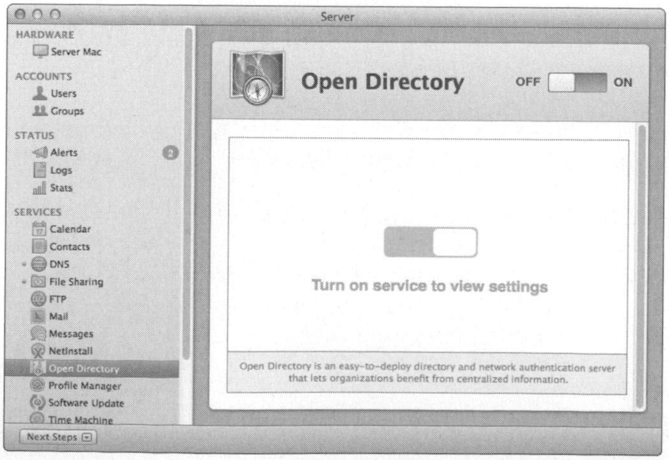

Figure 5-2:
The Open
Directory
pane of the
Server app.

2. **Click the big switch to the On position.**

   Open Directory Assistant launches.

3. **In the Configure Users and Groups dialog, shown in Figure 5-3, choose Create a New Open Directory Domain or Join an Existing Open Directory Domain as a Replica. Then click the Next button.**

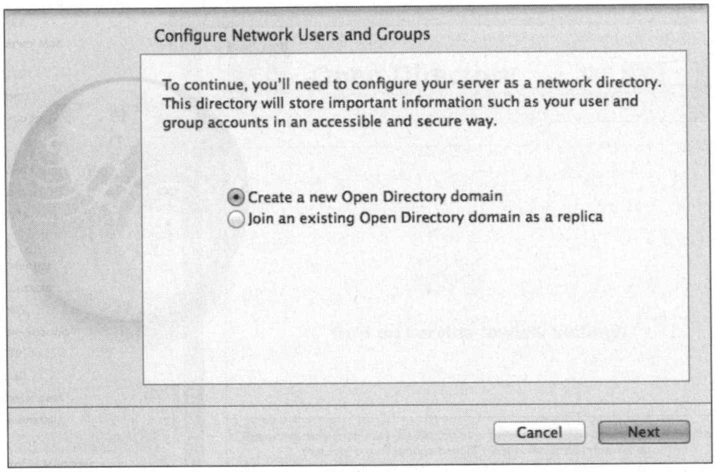

Configure Network Users and Groups

To continue, you'll need to configure your server as a network directory. This directory will store important information such as your user and group accounts in an accessible and secure way.

⦿ Create a new Open Directory domain
○ Join an existing Open Directory domain as a replica

Cancel   Next

Figure 5-3: Choosing to create an Open Directory master or a replica.

---

4. **Type a name and password for the directory administrator and then click Next.**

   The default is Directory Administrator (short name diradmin).

5. **In the next screen, enter an organization (or department) name to identify your server and then type an administrator e-mail address for users to contact. Click Next.**

6. **In the Confirm Settings dialog, click Set Up.**

   You may want to look over your settings and click the Back button if you need to change something.

At the end of this process, the Open Directory pane will display the Open Directory master, as shown in Figure 5-4.

If the Server app fails to create your Open Directory shared domain, DNS is a likely culprit. DNS service has to be set up before you create an Open Directory master. The Server app also doesn't allow you to change the LDAP search base path or the Kerberos realm name or to see the confirmation that these settings match the DNS server host name.

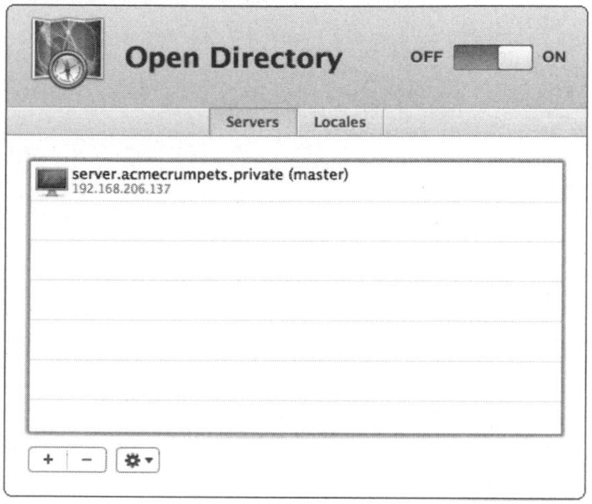

Open Directory   OFF ▮ ON

| Servers | Locales |

server.acmecrumpets.private (master)
192.168.206.137

+   −   ☸▾

Figure 5-4:
The Open
Directory
pane with a
master
configured.

If you decide that you've made a mistake, you can delete the domain master you created by selecting it in the Open Directory pane (refer to Figure 5-4) and clicking the Delete (–) button. Note that you will also delete any network user accounts you added after creating the Open Directory master.

You can add an Open Directory replica by clicking the Add (+) button and entering the information for the server hosting the Open Directory master (server address, server admin name and password, and directory admin name and password).

An Open Directory replica is essentially a clone of the Open Directory master with copies of the shared domain databases. Having one or more replicas on your network greatly helps reduce the load on any one domain server and adds peace of mind in case a server fails.

Considerations for DNS records and time synchronization are still valid for replica servers. Use the same DNS and time servers for all Open Directory servers in your shared domain. (See the sections "Checking for proper DNS setup" and "Synchronizing time for Kerberos reliability," earlier in this chapter.)

Just because you used the Server app to create the shared domain doesn't mean you can't also use Workgroup Manager to manage accounts. After the directory is created, you can switch between the two applications.

Importing directory information with the Server app

You can use the Server app to import user account information from another directory. If you don't yet have an Open Directory master, the dialog prompts you to create one when you turn on Open Directory service, as described in the preceding section.

You can import user accounts and group accounts. When you import a group, the Server app imports all the user accounts that are members of the group.

With an Open Directory master on your server, you first use the Server app to connect to another directory and then you import a user or group. First, follow these steps to connect:

1. **Click the Manage menu and choose Connect to Server.**

   The Choose a Mac dialog appears.

2. **Click Other Mac and then click the Continue button.**

3. **Type the IP address or host name of an Open Directory Active Directory server you want to connect to and then click the Connect button.**

4. **Enter the name and password of a user account for a directory and then click Next.**

   For an Open Directory account, you can use any user account. For an Active Directory account, the user must be an Active Directory administrator or the user account must be designated with Add Workstations to Domain permission. (See Chapter 6 for more on Active Directory.)

5. **In the Confirm Settings dialog, click Set Up.**

Now that your server is connected to the other network directory, you can import users and groups:

1. **In the Server app sidebar, click either Users or Groups under Accounts.**

2. **Click the Add (+) button to display the New User (or New Group) dialog.**

3. **Click the Type pop-up menu and select Imported User from *directory* (or Imported Group from *directory*), where *directory* is the network directory to which you are connected.**

   If you don't see the Type pop-up menu, Mountain Lion Server isn't connected to the other network directory.

4. **Begin typing the user or group account name you want to import, select the name when it appears, and click the Import button.**

5. **Click the Done button.**

Chapter 15 has more information about using the Server app to manage user and group accounts.

Binding to an existing directory

Instead of hosting Open Directory on your server, you can have Mountain Lion Server join an existing directory domain that exists on another server. This is called *binding* the server to the directory domain.

Follow these steps to bind a server to an Open Directory domain:

1. **In the Server app, choose Tools⊳Directory Utility.**

2. **Click the lock icon and authenticate as the local administrator.**

3. **In the Services tab, shown in Figure 5-5, double-click LDAPv3.**

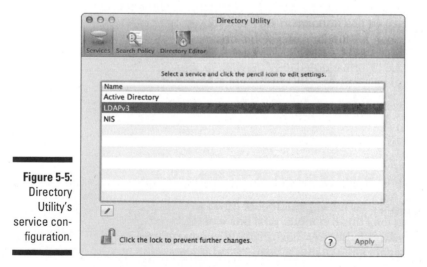

Figure 5-5: Directory Utility's service configuration.

4. **Click the New button, and in the Server Name or IP Address field, enter the fully qualified host name of the Open Directory master.**

By default, Secure Sockets Layer (SSL) is disabled.

5. **Click Continue.**

6. **In the dialog that appears, make your desired changes and then click the Bind button.**

   If desired, you can use the Security tab to enter the directory administrator username and password to create an authenticated bind. Otherwise, leave those fields blank for an anonymous binding.

7. **Click OK.**

8. **Review the configuration, click OK, and then close Directory Utility.**

Binding Clients to the Shared Domain

You share the directory by creating a binding between the client and the Open Directory domain. *Binding* creates a connection between the server and the client, enabling the client to read the LDAP database, send authentication requests, and interact with the Kerberos realm for service tickets. Regarding authentication, you see this interaction most frequently from the login screen in OS X, and most of that interaction is transparent to the user.

Any version newer than Mac OS X 10.2 can bind to Open Directory running on Mountain Lion Server. Your Mac OS X 10.7 and 10.8 client systems should not be bound to versions of OS X Server previous to 10.7 to best support the newest enhancements of Mac OS X.

Binding Mac OS X 10.6 and later clients

You can bind Mac OS X 10.6, 10.7, and 10.8 clients by using System Preferences. Follow these steps:

1. **Select the Apple menu and choose System Preferences. Then click the Users & Groups icon in Mac OS X 10.7 or 10.8 (or Accounts in Mac OS X 10.6).**

2. **Click the lock icon, enter a password, and then click Login Options.**

   If the client has never previously bound to a directory, you see a Join button next to Network Account Server at the bottom of the Login Options window. If a current binding exists, you see an Edit button.

3. **Click the Join or Edit button.**

4. **In the Server field, shown in Figure 5-6, enter the Open Directory master's fully qualified host name.**

   If you previously enabled service discovery on your Open Directory Master server, it will be listed.

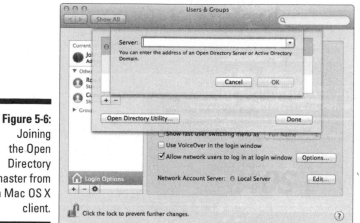

Figure 5-6:
Joining
the Open
Directory
master from
a Mac OS X
client.

5. **Click OK.**

6. **If prompted, enter the local administrator username and password, authorizing changes to the local directory structure.**

After your client is bound to the server, the OS X 10.7 and 10.8 Users and Groups preferences pane (or Accounts in Mac OS X 10.6) in System Preferences indicates this with a green dot and the server's host name. You can click the Edit button to modify the settings, and you can also access Directory Utility (in /System/Library/CoreServices) to make more advanced changes to the directory bindings.

Binding Mac OS X 10.5 and earlier clients

In previous versions of Mac OS X, you used Directory Utility, installed in the Utilities folder within the Applications folder, to bind to a network directory. To bind a Mac OS X 10.5.8 or earlier client, open Directory Utility and do the following:

1. **Click the lock icon and enter an administrator name and password.**

2. **Click the Add (+) button and select Open Directory from the pop-up menu.**

   Select Active Directory to bind to an Active Directory domain.

3. **Enter the fully qualified host name or IP address of the server hosting the domain, and then click OK.**

Binding Windows clients

Lion Server dropped the ability to act as a Primary Domain Controller (PDC) for Windows clients, so Windows clients cannot authenticate to a directory hosted on Lion Server or Mountain Lion Server. However, you can run an Open Directory master and a PDC on a separate Mac running Mac OS X Server 10.6.8 Snow Leopard and bind Lion or Mountain Lion Server to it.

To bind Windows clients to Snow Leopard Server's directory services, you connect it to a PDC, a Windows domain. With Windows Vista and Windows 7, you can bind only the Ultimate and Business editions. You can also bind Windows XP clients. Here's how to bind a Windows client:

1. **Log in to Windows as an administrator.**

2. **From the Start menu, open the Control Panel and then double-click the System icon.**

3. **Click the Change Settings button.**

   Note: Skip this step for Windows XP.

4. **Click the Computer Name tab and then click the Change button.**

5. **Enter a computer name, if none exists.**

6. **Click Domain, enter the Windows domain name of the OS X Server PDC, and then click the OK button.**

   If you don't remember the Windows domain name, you can view it in Server Admin in Snow Leopard Server: Select SMB in the list of services under your server, click the Settings icon, and then click the General tab.

7. **In the dialog that appears, enter the name and password for an LDAP directory administrator and then click OK.**

Chapter 6

Integrating Open Directory with Active Directory

*M*icrosoft Active Directory is a fact of life for most corporate networks. With Mountain Lion Server, you can provide native services to Mac clients within a larger Windows network.

Apple provides every Mac with an LDAP (Lightweight Directory Access Protocol) plug-in and an Active Directory plug-in that allows a Mac to receive authentication from Active Directory. The plug-ins also enable the Mac to access information from Active Directory, allowing for single sign-on. However, the client plug-ins alone don't provide the wealth of Access Directory policy features that enable administrators to set policies that enable the management of dozens or hundreds of computers at a time. Using Mountain Lion Server, however, you can truly integrate your Mac clients into Active Directory and provide other features.

One of the great things about Apple's implementation of Open Directory services is that your Active Directory administrator doesn't need to do anything special to support an OS X server. The Mac server manages and stores the information about the Mac network and exchanges the information with Active Directory in the format that it likes. For more information about setting up an Active Directory schema, check out *Active Directory For Dummies,* 2nd Edition, by Steve Clines and Marcia Loughry (John Wiley & Sons, Inc.).

The Magic Triangle

Windows servers use Active Directory to provide directory services on a network. Apple's Active Directory plug-in for OS X allows a Mac server to maintain information about Mac clients and allows access to enforce Active Directory policies and authentication.

In an Active Directory environment, Mac servers actually provide authentication of both Open Directory and Active Directory to the Mac clients. This dual authentication role allows policies to be implemented on the Mac server for Mac clients that are nonstandard in an Active Directory environment (such as Messages services or Contacts services), while allowing Active Directory to handle the network services that are common to Windows and Mac users on the network.

The Mac server's capability to manage both Open Directory and Active Directory separately (and never the twain shall meet) is known as implementing the *magic triangle,* as shown in Figure 6-1. The Mac server handles the Active Directory piece of the puzzle by using the Mac's Active Directory plug-in, which sets up a special account on Active Directory that translates network requests from Mac clients into the format that Active Directory expects from Windows clients.

Binding Your Server to Active Directory

The first step in integrating a Mac server into an Active Directory environment is to bind the OS X Server to the Active Directory domain. *Binding,* in this case, means creating the link between the Mac server and Active Directory.

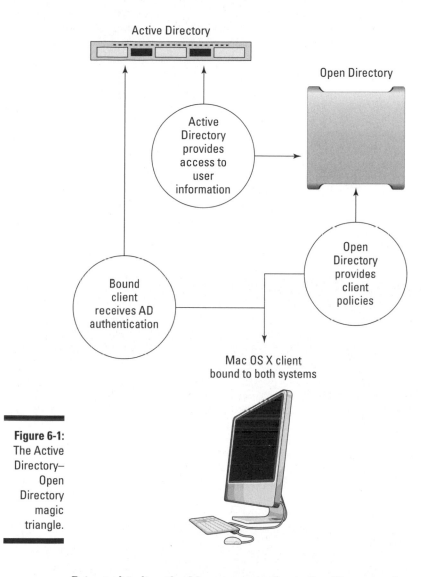

Active Directory

Open Directory

Active Directory provides access to user information

Open Directory provides client policies

Bound client receives AD authentication

Mac OS X client bound to both systems

Figure 6-1:
The Active Directory–Open Directory magic triangle.

Prior to binding the Mac server to the Active Directory domain, you need to have ready the following information (some of which must come from your Active Directory domain administrator):

- ✔ **Mac Server credentials:** You need to have your local server administrator login and password at the ready.

- ✔ **Domain administrator login credentials or rights:** An administrator login and password for the Active Directory domain to which the server will be bound (or having your credentials added to this administrative group in Active Directory).

✔ **Fully qualified domain name for the Active Directory (AD) domain:** If you don't know the fully qualified AD domain name, ask your AD administrator. Generally, the domain name is `domain.top-level-domain` — for example, `mycompany.com` in a simple structure or `NorthAmerica.BigCompany.com` in a larger network with multiple domains.

✔ **The host name or IP address of the time server used by the Active Directory domain:** The time setting for the Active Directory server must be within five minutes of the time setting for the OS X Server for the binding to be successful. The easiest way to ensure that the time settings are correct is to use the same time server for all servers and clients on your network. Select the same date and time server from the Date & Time System Preferences pane.

Checking DNS configuration

Active Directory requires that domain name services (DNS) be working properly so that the OS X Mountain Lion Server host name and IP address are linked. The linkage should work both in forward and reverse (meaning that if you check the IP, it resolves to the server's host name; and if you check the host name, it resolves to the correct IP address). The server's host name and IP address are stored as DNS service (SRV) records. The Mac and Windows clients must use the same DNS server, so typically, the DNS server is running on a Windows server, not the Mac server.

To check that DNS is configured properly, open Network Utility (located in the Utilities folder within the Applications folder). Click the Lookup tab and type the server's domain. If configured properly, the DNS server reports the IP address of the server. To check the reverse, type the IP address of the server. If configured correctly, the DNS server reports the host name for your OS X Server. If either of these methods fails, DNS isn't configured properly for your server.

You can also do the same lookup with the command line and the Terminal utility. Type **NSLOOKUP** *hostname.* to look up the server's IP address and **NSLOOKUP** *ipaddress.* to look up the server's domain name.

Binding the server

After you have the required information in hand and have ensured that DNS is working properly (see the preceding section), you're ready to bind the server. To bind your server to an Active Directory domain, follow these steps:

1. **Launch System Preferences and click the Users & Groups icon.**

   The Users & Groups pane opens, as shown in Figure 6-2.

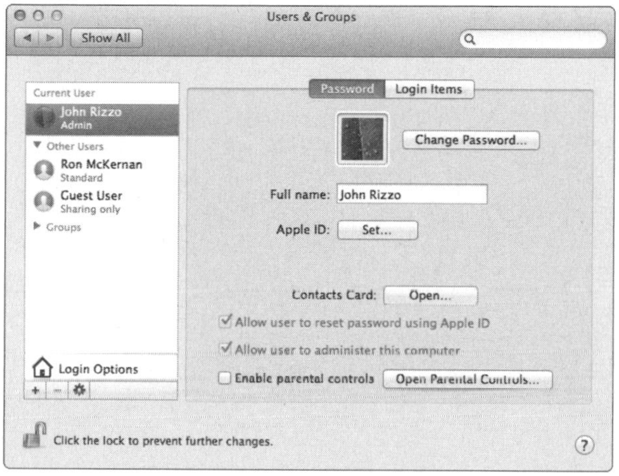

Figure 6-2: The Users & Groups pane of System Preferences.

2. **Click the lock icon, in the lower left, to display a login dialog.**

3. **Enter your administrator login and password and then click OK.**

4. **Click the Login Options icon at the bottom left of the Users & Groups pane.**

   The available options appear, as shown in Figure 6-3. This pane provides access to set network directory configuration.

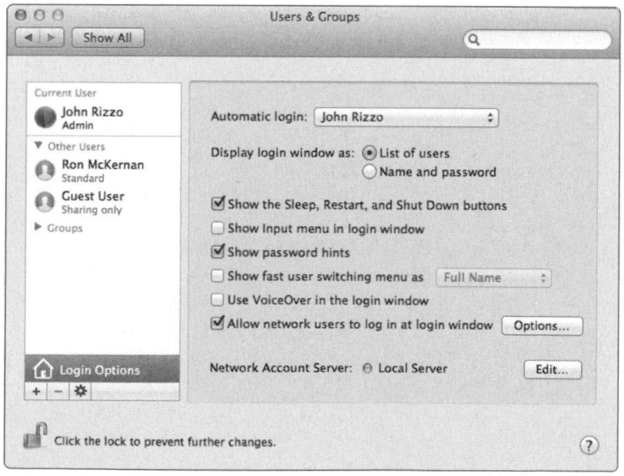

Figure 6-3: Configure network directories by clicking the Login Options icon.

5. Click the Edit button.

A sheet opens that displays all network directories that the machine has been set up to access. The first time you bind a directory, you see only the local directory server, as shown in Figure 6-4.

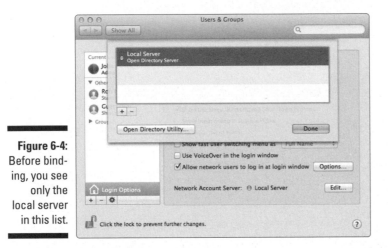

Figure 6-4:
Before binding, you see only the local server in this list.

6. Click the Open Directory Utility button.

The Directory Utility application opens, as shown in Figure 6-5.

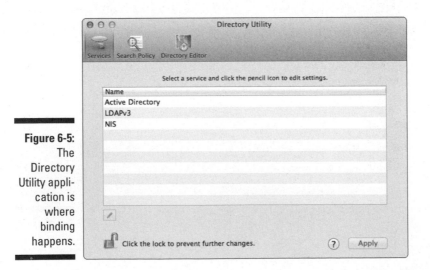

Figure 6-5:
The Directory Utility application is where binding happens.

7. **Ensure that the Services icon is selected in the toolbar. Then click the lock icon at the bottom left to access the login and password dialog.**

8. **Enter your administrator credentials again, and then click Modify Configuration.**

9. **Click the Active Directory line to *highlight* it. Then click the plug-in configuration button (the pencil icon, as shown in Figure 6-5).**

   The sheet shown in Figure 6-6 appears.

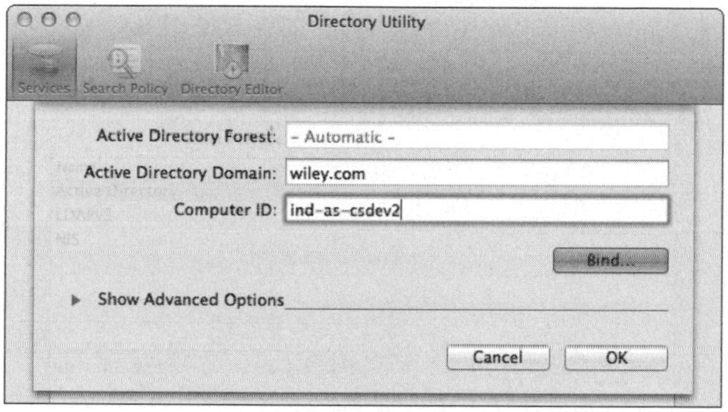

Figure 6-6:
Fill in the
Active
Directory
Domain text
box and
then click
Bind.

10. In the Active Directory Domain text box, type your fully qualified Active Directory domain name and then click the Bind button.

   The Network Administrator Required dialog opens, as shown in Figure 6-7.

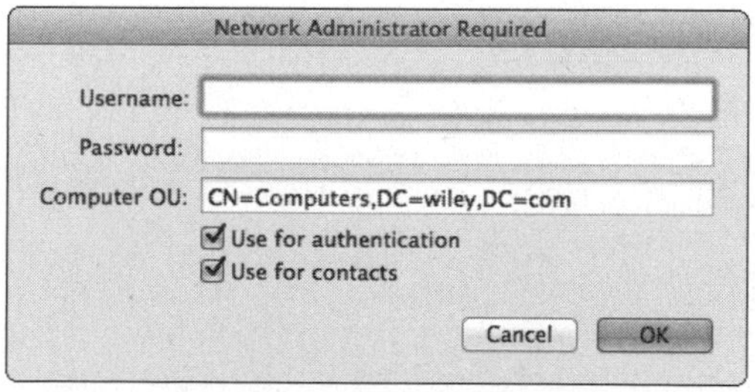

Figure 6-7:
Enter the
login
credentials
for a domain
administra-
tor.

11. Enter a network domain administrator login and password, and then click OK.

The login and password may not be the same as the local administrator credentials you entered earlier. The account you're using to log in must have rights to make changes to the Active Directory domain. If you're unsure, contact your Active Directory administrator.

The Computer OU (organizational unit) text box typically has the correct information by default. If you're unsure whether it's correct, or if this text box is blank, contact your Active Directory domain administrator for the correct organizational unit to enter.

Another authentication dialog appears that asks for the local server administration credentials.

12. **Enter your OS X Server administrator credential and password and then click OK.**

The Bind button in the Directory Utility dialog of Figure 6-6 changes to Unbind, which tells you that the binding has succeeded. The server is now bound to the Active Directory domain.

To test whether the binding is indeed successful, open a Terminal session to access the command line and type id *AD user shortname*. If the binding is successful, Active Directory returns the first 16 Active Directory groups of which the user is a member.

Deciding Whether to Muck Around with Advanced Configuration

In some cases, Mac administrators want to configure particular settings that appear in the advanced options of the Directory Utility to specify particular ways that the OS X Server interacts with Active Directory. In many cases, the default settings are fine, but in some cases, particularly when the AD schema is for a large company, you may need to make some specific changes to these settings.

All advanced options specify how the plug-in accepts information from Active Directory for the server itself. The configurations are not translated to clients and groups administered by the OS X Server on the Active Directory domain.

To access the advanced options for configuring the Active Directory plug-in, access the Directory Utility application by following Steps 1 through 9 in the previous section, "Binding the server." Click the triangle next to Show Advanced Options to expand the advanced options, as shown in Figure 6-8.

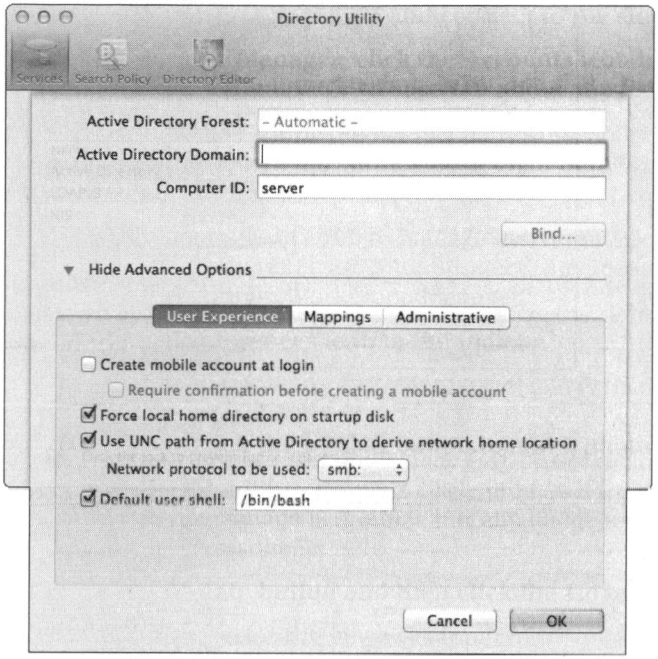

Figure 6-8:
Advanced
options
for Active
Directory
integration.

Three tabs are available in the advanced options:

- ✔ **User Experience:** This tab lets you change some default settings for users, including changing the location of the home directory to point to an external file server rather than the hard drive on the local OS X Server.

- ✔ **Mappings:** This tab allows the administrator to redirect default user and group ID settings to customized extensions in the Active Directory schema. These mappings may or may not come into play, depending upon the configuration of the Active Directory schema. Contact your Active Directory administrator for details.

- ✔ **Administrative:** This tab enables the administrator to direct contact between the OS X Server and Active Directory domain to a specific domain server. You can also allow domain administrators or other groups to administer without the need to log in with the server's login credentials. And you can allow the server to look up user and password information for domains administered by Active Directory that reside outside the local domain. (These domains are cryptically referred to as *other domains in the forest* in IT architecture parlance.)

Managing User Groups with Workgroup Manager

The important thing to remember about managing users in an Active Directory environment is that you need to add the users from Active Directory to your Open Directory domain on the Mac server. Doing so is necessary because Active Directory manages the permissions and policies of the users in an Active Directory environment. Active Directory user information isn't directly translatable to a Mac client. Open Directory serves as the mechanism to implement client management policies similar to the policies that Windows clients enjoy from Active Directory.

Adding users from Active Directory is as simple as dragging and dropping users into Open Directory, which you can do with Workgroup Manager, which you can download at `http://support.apple.com/kb/DL1567`. Follow these steps:

1. **Open Workgroup Manager.**

   Workgroup Manager asks you to authenticate with your local server manager username and password to connect to the local server.

2. **Enter your local admin username and password, and then click OK.**

   Workgroup Manager opens.

3. **Click the lock icon to bring up an authentication dialog to allow changes to Open Directory.**

4. **Enter the username and password for the Open Directory administrator, and then click OK.**

5. **Click the Accounts icon in the toolbar (the default) and then click the Groups icon directly below the Accounts icon.**

   The window now looks similar to Figure 6-9.

6. **Click the New Group icon in the toolbar.**

   Workgroup Manager creates a new group with a group ID (GID).

7. **In the Name text box, type a name for the group.**

   The name can include characters, numbers, and spaces. The short name is automatically created and will abide by Unix naming conventions, so you're free to name the group any way you like. You can also supply a path to an icon by entering the path in the Picture Path text box and a comment, but this isn't necessary.

8. **Click the Members tab.**

   A blank members table opens.

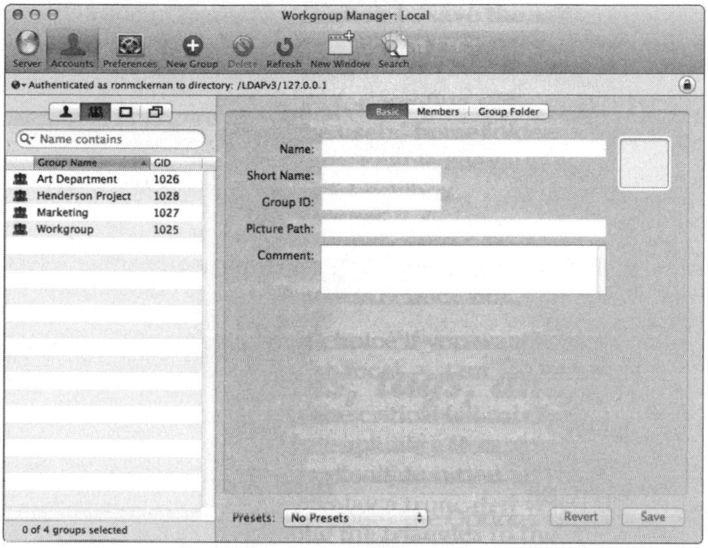

Figure 6-9:
The Group accounts area of Workgroup Manager.

9. **Click the Add (+) button near the upper right, as shown in Figure 6-10, to display the Open Directory users list.**

   A drawer slides open on the right or left, listing the names of Open Directory users.

Figure 6-10:
Accessing Open Directory users.

10. **Click the directory menu at the top of the drawer (refer to Figure 6-10) to access the Active Directory domain.**

    A list of Active Directory users for your domain is returned. All records may not appear in the list, but you can gain access to any user record in the domain via the search field.

11. **Drag the records you want to manage from the drawer list to the user list in the main window.**

12. **After you identify all records that you want to manage, click the Save button.**

    At this point, Active Directory is managing authentication for the users in the groups.

Configuring Single Sign-On for Mac Clients

After successfully binding the Mac server to the Active Directory domain (see the section "Binding Your Server to Active Directory," earlier in this chapter), another step to consider is to implement Kerberos on the server. Both Active Directory and Open Directory use Kerberos for authentication across various applications so that after a user logs in to the network, the user can access all network assets, such as file servers, for which he or she has permission without the need for further authentication. Doing away with the need for multiple passwords and authentications is called *single sign-on*.

Single sign-on in Active Directory works by AD's issuing a *ticket* when a user logs in to the domain. The ticket represents everything that the user can do. After a user logs in initially, the ticket handles all other authentication activities automatically.

For single sign-on to work for Mac clients on an Active Directory network, single sign-on must first be implemented in Active Directory. Single sign-on implementation in Active Directory is beyond the scope of this book.

To implement Kerberos and SSO for Mac clients in an Active Directory domain, you need to type a command in the Terminal application (in the /Applications/Utilities folder). Type this:

```
sudo dsconfigad -enablesso
```

Test that single sign-on is working properly by logging in as a user and attempting to access a resource to which the user has permission that's managed by Active Directory. In a working deployment, access is granted without the need to reauthenticate.

Troubleshooting and Getting Help

You've come to this section, so I can only assume that something went wrong with implementing OS X Server on Active Directory. This short section describes some areas known to cause problems and provides some troubleshooting tips. Because every Active Directory implementation is different, troubleshooting every possible scenario is impossible. If these tips fail, however, remember that Apple stands behind its products and will help you figure out what's going wrong.

The most commonly reported issues are

- **DNS service problems:** The Mac client must use the same DNS servers as all the Windows clients on the network. To ensure that the correct DNS server is being used, open a Terminal session, and type `dig -t SRV _ldap._tcp.`*yourDomainDNS*`.com`. If DNS service configured properly, you should receive, in response, the IP address of your domain server. If not, either the Mac systems are using a different DNS server than the Windows clients or DNS is set up improperly on your Mac server.

- **Time server issues:** If the times on the Mac server and the domain server are more than five minutes apart, you'll be unable to join the domain.

- **`.local` domain issues:** The `.local` domain used by Bonjour may conflict with a `.local` Active Directory domain. If so, add the `.local` domain to the search domain settings in the Network preferences pane.

- **Replication issues:** In the past, binding a Mac to a large AD domain has resulted in the computer account being created on one domain and the computer account's password on another domain. If the replication interval isn't fast enough, the set password request fails, and the Mac isn't bound to the domain. Ensure that the same server is being used for both Kerberos and LDAP connections.

If you're still having problems, check out my MacWindows.com site. On the web since 1997, `www.MacWindows.com` features bug reports and tips regarding Mac integration with Active Directory, among other topics.

Part III
Serving Up Files and Printers

In this part . . .

Meat and potatoes. For many, network file and print sharing makes up the basic work of a server. Mountain Lion Server's roots go back to file-sharing software, Apple's 1985 release of AppleShare. Apple thought it would help Mac sales to businesses by providing a central repository for files that all Mac users could access. Today, file and print sharing are only two of many functions that the server provides to users, but they still play a central role in networks. Mountain Lion Server's file and print services support client computers running any operating system, as well as iPhones, iPads, and iPod touches. This part covers everything you need to know about file service.

You can easily share printers without a server, but print serving goes beyond giving users access to printers. It juggles multiple printing requests to any single printer and manages all your printers. And it provides user features, such as automatically sending a print job to a free printer rather than sitting in a queue. This part includes a chapter on how to use the built-in printer sharing software of Mountain Lion Server.

I also throw in a chapter on *permissions*, settings that determine who can do what to which files. Mountain Lion Server supports a set of easy-to-use permissions that you can configure in minutes. It also supports high-end, enterprise-level permissions for large and complex network situations. Use one or the other or mix and match.

Chapter 7

Setting Up File Sharing

. . . .

In This Chapter

▶ Looking at types of file sharing for Mac, Windows, and Linux clients

▶ Setting up file sharing

▶ Setting user and group permissions for share points

▶ Using FTP file service

. . . .

For many organizations, file sharing is the *raison d'être* for a server. It enables users to quickly and securely move files between computers sitting next to each other or in different buildings. Mountain Lion Server uses the native file-sharing methods of OS X, Windows, Linux/Unix, and iOS (IPad, iPhone, and iPod touch). Apple refers to shared folders as *share points;* Microsoft calls them *shares.* But they're the same thing in OS X Server.

The Server app provides a simple way to quickly set up file sharing and grant users and groups access. This chapter describes how to do this setup, and describes the file-sharing protocols and permissions involved in the setup. (Chapter 8 describes permissions in much more detail.) Apple's approach is to keep the more complex tasks out of the way. In fact, you may never need to use them. If that's the case, congratulations — you don't have to read most of this chapter.

Protocol Soup: AFP, SMB, and Other File-Sharing Methods

OS X Server can share files by using several standard *protocols* — sets of rules that the server and client use to share the files. Each protocol is known by its three-letter acronym. Because the acronyms are more widely used than the full names, Apple uses the acronyms in OS X Server and in the Help system.

File-sharing protocols 101

The different protocols are native to different operating systems, though Macs have the capability to use all these protocols. You can use multiple file-sharing protocols at the same time to support clients running OS X, Windows, and iOS:

✔ **For Macs—Apple Filing Protocol (AFP):** AFP is the native file-sharing protocol for Macs and should be your first-choice file-sharing protocol for Mac clients. It can be faster than SMB, and your Mac clients will have fewer file-sharing glitches. AFP also provides Mac users with special features that the other protocols don't support, such as the capability to search server folders with Spotlight. (Users need read permissions for a share point to search it.) AFP also supports Kerberos authentication, access control lists, and the extended attributes of some Mac files.

AFP also provides automatic reconnect: When a Mac client goes into sleep mode, OS X Server disconnects its AFP session. AFP can automatically reconnect to Mac clients after they wake, enabling users to resume working on open files from where they left off. Clients that wake up within a 24-hour period can reconnect automatically after waking. If the client Mac wakes after 24 hours, the user will need to log in.

Windows clients don't use AFP.

✔ **For Windows—Server Message Block (SMB):** SMB is the native protocol that Windows clients use to access file servers. Many Linux and Unix clients also use SMB. Mac clients running Mac OS X 10.6 or later can also access files by using SMB in Mountain Lion Server, but they get better results with AFP.

SMB is also referred to as Samba or CIFS (Common Internet File System). Samba is used in Linux, whereas CIFS comes from the Windows world. Although often used interchangeably, SMB and CIFS aren't actually the same thing, but the two technologies are often used together. OS X Server's SMB service is technically SMB/CIFS.

When OS X Server runs these protocols, the user can't tell that the shared files are on a Mac. To Windows clients, SMB share points hosted by Mountain Lion Server behave just as they do on a Windows server.

✔ **For iOS—WebDAV (Web-Based Distributed Authoring and Versioning):** Mountain Lion Server uses WebDAV for file sharing with iPads running a WebDAV-enabled app, such as Apple's Pages, Numbers, and Keynote. You'll also find plenty of free or inexpensive WebDAV file-sharing apps in the App Store. Just search for WebDAV.

✔ **For all OSs—File Transfer Protocol (FTP):** FTP is a different animal from AFP, SMB, and WebDAV. FTP volumes don't mount on a user's machine, and you can't open a document while it resides on an FTP server. A benefit of FTP is that any computer operating system can download files from an FTP server with a web browser. FTP is often used to serve files across the Internet, but it isn't secure. FPT is also a common way to remotely upload files to a web server hosted on your Mac server. Add an FTP client app to your iOS device, and iPads and iPhones can also move files to and from the server.

✔ **Network File System (NFS):** Mountain Lion Server has the capability to use NFS to host home directories, typically for Linux and Unix clients. However, you won't see anything about NFS in the Server app. If you know Unix commands, you can configure NFS with Terminal to share files and create NFS home folders. For more information, see Apple's *Mac OS X Server Command Line Administration* manual at `www.apple.com/server/docs/Command_Line.pdf`.

Security in file-sharing protocols

File sharing can work with or without encryption of passwords. No encryption, or *cleartext,* sends the straight characters of a password over the network. AFP is the most secure file-sharing protocol, and FTP is the least secure. Here's the security lowdown for each protocol:

✔ **AFP** can send login passwords to the server as cleartext or with Kerberos encryption. Cleartext is disabled by default in Mountain Lion Server but can be turned on via the command line. (See `http://support.apple.com/kb/HT4700` for directions.)

If you upgraded your Snow Leopard Server to Mountain Lion Server, your Macs may not be able to authenticate using Kerberos. You can fix the problem by typing this command in Terminal:

```
sudo sso_util configure -r REALM_NAME -a diradmin afp
```

The realm name is usually the same as the fully qualified domain name of the Open Directory master, but in all capital letters. Restart the server when you are finished.

✔ **SMB** supports sending passwords as cleartext or with Kerberos encryption, as well as with some older Windows encryption methods. SMB does not support encryption of transmitted data, however.

✔ **WebDAV** requires a user to enter a name and password (authentication) and uses SSL encryption.

✔ **FTP** sends all data as cleartext. It doesn't provide for encryption of passwords or data transmission. (The command line also supports FTP over `ssh`, or `sftp`, which is a secure connection.)

✔ **NFS** authentication always uses Kerberos but is less secure than the other protocols. NFS doesn't ask the user for a username and password. Instead, the client computer tells the server what the computer ID is. This means that anyone using that computer has access to whatever the user account has. This is what makes NFS authentication less secure than AFP and SMB. Like AFP, NFS file transmission can be cleartext or use Kerberos encryption. NFS is available only from the command line.

Configuring File Sharing

Unlike some other services, file sharing doesn't require much in the way of prerequisites on your network. You can use either a shared network directory or local user accounts. For a small network not connected to a larger network (where your server has a `.local` host name) you even can do without DNS.

You can use the Server app running on the server Mac or remotely from another Mac running Mountain Lion on the network. With just a few mouse clicks, you can turn on file service with several folders already shared. You'll want to designate your own folders as share points, set what types of computers can access them, specify who can access the shared folders, and control what users can do. The next few sections describe how to perform these tasks.

Logging in and turning on file sharing

If you're logging in to your server for the first time or if you're configuring it remotely, you may have to log in to the Server app before turning on file sharing. Here's how:

1. **Launch the Server app from the Dock.**

   If the Server app launches, go to Step 2. If the Choose a Mac window appears, go to Step 3.

2. **If your server doesn't appear in the sidebar under Hardware, choose Manage⇨Connect to Server.**

   If your server is listed under Hardware, you're already logged in and don't need to do anything else.

3. **Select a server from the Choose a Mac dialog and click the Continue button.**

   If you're running the Server app from your server, it will be listed as This Mac. To log in to another Mac on the network, select Other Mac.

4. **In the login dialog that appears, type a name and password. If the Server field appears, type the server's DNS name or its IP address.**

The username and password are those of the administrator account, which is the account you created when you installed the server.

If you chose This Mac in Step 3, the Server app enters the host name for you.

5. **Click the Connect button.**

When you're logged in, you can turn on file sharing by using the Server app:

1. **Click the File Sharing icon.**

2. **If the File Sharing switch is set to Off, click it to turn it on (see Figure 7-1).**

Figure 7-1:
You can turn file sharing on and off by clicking the big switch.

With File Sharing turned on, the Share Points tab will be selected. Note in Figure 7-1 that several share points have been created already. You'll probably want to create your own share points, but here's a description of the default share points:

✔ **Backups:** This share point appears if you've enabled Time Machine backup in the Server app. Macs set it for access because Time Machine is a Mac-only feature. The path for this folder is /Shared Items/Backups.

✔ **Groups:** When you create a new group in the Group pane and select the Give This Group a Shared Folder check box, a shared folder is created inside the Group folder. The folder is named after the group, and the users in the group have access to their group folder. This folder is located at the root level (/Groups).

✔ **Public:** This is a default share point. By default, administrators have read and write access. Other users can open items in the Public folder and copy items from it, but they can't put files and folders into it. The path for this folder is /Shared Items/Public.

✔ **Users:** This folder contains the home folders for administrators of the computer. It is located at the root level (/Users).

If the automatically created group folders fulfill your needs, you're finished. To share another drive, partition, or folder, read the following section.

Keep in mind that these default folders are all located on the server Mac's startup drive. It's a good idea to keep shared files on another storage device, such as another partition, a second hard drive, or RAID storage. To do so, you can add a location to share, as I describe in the next section.

Creating a share point

You can designate a folder or an entire hard drive as a share point to enable access by users. Here's how:

1. **Open the Server app, and then click File Sharing in the sidebar.**

2. **Click the Add (+) button (refer to Figure 7-1).**

3. **In the new dialog that appears, navigate to the folder or hard drive that you want to share; select it, and click the Choose button.**

   If you want to create a new folder to share, navigate to a folder or hard drive, click the New Folder button, and then type the name of the new folder. Select the new folder before clicking the Choose button.

After a few seconds, the new share point appears in the Share Points list in the File Sharing pane, ready for further configuration.

 There's a second method for creating a share point that uses the Finder's Get Info box rather than the Server app. In the Finder, select a folder and press ⌘-I. Under General, select the Shared Folder check box. Here, you can also set permissions.

With your new share point created, you'll want to decide which file-sharing protocols you want to use, depending on whether you have Macs, Windows PCs, or iOS devices.

Assigning file-sharing protocols to a share point

When you create a share point, it's shared automatically with the file-sharing protocols that Mac and Windows computers can access, AFP and SMB. You can turn off either of these protocols and add WebDAV access for iOS devices that have a WebDAV-enabled app. (Turning on FTP is different process, however, and is described in the section called "Setting Up and Using FTP File Service.")

To conserve hardware resources and increase security, turn off file-sharing protocols you're not using for any given share point. For example, if you have a folder that only your Windows users access, turn off AFP for that folder.

To enable and disable file-sharing protocols for any given share point, follow these steps:

1. **In the Server app, click File Sharing in the sidebar.**

2. **In the Share Points list, double-click the folder you want to configure.**

   A settings pane appears for that share, as shown in Figure 7-2. The path to the shared folder is displayed at the top under the folder name.

   In Figure 7-2, because the path starts with /Volumes, you can tell that the folder resides on a drive or partition that is not the boot drive. On any Mac, the path for a nonbooted volume starts this way. The *V* is always capitalized.

3. **Turn off a protocol for the share point by deselecting a check box next to Share with Mac Clients (AFP) or Share with Windows Clients (SMB).**

   Note that SMB shares not only with Windows clients but also with most Linux clients.

4. **To give iPad, iPhone, and iPod touch devices access to the folder, select Share with iOS Devices (WebDAV).**

5. **Click the check box to allow guest access if you want to permit anonymous users to access the share point without logging in.**

   This check box enables guest access for each of the protocols enabled.

6. **If you want the server to host users' home folders, select the check box called Make Available for Home Directories Over, and select AFP or SMB (for Macs or PCs) in the pop-up menu to the right.**

   Server-based home folders, which are used in larger organizations, enable users to access their documents and settings from different computers. Chapter 16 has more about server-based home folders.

7. **Click the Done button when finished.**

With the new point created, you can now determine who can access it. The next section describes this process.

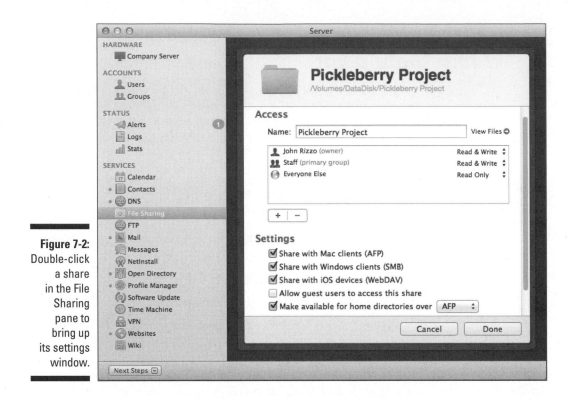

Figure 7-2:
Double-click
a share
in the File
Sharing
pane to
bring up
its settings
window.

Assigning groups to access the share point and setting permissions

While still in the pane of the share point you just created (refer to Figure 7-2), you can add users and groups to the Access list for that share point to restrict access to certain people or groups.

For a home or small network, the easiest method is to give everyone on the network read and write access (that is, the ability to create, edit, or delete anything in the share point). You do this by clicking the double arrows next to Read Only in the Everyone Else line, and selecting Read & Write, as shown in Figure 7-3.

Note that you can also select No Access, which you might do if you want only a few people to access the share point. The other option, Write Only, is sometimes called a *drop box* — users can copy files into a folder but can't open it.

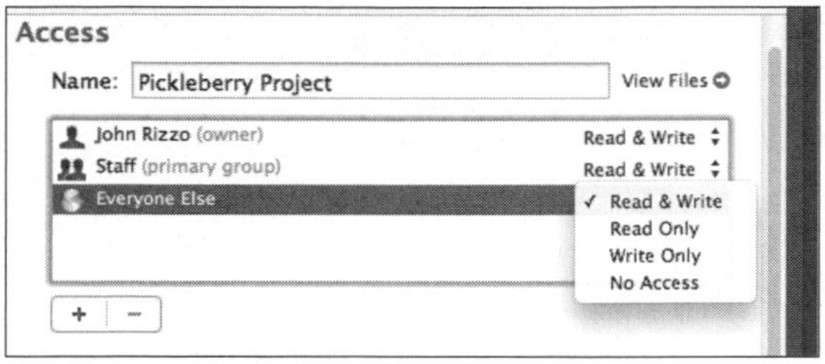

Figure 7-3:
Changing
Everyone's
access to
Read &
Write for a
share point.

Giving everyone access to everything may work with a handful of users, but in mid-to-large networks, you may want to assign different permissions to individual users. You do this by adding user and group accounts to the Access list in Figure 7-3 and set permissions for each. It's easier to keep track of permissions, however, if you add groups rather than individual users.

To add a user or group, follow these steps:

1. **Click the Add (+) button.**

   A new field appears in the Access list.

2. **Start typing the name of a user or group.**

   A drop-down list appears, listing users and groups that begin with (or are close to) the letters you've typed, as shown in Figure 7-4. Included in the list is Browse.

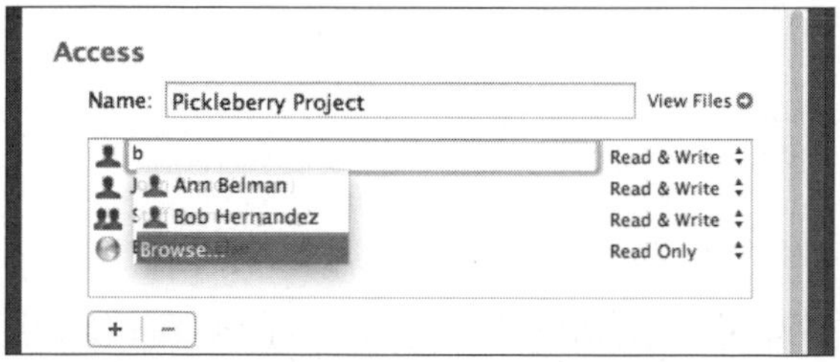

Figure 7-4:
Start typing
in the new
field to bring
up a list of
users and
groups.

3. **Select a user or group from the drop-down list or select Browse.**

   Selecting a name adds the user or group to the Access list, giving them read and write access to the folder. Selecting Browse brings up the dialog in Figure 7-5. To make multiple selections, ⌘-click on each name.

Figure 7-5:
Select a
group or
user to
which you
want to
assign
permissions.

4. **(Optional) If you selected Browse, select a name or add multiple users and groups by ⌘-clicking multiple names.**

   Groups are indicated with a two-headed icon.

5. **Click the OK button.**

   The users and groups you selected now appear in the Access list (refer to Figure 7-2), with full access (read and write permissions).

To change the permissions of any user or group, click the double arrows to the right and select a permission (refer to Figure 7-4). If you don't need to change the permissions of the users and groups in the list, click the Done button in the lower right of the File Sharing pane. For users and groups that you add to the Access list, you have three choices of permissions: Read and Write, Read Only, and Write Only. (See Chapter 8 for more information on these permissions.)

For the default users and groups — Owner, Primary Group, and Everyone — you have a fourth choice, No Access. This setting is a complete ban and over-rides other settings. You can use this setting to prevent access by a user who is a member of a group that has access to the shared folder.

If you see the word *Custom* listed as a permission for a user or group, it means that the permissions are set by ACL permissions in the server's pane. (See the next section, "Configuring ACL permissions (advanced)," for more on configuring ACLs.)

When you're finished making changes to permissions, click the Done button.

Configuring ACL permissions (advanced)

The permission settings described previously may be sufficient for most readers. But if you're in an enterprise environment, you may also want to use access control list (ACL) permissions for share points shared with AFP or SMB or both. ACLs give you a finer degree of access control. An ACL is the server's list of all permissions for all users and groups and for a share point. You add names of users and groups to the list and then use pop-up menus to assign permissions. ACLs are more complicated than POSIX permissions because they give you up to 17 choices: 13 permissions grouped by type, as well as 4 types of inheritance. I describe what they all do and how they work in Chapter 8.

With almost 100,000 possible combinations of ACL permissions, it's best to set permissions for groups and add user permissions only for exceptions.

Setting ACL permissions for a folder

The ACL permissions settings are well hidden in the Server app. Here's how to access them:

1. **Click the name of your server in the sidebar under Hardware.**

2. **Click the Storage tab and browse for and select a shared folder, as shown in Figure 7-6.**

Figure 7-6: Selecting a shared folder to configure ACL permissions in the Server app.

3. **Click the gear icon and select Edit Permissions from the pop-up menu, as shown at the bottom of Figure 7-6.**

   A list of users and groups that have access to the share point appears.

4. **If you want to add a user or group, click the Add (+) button and start typing the name of an existing user or group.**

   Users and groups you have added in the File Sharing pane have a triangle to the left. The default owner and group do not have a triangle.

5. **To configure ACL permissions, click the triangle to the left of the user or group name.**

   The first level of ACL permissions is exposed, as shown in Figure 7-7. You have four choices: Administration, Read, Write, and Inheritance. You can make choices here. A hyphen in a check box means that some, but not all, subordinate items for that category are selected. Selecting or deselecting a check box selects or deselects all subordinate items.

	Server	
User or Group	Permission	
▼ 👤 Ron McKernan	Custom	⇕
▶ ☐ Administration		
▶ ☑ Read		
▶ ⊟ Write		
▶ ☑ Inheritance		
▶ 👥 Art Department	Read	⇕
▶ 👤 Spotlight	Custom	⇕
👤 johnrizzo	Read & Write	⇕
👥 staff	Read & Write	⇕
🌐 Others	Read Only	⇕
+ − ⚙·	Cancel	OK

Figure 7-7: The first level of ACL permissions.

6. **(Optional) If you want to go even deeper into ACL permissions, click the triangles next to the choices to expand them.**

   The expanded choices are shown in Figure 7-8. (I explain all ACL permission choices, including inheritance, in Chapter 8.)

7. **Make any changes that you need and click OK.**

If you decide to share an application, set permissions so that very few people can change permissions for shared applications. In the ACLs, under Administration, few people should have the Change Permissions and Change Owner permissions. Malware such as viruses often targets permissions in applications.

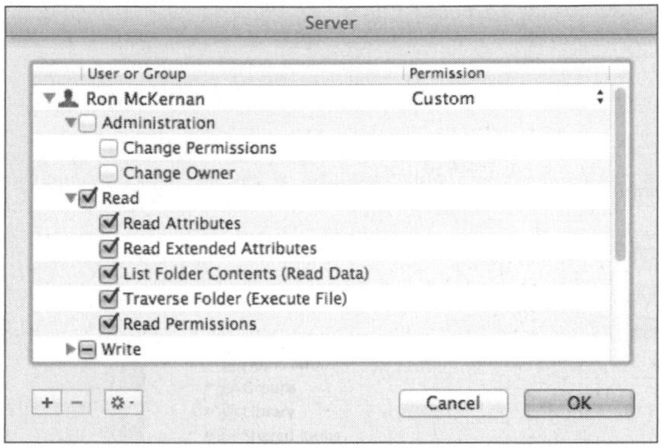

Figure 7-8:
Expanded
ACL permis-
sions.

Removing or adjusting a specific folder's inherited ACL permissions

When you use ACL inheritance settings, subfolders created inside a folder will inherit the permissions of the original folder. If you have a subfolder or file that you don't want to have those permissions, you can remove or edit them for just that folder without changing the inheritance settings for the other subfolders.

Editing these permissions for a particular user or group is referred to as *making the inherited permissions explicit.* Removing a user's or group's permissions for a folder with inherited permissions is called *removing an ACL entry.*

The procedure for both takes you to the same permission-editing dialog described in the previous section. Open the Server app and do the following:

1. **Click the name of your server in the sidebar under Hardware.**

2. **Click the Storage tab and browse for and select the shared folder (refer to Figure 7-6).**

3. **Click the Action menu (gear icon) and select Edit Permissions from the pop-up menu.**

   A list of users and groups with permissions appears. If permissions appear dimmed, they are inherited from a higher-level folder.

4. **Click the Action menu in the permissions dialog and select one of these options from the pop-up menu:**

   • *Make Inherited Entries Explicit:* When you choose this option, the formerly inherited permissions will no longer appear dimmed and are editable.

   • *Remove Inherited Entries:* The dimmed inherited permissions disappear from the list.

5. **Click the Cancel button to redo your selection or the OK button to approve.**

Chapter 8 has a thorough explanation of how inheritance works and how it can affect access.

Propagating permissions to subfolders

With either standard POSIX or ACL permissions, you can manually propagate them down through a folder hierarchy. That is, you can give folders inside a folder the same permissions of the parent folder. With POSIX permissions, you can choose to propagate the Owner, Group, or Others permissions, or any combination. With ACLs, you can propagate only a folder's entire ACL, not entries for individual groups or users.

To propagate folder permissions to all the folders and files inside, open the Server app and do the following:

1. **Click the name of your server in the sidebar under Hardware.**

2. **Click the Storage tab and browse for and select the shared folder (refer to Figure 7-6).**

3. **Click the Action menu (gear icon) and select Propagate Permissions from the pop-up menu.**

   The dialog shown in Figure 7-9 appears.

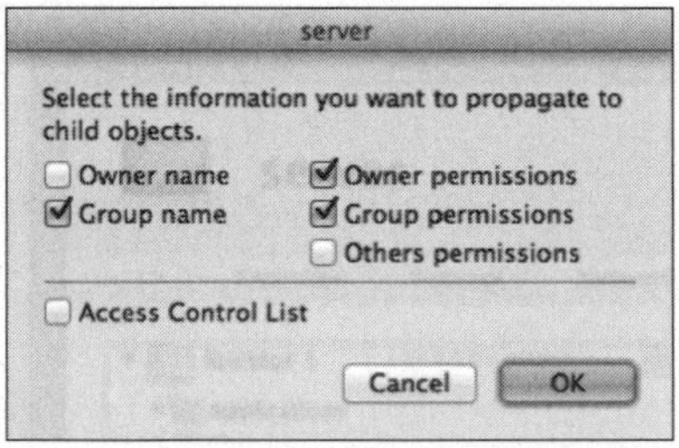

Figure 7-9:
Propagating
POSIX and
ACL permis-
sions with
the Server
app.

server
Select the information you want to propagate to child objects.

☐ Owner name   ☑ Owner permissions
☑ Group name   ☑ Group permissions
                   ☐ Others permissions

☐ Access Control List

     Cancel   OK

4. **Select the Access Control List check box to propagate ACLs, select the POSIX permissions in the top half of the dialog, or make both selections.**

5. **Click the OK button when done.**

   There is no undo here. Make sure that you've selected the right permissions before clicking OK.

Setting Up and Using FTP File Service

FTP file sharing has its own pane in the Server app, as shown in Figure 7-10. Configuring the FTP server involves two tasks:

1. **Choose a folder or share point to share with FTP from the Share pop-up menu.**

   The default share point is called Websites Root. This is the folder where the web service will store website contents. The Share pop-up menu lists already created share points, as well as a choice called Custom for selecting another folder.

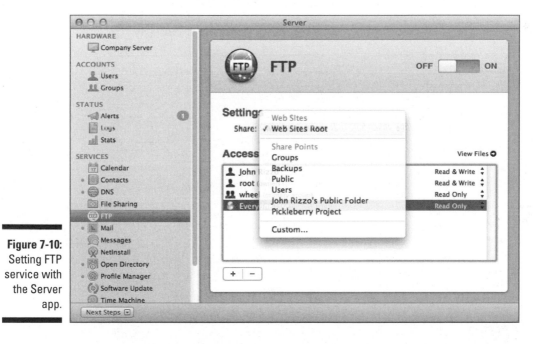

Figure 7-10: Setting FTP service with the Server app.

2. **Set permissions in the Access box, if it appears.**

   The Access box appears only if you select a folder that isn't already a share point, as in Figure 7-11. Here, you can add users or groups with the Add (+) button, and use the double arrows to the right to grant or deny access.

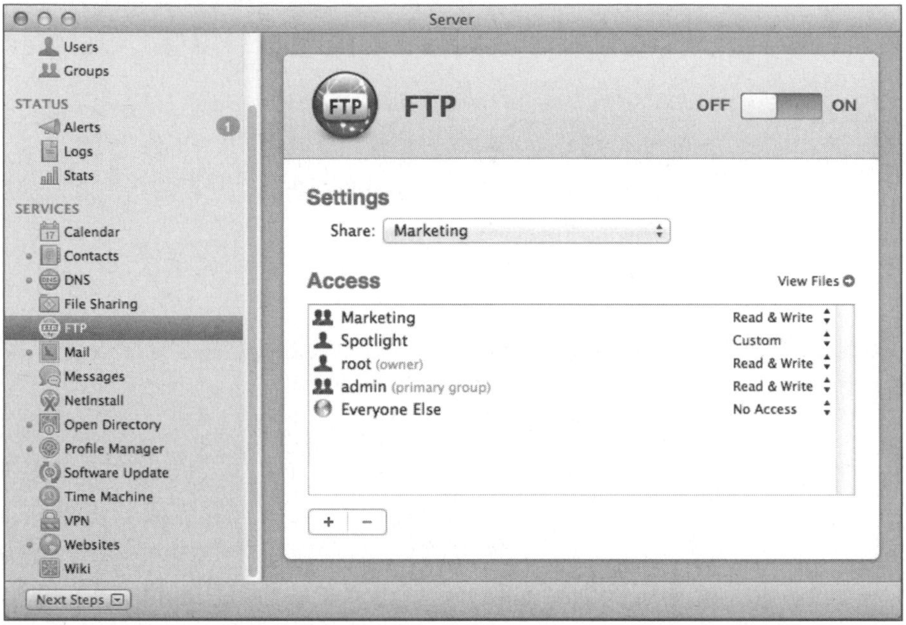

Figure 7-11:
Setting
permissions
with the
Access box
for a folder
that is not
shared.

Using the Server app, you can share only one folder or volume with FTP.

To access the FTP share point, clients can specify the IP address or the host name and path in their FTP client.

FTP is a great way to have your iPads, iPhones, and iPod touches move files to and from the server. Simply load your iOS device with an FTP client app, which you can find in the App Store. Two of the best are FTP On the Go Pro ($10) and FTP Client Pro ($2).

While you're at it, if you're looking for a good FTP client for users running OS X, Windows, or Linux, try the free, open-source FileZilla (http://filezilla-project.org). FileZilla is dependable and easy to use. Macs can also use the Connect to Server command in the Go menu to access an FTP server.

Chapter 8

Controlling Access to Files and Folders

*I*f you're a strict egalitarian, you may be inclined to give everyone on the network complete access to everything on the server. This approach might work at home or in a small office with a handful of users. With large networks, however, you'd run into problems of people changing things they shouldn't and having to sift through everyone's files and folders to find what they need.

Mountain Lion Server lets you control access by users to shared folders, files, and applications by setting *permissions*. You can also control who has access to entire services, such as file sharing, Calendar service, and Mail.

Chapter 7 describes some basic file-sharing permissions and how to set them. In this chapter, I delve deep into the two kinds of permission schemes, standard POSIX and access control lists, and their more advanced options. The topics in this chapter get progressively more advanced, so you can stop when you've have enough.

Defining Owner, Group, and Others (and Sometimes Everyone)

In the most basic file sharing, you set permissions for three user categories: *Owner, Group,* and *Others.* (There's also *Everyone,* which is similar to Others.) You can use the Owner, Group, and Others categories to restrict access to a certain set of users, provide different levels of access to different users, or prevent access. When you create shared folders (called *share points*), Mountain Lion Server assigns default permissions to these three classes of users. Owners get read and write permissions, and Groups and Other get read-only.

These user categories are hierarchical; a user gets the permissions of the highest level to which he or she is a member. So, if a user is both the owner and in a group, the user gets the read and write permissions of the owner, not the lesser permissions of the group.

You can change the default permissions for a Group and Others to give them read and write permissions. In more complicated setups, you can also set different permissions for each individual user. This is described in the section "Working with Access Control Lists."

But first, here's a little more about the user categories.

Owner

The *owner* can be a user with a local account or one with a directory domain account. By default, the owner of a file or folder is the user who created it. The owner could also be the administrator.

The owner usually has the highest level of permissions: the ability to do anything to a file, such as edit, delete, or copy it. The owner is the only entity that can change permissions for groups or for Others. The owner can also change the owner — that is, transfer ownership to another user.

The owner doesn't have to be a person — the owner can be an entity of the operating system or the operating system itself. In the latter case, this owner is system, the equivalent of the Unix root user.

Group

A *group* is a collection of users for which you create accounts. When a folder on the server has permissions for a particular group, all members of the group can access the folder. I describe creating groups with the Server app in Chapter 16.

Others, Everyone, and Guests

Others, Everyone, and Guests share some similarities: They all refer to users who aren't an owner or in a group. By default, these users get the lowest level of permissions, which may mean no access at all.

But there are differences. *Others* are users who are logged in to the file server but are not owners or members of a group for a particular file or folder. *Everyone* includes anonymous users who are not logged in to the file server. You never have to choose between Others and Everyone in a dialog because they are used in different places. *Guest* is like Everyone, but is found only in the settings for file services (not for individual shared folders), where you can choose to Allow Guest Access. Doing so allows anonymous users who aren't logged in to access that file service or protocol without using a password. Guests have access only to files and folders with privileges for Everyone.

Standard POSIX Permissions versus ACL Permission Schemes

Mountain Lion Server offers two different kinds of permissions for files and folders. The first, standard POSIX (Portable Operating System Interface for Unix), is from the Unix world. Access control lists (ACLs) are from the Windows world.

Here's the basic difference between the two: For any share point or shared folder or file, POSIX permissions allow you to set permissions only for the Owner, one Group, and Others. ACLs give you the additional option to set permissions for multiple individuals and multiple groups for a shared item. ACLs also have more types of permissions.

POSIX permissions are easier to use and may be all that a home user needs. ACLs give you a finer degree of control over access to files and folders but can quickly become complicated to manage. ACLs can be useful if you have several departments in an organization that need different levels of access for the same shared folder.

Note, too, that although POSIX permissions can be used with any method of file sharing, ACLs can be used only with the most common file-sharing protocols (which I describe in Chapter 7). Table 8-1 shows the permission types that each file-sharing protocol can use.

Table 8-1 . Permission Types Available to File-Sharing Protocols		
File-Sharing Protocol	*POSIX Permissions*	*ACL Permissions*
AFP (Mac only)	Yes	Yes
SMB (best for Windows)	Yes	Yes
WebDAV (iOS devices)	Yes	Yes
FTP	Yes	No
NFS	Yes (files only)	No

You won't find NFS (Network File Sharing) in the Server app. Advanced administrators with knowledge of Unix can configure NFS from the command line in the Terminal application.

The following sections look more closely at POSIX permissions and ACLs.

Working with Standard POSIX Permissions

Among other things, POSIX permissions define a permission structure for accessing files and folders. POSIX permissions are used not only in file sharing on a network but also on the Unix computer itself. Because OS X (and, therefore, Mountain Lion Server) has Unix at its core, POSIX permissions are used on all files and folders on every user's Mac.

Because these permissions are used throughout OS X, POSIX permissions are often referred to as *standard* permissions (or standard POSIX) in Apple documentation and elsewhere.

For any given file, folder, or volume, standard POSIX permissions have only four types of access that you can set for Owner, Group, and Others or Everyone:

- ✔ **Read and write:** Gives full access to a shared folder or file. A user can open and save files located on the server-based folder and can copy files to the folder.

- ✔ **Read-only:** Users can open the shared folder and files as well as copy a file or folder to their computer. But users with read-only access can't save changes to files that they open in the shared folder, and they can't add files to the shared folder or delete files.

- ✔ **Write-only:** Users can only copy a file into a write-only folder. They can't open the folder to see what's in it or access the files. A write-only folder on a server is sometimes referred to as a *drop box* or *drop folder*.

✔ **None (No access):** Users have no access to the folder or file and can't copy files to or from it.

Figure 8-1 shows these settings in the Server app. To display this window, click File Sharing in the left sidebar, double-click a shared folder, and then click the double arrows to the right. (Chapter 7 has more about configuring file sharing.)

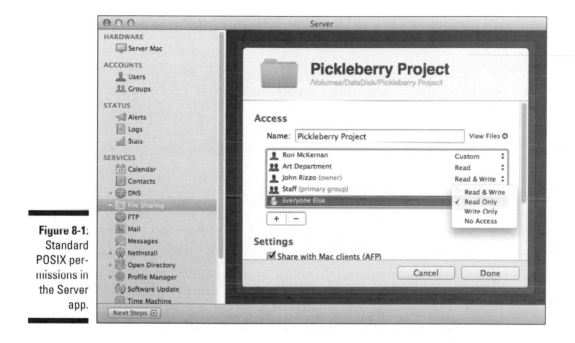

Figure 8-1: Standard POSIX permissions in the Server app.

In Unix, another POSIX permission is *execute.* This permission enables a user or group to run a program. In a Unix command-line shell, the execute permissions also allow you to list the files in a directory. Execute permissions are similar to read permissions, which let you open folders to see what's inside. The execute permission isn't used in the Server app.

When you configure file sharing, you generally set permissions for one or more shared folders *(share points).* Folders inside a share point are called *child folders.* By default, the server uses a set of rules to set Owner and Group permissions on new or existing child folders. This process is called *propagating permissions through the folder structure.*

In addition to this default behavior, the AFP and SMB file-sharing protocols have another option for propagating POSIX permissions, dubbed *inherit permissions from parent* or just *inherit permissions.* With this method, new files and folders inherit certain permissions from the *parent* folder (the folder in which the files and folders are created).

These two ways of propagating permissions are described in the next two sections.

Standard POSIX permission propagation behavior

In the standard behavior, permissions are assigned for new files and folders on a share point, *regardless of the permissions on the parent folder*. New files or folders get these permissions:

- ✔ **Owner:** The user who created the new folder or file becomes the owner and is assigned read/write permissions.
- ✔ **Group:** The new file or folder inherits the group assigned to the parent folder; however, the group is assigned read-only permissions.
- ✔ **Everyone/Other:** Everyone/Other is assigned read-only permissions.

Files and folders copied to the share point or duplicated don't inherit any permissions from the parent folder. Copied or duplicated files or folders get these permissions:

- ✔ **Owner:** The user who created the folder or file remains the owner and is assigned read/write permissions.
- ✔ **Group:** Retains the group and permissions of the *original* file or folder.
- ✔ **Everyone and Other:** Retains permissions of the *original* file or folder.

These rules are only the default ones. Administrators can change the permissions of new or copied files and folders.

Inherit permissions from parent

In addition to the standard POSIX permissions propagation described in the preceding section, the AFP and SMB protocols support an inheritance model for propagating POSIX permissions. In the inheritance model, certain permissions are inherited from the parent folder. This behavior can be more convenient.

Inheritance for folders works differently than inheritance for files:

✔ **Folders:** New folders and folders created in or copied to the share point (parent folder) inherit the Owner, Group, and Everyone permissions from the parent folder.

✔ **Files:** For files created in or copied to the share point, the Owner inheritance is different than that for Groups and Everyone. In particular:

- *Owner:* The user who created the file or copied it to the shared folder remains the owner.

- *Group and Other/Everyone:* The Group and Other/Everyone permissions are inherited from the parent folder. In other words, if a user copies a file or folder to a share point that uses the inheritance model, the Group permissions change to that of the parent folder. This behavior is different than the standard POSIX permissions behavior described in the preceding section.

The standard POSIX permissions propagation and the inheritance model rules are both applied to POSIX permissions. ACLs, described in the next section, have their own permissions propagation models.

Working with Access Control Lists

For more advanced, more flexible permissions, you can create an access control list (ACL). Windows clients and servers also use ACLs, which can give you compatibility in mixed-platform networks.

An *ACL* is a list of users and groups that have access to a share point and its permissions and inheritance settings. Each entry in the list is an access control entity (ACE), which consists of a user or group and its associated permissions and inheritance settings.

Here's a simple ACL with two ACEs you might set for a share point:

	Permission	*Applies To*
User: ronmckernan	Read/write	This folder
Group: students	Read	This folder

Look familiar? That's because this ACL reproduces the standard POSIX permissions for a folder. One user (like the owner) has read/write permissions, and one group has read permissions. "Applies to this Folder" means no inheritance, as with POSIX permissions.

A limitation of POSIX permissions is that you can assign only one group and one user (the owner) access to a shared folder. With an ACL, however, you can continue to add users and groups to the list. In the following, I added a teachers group with read/write privileges and a second user with write-only access:

	Permission	*Applies To*
User: ronmckernan	Read/write	This folder
User: Tim Constanten	Write	This folder
Group: teachers	Read/write	This folder
Group: students	Read	This folder

Further deviating from POSIX permissions, you can refine the ACL by setting more specific permissions, in addition to read and write and adding inheritance. I made this change for the first user in the following:

	Permission	*Applies To*
User: ronmckernan	Read/create files/create folders/write extended attributes	This folder/child folders/child files/all descendants
User: Tim Constanten	Write	This folder
Group: teachers	Read/write	This folder
Group: students	Read	This folder

I describe these more specific ACL permissions in the next section.

ACL permissions

ACLs provide finer shades of what read and write mean. For example, you can set write permissions to enable a group to edit files but not to create new folders. You can also enable users to edit a file but not to delete it, as shown in Figure 8-2.

Apple's implementation of ACLs contains 13 permissions. You access these permissions in the Server app:

1. **Click the name of your server in the left column under Hardware.**

2. **Click the Storage tab and browse for and select a shared folder.**

3. **Click the Action menu (gear icon) and select Edit Permissions.**

4. **Click the Add (+) button and start typing the name of an existing user or group.**

    The Server app finishes the name.

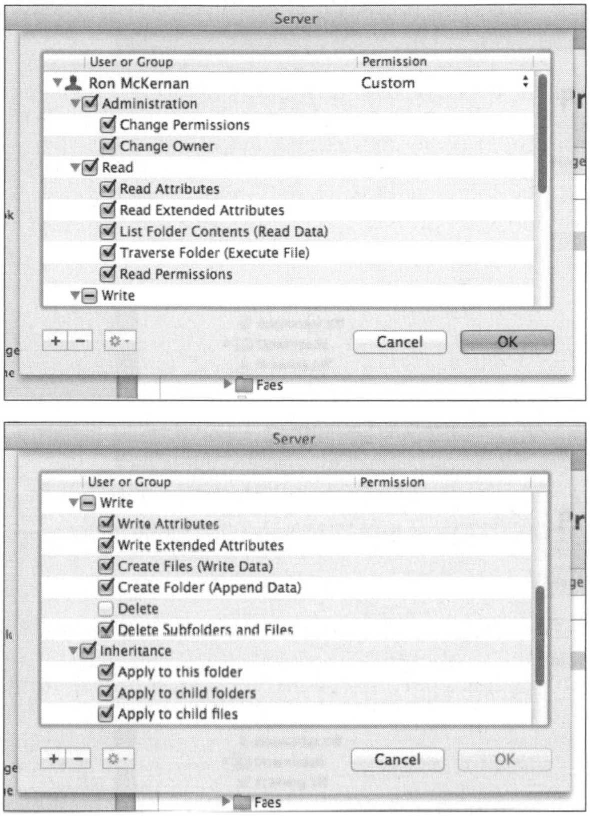

Figure 8-2:
The full set
of ACL per-
missions in
the Server
app.

5. **Click the triangle to the left of the user or group name.**

   You see four types of permissions listed. Click the triangle next to each
   to expand the list, to display the permissions under each type.

The permissions are as follows:

✔ **Administration:**

   • *Change Permissions:* Users can change standard POSIX permissions
     even if the users aren't owners.

   • *Change Owner:* Users can change the file's or folder's ownership to
     themselves or to someone else.

✔ **Read:**

   • *Read Attributes:* Users can view the file's or folder's attributes,
     including filename, date created, and size.

   • *Read Extended Attributes:* Users can view the file's or folder's meta-
     data added by third-party developers.

- *List Folder Contents (Read Data):* Users can view the folder's contents and open files.

- *Traverse Folder (Execute File):* Users can open subfolders and run programs in the folder.

- *Read Permissions:* Users can view the standard POSIX permissions of the file or folder with the Mac Finder's Get Info window (select the file or folder and choose Finder⇨Get Info) or with Terminal commands.

✔ **Write:**

- *Write Attributes:* Users can change the file's or folder's standard attributes.

- *Write Extended Attributes:* Users can change the file's or folder's other attributes.

- *Create Files (Write Data):* Users can create and edit files.

- *Create Folder (Append Data):* Users can create subfolders.

- *Delete:* Users can delete files or folders.

- *Delete Subfolders and Files:* Users can delete subfolders and files within the selected folder. You set these permissions on folders only. Files inherit permissions from the folder they're in.

With this staggering array of permissions, you can easily lose track of who gets access to what and how. Using a lot of these different ACL permissions can result in users being mysteriously being locked out of a folder and can be difficult to troubleshoot, especially when using inheritance. The best practice is to base your permission structure on group permissions. Set individual user permissions only when you need an exception, either with more permissive or more restrictive access. A good plan is to try to assign permissions to groups only once. Then if you need to change the access of individuals, just add or remove them from groups.

You can use ACLs only on storage devices formatted in the HFS+ file system, which is the Mac native format. If you want to use ACLs on a particular storage device that's formatted differently, you must first reformat that drive in HFS+.

ACL inheritance

You can apply one or more of the 13 ACL permissions to a folder. You can also set up to four types of inheritance to propagate these permissions to files in the folder and to folders within the selected folder. (Figure 8-2 shows three of the four choices for inheritance.) Each type applies to a particular level of folder hierarchy:

- ✔ **Apply to This Folder:** Applies permissions to the selected folder (the folder for which you're setting the permissions).

- ✔ **Apply to Child Folders:** Applies permissions to subfolders (folders one level below the selected folder).

- ✔ **Apply to Child Files:** Applies permissions to the files in the selected folder.

- ✔ **Apply to All Descendants:** Applies permissions to folders and files that are inside subfolders — that is, to items that are two or more levels below the selected folder (see Figure 8-3). By itself, this setting doesn't apply to the subfolders.

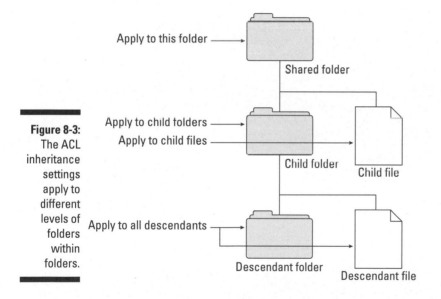

Figure 8-3: The ACL inheritance settings apply to different levels of folders within folders.

Apply to this folder → Shared folder

Apply to child folders → Child folder

Apply to child files → Child file

Apply to all descendants → Descendant folder

Descendant file

You can use the four inheritance settings in combination. If you select only Apply to This Folder, the ACL permissions settings wouldn't propagate but would apply only to the selected folder (and not folders inside this folder).

If you check both Applies to Child Folders and Applies to Child Files, the permissions would apply to the files and folders inside the selected folder but would not apply to the selected folder itself. Also, any folders inside the subfolders wouldn't get the permissions.

If you select Applies to This Folder and Applies to All Descendants, the permissions propagation would *skip a generation,* applying to the selected folder and to all folder levels below the first subfolder level.

Removing or editing inherited permissions

You can remove all inherited permissions from an individual folder or file that is inside a folder structure with inheritance settings. Just do the following in the Server app:

1. **Click the name of your server in the sidebar under Hardware.**

2. **Click the Storage tab and browse for and select a shared folder.**

3. **Click the Action menu (gear icon) and select Edit Permissions.**

   A new dialog appears.

4. **Click the Action menu, choose Remove Inherited Entries, shown in Figure 8-4, and then click OK.**

Figure 8-4: Removing inherited permissions from a file or a folder.

Instead of removing all inherited ACL permissions from a nested folder or file, you can edit them, similar to the way you create them in the parent folder.

(See the section "Working with Access Control Lists," earlier in the chapter.) However, before you edit them, you need to convert them from inherited permissions to *explicit permissions,* which are permissions you set manually without inheritance.

In Figure 8-4, a choice called Make Inherited Entries Explicit converts the inherited ACL permissions to explicit entries that are set for that folder or file. Explicit permissions are described in the next section.

Using inherited and explicit ACEs together

As mentioned, permissions that you set for a file or folder are called explicit permissions. Permissions that are inherited from a higher-level folder are called *inherited permissions.* You can use inheritance to automatically assign ACLs together with explicit permissions.

As an example, say that you have a share point called Publications. You've assigned a Marketing group with certain ACL permissions that propagate down through all the subfolders. For only two subfolders, you want to grant access to a second group, Art Department. For the contents of those two subfolders, both the Marketing and Art Department groups can have permissions for the files and folders in those subfolders. Within other subfolders, only Marketing has permissions.

Explicit permissions can also be propagated down through subfolders by inheritance settings. (Use the Propagate Permissions item in the gear icon under the permissions area.)You can set explicit permissions that propagate through a portion of the folder structure — useful for changing permissions for hundreds of folders and files all at once.

Troubleshooting with Rules of Precedence

If a user complains that he or she can't access a certain share or save a file, look at your permission structure and the inheritance. You may have one type of inheritance unexpectedly taking precedence over another. For example, check the permissions of the groups that the user belongs to. If you have multiple sets of permissions and inheritance, only one can apply for any given shared folder and user or group. Some permissions take precedence over others.

Here are some rules that define which permissions take precedence:

- **Standard POSIX permissions apply automatically if no ACL exists for a certain file or folder.** If you don't specify any permissions to a newly created share point (and none are inherited), the default POSIX permissions and inheritance rules are applied.

- **Deny permissions take precedence.** When the server sees a Deny permission, it applies it regardless of other rules or precedence. This behavior can unintentionally block access for a user.

- **ACL entries are first-come, first-served.** The order in which users and groups are listed in the ACL matters. If a user belongs to multiple groups in the list, the group listed higher takes precedence over one listed lower. If the first entry doesn't give a user the right to delete a file even though another permission farther down in the list does, the user can't delete a file in the folder.

- **OS X Server adds all Allow permissions.** OS X counts all the permissions that allow the user to do things and gives them to the user. If a user has one set of permissions and belongs to a group that has different permissions, the user gets the Allow permissions of both.

  After looking at all the ACL permissions that might apply to a user for a given folder, the server looks at the POSIX permissions for any Allow permissions that might apply. OS X Server then adds them to create the access to the file for the particular user or group.

Chapter 9

Sharing Printers over a Network

• •

In This Chapter

▶ Understanding printer sharing

▶ Creating shared printer pools for balancing loads

▶ Using System Preferences and CUPS to share and manage printers

▶ Keeping track of print jobs and printers

▶ Helping Mac, Windows, and Linux/Unix clients print

• •

*P*rinter sharing, or print serving, is a useful feature for both users and network administrators. For users, a print server eliminates waiting for a printer when it's busy. For administrators, a print server provides management tools that can keep track of how often different printers are used and who's using them, as well as keep track of print errors.

OS X Server allows you to set up a shared print queue for any printer. When a user presses the Print button, the print job goes not to the printer but to the shared print queue on the server. The print server feeds print jobs in the queue to the printer one at a time. You can also schedule printing and assign priority.

Mountain Lion Server includes the same print server and management interfaces found in every client copy of OS X. In this chapter, I describe using the two ways you can manage printer sharing: with System Preferences and with the CUPS web-based interface. I also describe how to limit access to printers using Workgroup Manager.

Listing Printer Sharing Features in Mountain Lion Server

The print server built into every copy of OS X is quite capable. These are its main features:

✔ Printers accessible by users on the same local network as the server

✔ Print queues stored on the server

✔ Sharing of network printers, not just printers connected to the server

✔ Support of Windows and Linux clients

✔ Automatic connections to the network directory

✔ Printer load balancing with pooling

✔ Remote administration from any computer and any OS with a web browser

✔ Kerberos authentication for printing

In the following section, I go through some of the terminology you encounter when setting up shared printing.

Printer Sharing Technology and Terminology

Centralizing printing with a server enables any client to print to any printer connected to the server. Without a server, the user's computer communicates directly with the printer, and the computer and the printer both need to support the same technology. When you throw a print server into the mix, you have two steps of communication — client to server and server to printer. The two steps don't have to use the same technology.

Mountain Lion Server supports a variety of types of printers. But in printing parlance, *printer type* can mean different things: USB, LPR (Line Printer Remote), inkjet, Ethernet, PostScript, IPP (Internet Printing Protocol), or laser printer. These sometimes-cryptic terms aren't equivalent, however. We're talking apples and oranges, with some cherries and pomegranates thrown in for good measure.

Communicating with the printer

Mountain Lion Server works with hundreds of new and old printer models. Here are the supported printer types:

✔ **Printer technology (laser, inkjet, others):** OS X Server doesn't care about how the ink's put on the paper. More exotic technologies may also work, depending on drivers and the other factors noted later in this list. Inkjet printers typically use USB to connect to the server.

✔ **Physical connection (USB, Ethernet, Wi-Fi, or Bluetooth):** You can share a printer that's plugged into the server Mac or a printer that connects directly to the network with its own Ethernet port.

Ethernet printers use a print protocol to communicate with the server over the network; directly connected USB printers do not. USB printers are easier to configure in OS X Server, but Ethernet printers are more convenient because you can locate them where the users are, not just where the server is located.

You can also share a wireless printer with built-in Wi-Fi (802.11 networking) or Bluetooth. Sharing a wireless printer isn't the same, however, as connecting a USB printer to a box that puts the printer on the Ethernet network. Apple's Time Capsule does this, as do some wireless routers and DSL modems. For the purposes of the OS X Server's print service, USB printers connected to wireless network devices are treated as Ethernet printers.

✔ **Page description language (PostScript, raster, or proprietary):** The page description language is what the client uses to describe the page; the printer reads the description to re-create the page in printed form. PostScript is a standard page description language for Ethernet printers. Some inkjet printers also use PostScript, though many describe a page with *raster* printing, which simply defines where dots are applied on a printed page. Proprietary page description languages are also used for specific printers.

✔ **Network printing protocol:** Mountain Lion Server uses Line Printer Remote (LPR) to communicate with printers and servers. These network protocols aren't used for USB printers-to-server communications. In that case, the USB data transmission standards are used to move print data from server to printer.

The server can use one printing protocol to communicate with the printer and another protocol to communicate with clients.

Communicating with the client

The print service in OS X Server can communicate with user client computers with one of three network printing protocols, which you set up a print queue to use:

✔ **Internet Printing Protocol (IPP):** Mac, Windows (XP and later), and Unix/Linux clients can all use IPP to print. When OS X clients print to a non-PostScript printer, they can use the printer's native driver installed on the client to have access to the printer's special features, which isn't available with LPR.

✔ **Line Printer Remote (LPR):** Mac, Windows (XP and later), and Unix/Linux clients can all use LPR to print.

✔ **Server Message Block (SMB):** Only Windows clients use this.

Client computers can use any of these protocols to transfer PostScript print jobs to the server. If you have a printer that uses a proprietary non-PostScript print driver, the printer will use IPP to send print job data.

A USB printer connected to the server Mac is a network printer as far as the client computers are concerned. So, although a USB printer doesn't use a network printing protocol to talk to the server, the clients do use a network printing protocol to send jobs to the server. Therefore, even if the USB printer is a raster (non-PostScript) inkjet printer, the client computers can use any printing protocol to send a PostScript job to the server. The server converts the PostScript job to what the inkjet printer expects to receive.

Mountain Lion's Print Management Software

OS X provides two choices of software that you can use to start and manage network printer sharing. The simpler and easier of the two is System Preferences, and it may be all that you need. System Preferences is the first place you'll go to turn on print sharing. The more powerful choice is the web interface to the Common Unix Printing System (CUPS). You can use either or both.

You can share printers connected to the Mac, or you can share network printers. For the latter, the print queue must be hosted on the server rather than the printer. Although System Preferences has limited capabilities, you can use it to restrict print sharing to certain users or groups in the network directory. You can also use Workgroup Manager to further limit which users and groups can access specific printers. Workgroup Manager is a separate download available at http://support.apple.com/kb/DL1567.

Looking at System Preferences for printer sharing

System Preferences, which is the equivalent of the Control Panel in Windows, is on the Dock by default and also accessible from the Apple menu. Found on all Macs — clients and servers — System Preferences generally is the place for user settings on a local Mac.

To set up printer sharing, you access two areas: the Sharing pane and the Print & Scan pane, as shown in Figure 9-1. I have more on System Preferences later in this chapter, in the section "Setting Up Shared Printing."

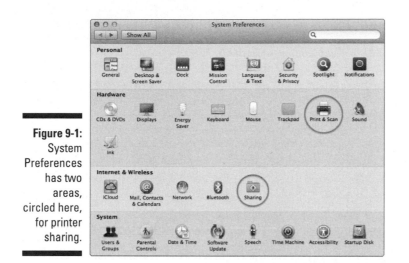

Figure 9-1:
System
Preferences
has two
areas,
circled here,
for printer
sharing.

Accessing the CUPS print engine from a browser

CUPS is actually the print engine in OS X and has been since 2002. Apple adopted CUPS soon after it was created as a print system for Linux in the late 1990s. Apple became a major developer and, in 2007, purchased the CUPS code and hired the creator, Michael Sweet. Apple continues to offer the CUPS code under open source licensing, so it continues to be part of many Linux distributions.

In OS X, System Preferences provides a simple front end to the CUPS printing system, and it may be all you need. OS X also includes a more detailed web-based interface to CUPS that you can access by typing one of these URLs in your web browser:

- ✔ `http://127.0.0.1:631`
- ✔ `http://localhost:631`

Use these URLs if you're logged in to the server Mac that is hosting the printing. If you're accessing your server from another computer, use instead a URL in this form: `http://server-ip-address:631`, where *server-ip-address* is the IP address of the server on which you have printer sharing enabled.

If you want to access CUPS from another computer (running any OS), you must enable Remote Administration. Open the CUPS web portal (the first page), click the Administration tab, and select the Allow Remote Administration check box.

The web interface of CUPS allows you to add printers and perform some tasks that you can't in System Preferences, including creating *printer pooling* (a type of load sharing) and print queues for network printers.

Figure 9-2 shows the home page of the CUPS web portal. The Online Help tabs take you to help and information pages. Much of the help information, however, is about the command-line interface.

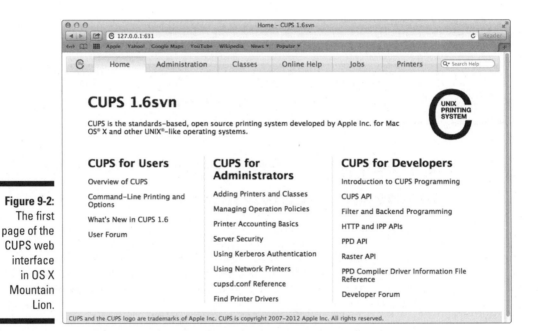

Figure 9-2:
The first page of the CUPS web interface in OS X Mountain Lion.

Setting Up Shared Printing

This section describes how to set up print service in OS X Mountain Lion by using System Preferences and then how to configure print sharing by using the CUPS web interface. This section includes balancing the printers' workload by creating printer pools and by managing printers and print jobs. I also describe how to use System Preferences and Workgroup Manager to restrict access to specific printers and to specify which printers show up in a user's list of printers.

Setting up your printers

Before you configure print services in OS X Server, make sure that your printers are connected to the network or plugged into the server. For network printers, it's a good idea to configure them by using a static IP address so that they have a consistent location on the network.

Some printers have print serving or spooling features built in. Turn *off* these features if you want your users to go through the OS X Server. Using two print queues (one in the printer and one on the OS X Server) can cause users to wait longer before their documents are printed.

Some printers also come with protocols that can advertise the printer over the network, such as SMB and Bonjour. You may consider turning off these features in these printers to prevent users from directly accessing the printers and avoiding the server-hosted print queues.

A good idea is to test print to the printer from a Mac and a Windows PC (if you have them) before you configure printer sharing on your server. This way, you can spot any trouble that the printer may be causing.

Turning on print sharing

You use System Preferences to turn on printer sharing:

1. **Open System Preferences and click the Sharing icon.**

2. **Select the Printer Sharing check box in the left column, as shown in Figure 9-3.**

   Printer sharing is now turned on, and you can select a printer to share (described in the next section). You may see printers listed in the lower right. If not, don't worry about it now.

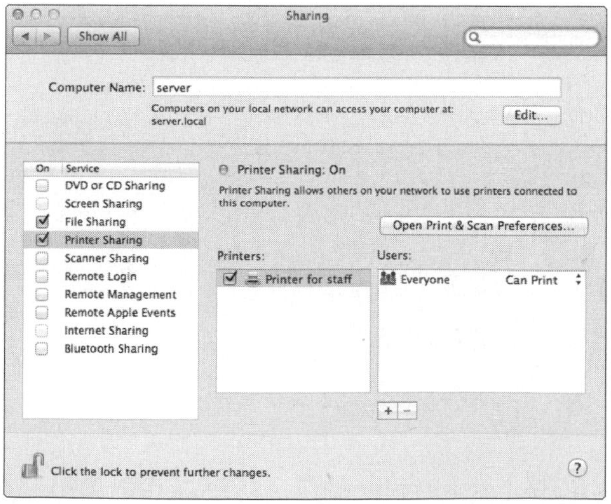

Figure 9-3:
The Sharing pane of System Preferences.

Checking the workgroup name for Windows clients

After you turn on printer sharing, check the workgroup name for your Windows clients. OS X has assigned a workgroup name of Workgroup, which is the default name on all your Windows PCs. If you have an existing network set up and have changed the Windows workgroup name, you can edit it by doing the following:

1. **In System Preferences, click the Show All button and then click the Network icon.**

2. **Select the network port on which your clients reside and then click the Advanced button in the lower right.**

3. **Click the WINS tab, as shown in Figure 9-4.**

4. **Type a new WINS name, if necessary, and then click the OK button (not shown in Figure 9-4).**

   The NetBIOS name is the same as the server Mac's computer name.

These settings help Windows PCs discover the server acting as a print server. Alternatively, you can install Apple's Bonjour for Windows on the PC, a free download at `http://support.apple.com/kb/DL999`.

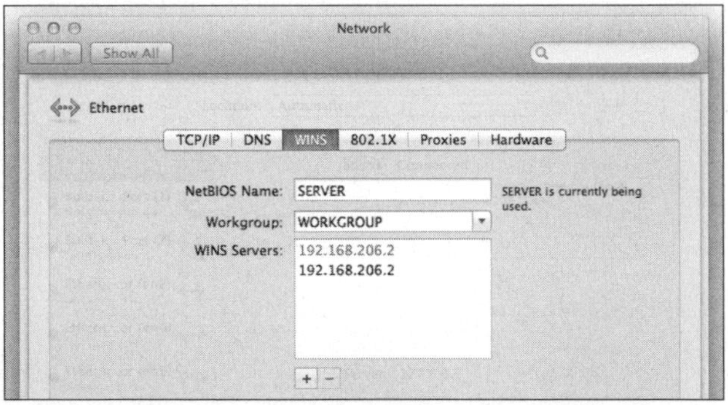

Figure 9-4:
You can change the default settings for Windows clients.

Sharing printers by using System Preferences

With printer sharing turned on, you can now designate printers to share. Start with System Preferences:

1. **In the System Preferences Sharing pane, make sure that Printer Sharing is selected and turned on.**

You may see one or more printers listed (refer to Figure 9-3).

2. **If a printer you want to share appears in the list, select the check box next to its name, and you're done.**

   If the printer isn't listed, proceed to the next step.

3. **If the printer you want to share doesn't appear in the list, click the Open Print & Scan Preferences button.**

   The Print & Scan pane appears, as shown in Figure 9-5.

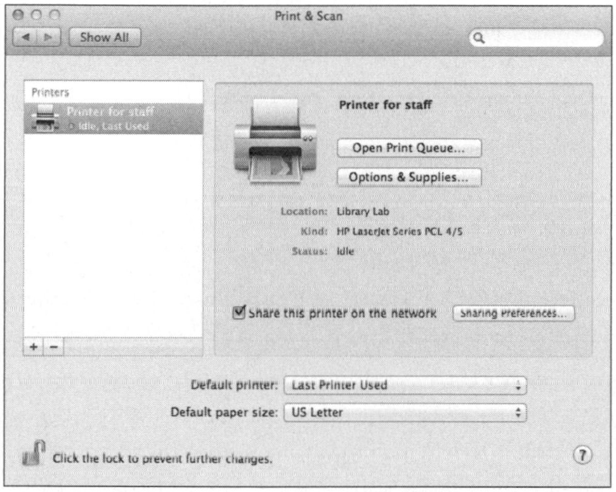

Figure 9-5: Selecting a printer to share in the Print & Scan pane of System Preferences.

4. **Select a printer in the Printers list and then select the Share This Printer on the Network check box.**

5. **(Optional) To give the printer a new name that is more recognizable to users, click the Options & Supplies button, enter a name and location in the corresponding fields, and click OK.**

   You return to the Print & Scan pane.

If you don't see your printer in the list, it is probably an IP network printer (not attached to the Mac) and probably doesn't support Apple's Bonjour technology. You can add your printer manually from this same Print & Scan pane. You need to know the printer's IP address and the print protocol that it uses.

Follow these steps to add a printer that doesn't appear in the Print & Scan pane:

1. **In the Print & Scan pane, click the Add (+) button, below the Printers list.**

   The Add window appears, as shown in Figure 9-6.

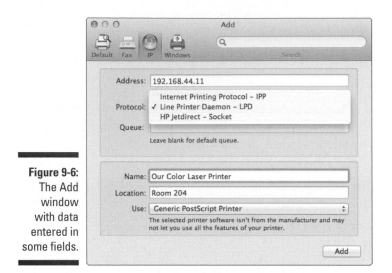

Figure 9-6:
The Add
window
with data
entered in
some fields.

2. **Click the IP icon in the toolbar.**

3. **Click the Protocol pop-up menu and then select your printer's connection method: IPP, LPD, or HP Jetdirect (refer to Figure 9-6).**

4. **In the Address field, type an IP address or a DNS name.**

   After you type an IP address or a DNS name, the Mac searches the network to find the printer. If the printer is turned on and is found, the Mac adds the correct PostScript Printer Description file (PPD) in the Print Using pop-up menu. Otherwise, the Mac selects Generic PostScript Printer for you. You can also select a printer from the menu.

5. **Type a name and location for the printer.**

6. **Click the Add button.**

   The printer appears in the Printers list of the Print & Scan pane.

7. **Share the printer by selecting it in the Printers list and then selecting the Share This Printer on the Network check box.**

You can add a printer also by using the CUPs web interface (described next).

Sharing printers by using the CUPS interface

The CUPS web interface isn't as simple to use as System Preferences (see the preceding section), but if you're doing other work with CUPS, you can use it to designate printers to share. The CUPS web interface also provides more choices when you're manually configuring printers to add.

Here's how to designate printers to share with the CUPS web interface:

1. **Open a web browser and go to the CUPS web interface by typing `http://localhost:631`) in the address bar.**

   You can also type `http://127.0.0.1:631`, or `http://server-ip-address:631`.

2. **Click the Administration tab.**

   The web page shown in Figure 9-7 appears.

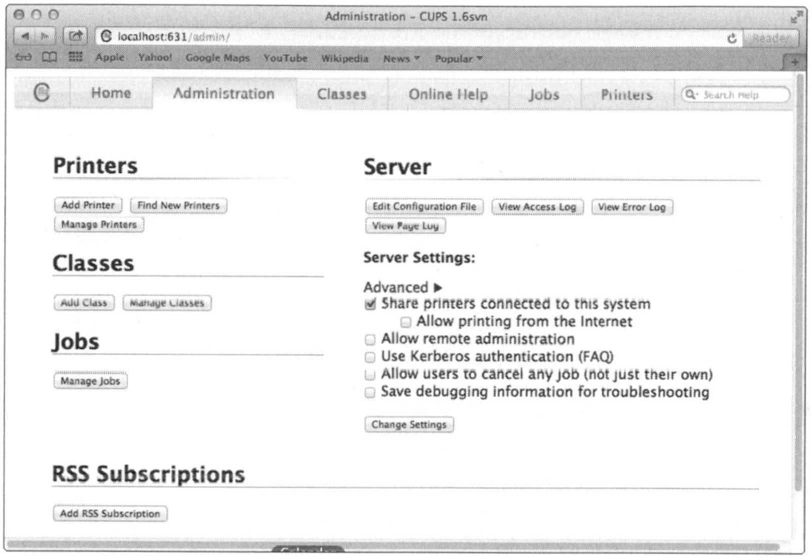

Figure 9-7: The Administration page of the CUPS web interface.

3. **If you haven't turned on printer sharing in System Preferences, turn it on now.**

   To do so, select the check box next to Share Printers Connected to this System and then click the Change Settings button.

4. **Click the Find New Printers button.**

   If CUPS finds any printers, they appear in the list.

5. **If you see your printer in the list, click Add This Printer and skip to Step 9.**

   Chances are, your printer will appear. If not, proceed to the next step.

6. **If you don't see your printer, click the Administration tab and then click the Add Printer button.**

   You may be prompted for your administrator name and password. If so, enter them and click the Log In button.

7. **Select one of ten types of printer, local, and network connections, and then click the Continue button.**

   Your choices include Bluetooth, fax, http, ipp (and the secure versions, https and ipps), and Windows printer via spools.

8. **If you choose a network printer connection, type the correct form of a URL identifier, using a host name or IP address; then click the Continue button.**

9. **Type a user-friendly printer name, description, and location and click the Share This Printer check box; click the Continue button when finished.**

   The printer appears in the Printers list.

Creating a printer pool by using classes

Here is something you can do with the CUPS web interface that you can't do with System Preferences: In a situation when a printer is heavily used, you may want to group two or more printers in a pool to share the load. A *printer pool* is basically a queue that contains multiple printers. When a user prints to the pool, the job gets printed to the first available printer. Often, administrators place the pooled printers next to each other so that users can easily find their printouts.

It's best to use printers of a similar model in a printer pool to ensure that printouts from the machines are the same and the printer features are consistent. If you have printers with different features, a user could select a print feature in his or her Print dialog that doesn't exist in one of the printers. This could lead to a situation where a print job won't print on one of the printers in the pool.

CUPS refers to printer pools as *classes*. To set up a printer pool, you use the CUPS web interface to create a class and assign printers to it:

1. **Open a web browser and go to the CUPS web interface by typing one of the URLs (such as `http://localhost:631`) listed in the section "Accessing the CUPS print engine from a browser," earlier in the chapter.**

2. **Click the Administration tab (refer to Figure 9-7).**

3. **Click the Add Class button under the Classes heading.**

4. **Type a name, a description, and the location of the class (or pool).**

   The name can't include spaces, slashes, or hash marks.

5. **In the Members list, select the printers you want to include in the pool. Then click the Add Class button.**

   The CUPS interface now takes you to a new management page for the new class, as shown in Figure 9-8.

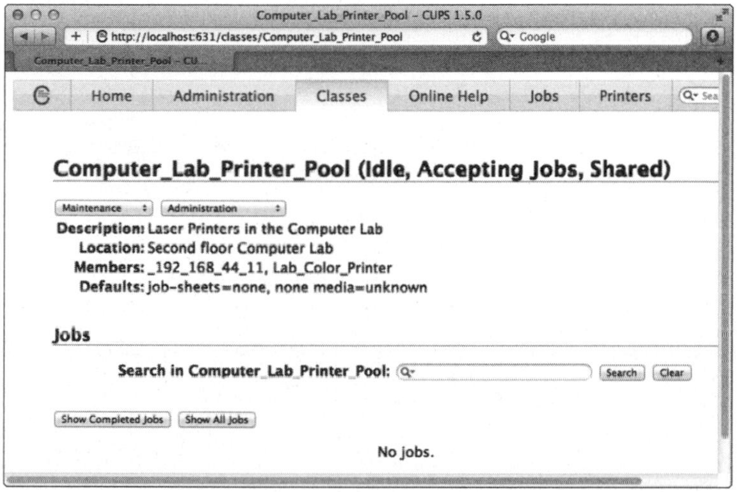

Figure 9-8:
The CUPS management page for a printer pool.

Computer_Lab_Printer_Pool – CUPS 1.5.0

http://localhost:631/classes/Computer_Lab_Printer_Pool

Computer_Lab_Printer_Pool – CU

| Home | Administration | Classes | Online Help | Jobs | Printers |

Computer_Lab_Printer_Pool (Idle, Accepting Jobs, Shared)

Maintenance | Administration
Description: Laser Printers in the Computer Lab
Location: Second floor Computer Lab
Members: _192_168_44_11, Lab_Color_Printer
Defaults: job–sheets=none, none media=unknown

Jobs

Search in Computer_Lab_Printer_Pool: [Search] [Clear]

[Show Completed Jobs] [Show All Jobs]

No jobs.

The management page for the class you just created is identical to the management page for an individual printer, accessible from the Printers tab. The Maintenance pop-up menu (refer to Figure 9-8) lets you manage jobs, giving you options to pause and resume all print jobs, as well as reject or accept all jobs and print a test page.

A useful option is Move All Jobs, which shifts current jobs in the pool to one printer, letting you take other printers offline without disturbing any printing.

The new printer class now appears in the print dialog of users' computers. You'll also see it in the System Preferences Print & Scan pane of the user and the server, with an icon showing three printers rather than one.

Restricting access to shared printers

When you first share a printer, all users on your local network can use it by default. You can restrict access to certain users and groups by using System Preferences or the CUPS web interface. System Preferences is easier to use for this purpose. After you share a printer on Mountain Lion Server, it automatically has access to the user and group accounts of your network directory, such as Open Directory; you don't need to do anything to connect the printer to the directory.

Although you can specify individual users who can access each printer or printer class (or pool), assigning groups to printer access is an easier option. You can create groups specifically for the purpose of printer access. (To create groups, use the Server app or Workgroup Manager , as described in Chapter 16.)

Restricting printer access by using System Preferences

To use System Preferences to restrict user or group access to a printer or printer class, follow these steps:

1. **Open System Preferences and click the Sharing icon to bring up the Sharing pane.**

2. **In the left column, select the Printer Sharing line.**

   Be careful not to uncheck the Printer Sharing check box.

3. **In the Printers list, select a printer or printer class (or pool).**

   By default, the Users field displays *Everyone Can Print.*

4. **Click the Add (+) button under the Users list.**

   A dialog appears, shown in Figure 9-9, listing four categories of users in the left column:

   • *Users & Groups:* This category consists of users and groups with *local* accounts. Use this category if you don't have a network directory, such as Open Directory.

   • *Network Users* and *Network Groups:* These two selections each display shared network accounts.

   • *Contacts:* This category consists of accounts listed in Contacts Server (see Chapter 10).

5. **Select a user category in the left column and one or more users or groups in the right column, and then click the Select button.**

   Hold down the ⌘ key to select multiple entries.

   The user or group you selected appears in the User list in the Printer Sharing pane, as shown in Figure 9-10.

6. **(Optional) To add more users or groups, repeat Steps 4 and 5.**

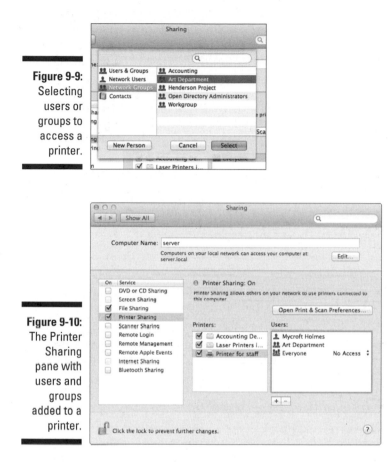

Figure 9-9:
Selecting users or groups to access a printer.

Figure 9-10:
The Printer Sharing pane with users and groups added to a printer.

The users and groups you add are able to access this printer or class. All other users will no longer have access. Also, any users you add to the Users list must have passwords in their directory accounts. User accounts without passwords won't be able to print to a printer that has restricted use.

Restricting printer access by using the CUPS web interface

Using CUPS to restrict access to printers takes a few more clicks and requires some typing, but it does give you a little more flexibility than System Preferences provides. Follow these steps:

1. **Open a web browser and go to the CUPS web interface by typing one of the URLs (such as `http://localhost:631/`) listed in the section "Accessing the CUPS print engine from a browser," earlier in the chapter.**

2. **Click the Printers tab (or Classes tab for printer pools), and then click the name of a printer (or class).**

3. **Choose Select Allowed Users from the Administration pop-up menu.**

   A page called Allowed Users for *printername* appears.

4. **Select either Allow These Users to Print or Prevent These Users from Printing.**

   Here's the extra flexibility that you don't get with System Preferences: By using Prevent These Users from Printing, you can easily give access to everyone except a few people or groups.

5. **In the Users field, type the names of users and groups, separating them with a comma and a space, and then click the Set Allowed Users button.**

Restricting access with Workgroup Manager

For a different take on restricting access to printers, you can use Workgroup Manager's *managed preferences.* (See Chapter 16 for more on managed preferences.) Instead of setting which users can access a particular printer, Workgroup Manager does the opposite, letting you set which printers can be accessed by a particular user or group. Follow these steps:

1. **Open Workgroup Manager, log in if necessary, and click the Preferences icon in the toolbar.**

2. **On the left side, just below the toolbar, click the Users or Groups icon in the short tab bar.**

   It makes more sense to set allowed printers for a group.

3. **Select one or more groups (or users) from the list on the left, and then click the Overview tab on the right, as shown in Figure 9-11.**

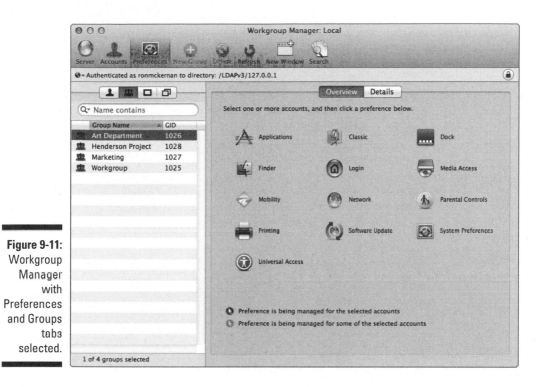

Figure 9-11:
Workgroup
Manager
with
Preferences
and Groups
tabs
selected.

4. **Click the printing icon.**

5. **Click the Always radio button next to Manage, as shown in Figure 9-12.**

6. **Under the Printer List tab, select one or more printers from the Available Printers field and then click the Add button.**

   Note: Printer pools (or classes) do not appear in Workgroup Manager and can't be used with managed preferences.

   In Figure 9-12, I've assigned the Art Department group access to the Accounting Department printer. This is the only printer users in the group will be able to print to.

7. **(Optional) If you want require a password to access the printer, click the Access tab and then select the Require an Administrator Password check box.**

   You can also select a printer and click the Make Default button to set the printer as the user's or group's default printer.

8. **Adjust any other settings, and then click the Apply Now button to accept all your changes.**

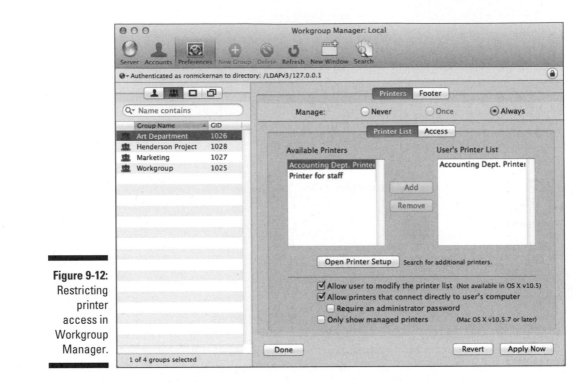

Figure 9-12:
Restricting
printer
access in
Workgroup
Manager.

Managing Printers and Print Jobs

With multiple printers shared on the network, you can use either Server
Preferences or the CUPS web interface to manage print jobs and printers.
Print pools (classes) are treated exactly like printers. The next few sections
describe some of these activities.

Using System Preferences to manage printers and jobs

Designating a printer to share automatically creates a print queue on the Mac
you're configuring. This is true even for network printers. The queue stores
users' documents waiting to be printed and feeds them to the printer when
ready.

You can see a list of the print jobs and users in the Print & Scan pane of
System Preferences (refer to Figure 9-5). Select a printer or a printer class

on the left and then click the Open Print Queue button. You can then hold or delete print jobs, see a printer status message (such as Paused or Out of Paper), and view the print queue's log file.

After you click the Open Print Queue button for a selected printer or class, you also see some additional menus in the menu bar at the top of the screen. For example, the Completed Jobs item in the Jobs menu displays a list of printed jobs.

One of the most interesting tasks is moving print jobs between printers. If a print job can't wait for the queue it's in, you can move the job to another printer by simply dragging and dropping it. Here's how:

1. **Open System Preferences and click the Print & Scan icon.**

2. **Select a printer that has the job to be moved, and then click the Open Print Queue button.**

   A separate print queue window opens. Move it to the side.

3. **In the Print & Scan pane, select the printer to which you want to move the job and then click the Open Print Queue button.**

   A print queue window opens for the second printer.

4. **Drag the print job from one printer's queue window to the other.**

A pretty neat trick!

Using the CUPS web interface to manage printers and jobs

The section "Creating a printer pool by using classes," earlier in this chapter, is the most useful example of what you can do with the CUPS web interface that you can't do in System Preferences. This section describes the rest of the CUPS web interface and some of the things you can do with it.

Keep tabs on the print server with RSS

You can set up Really Simple Syndication (RSS) feeds for individual printers, printer pools, or all your printers. When something happens to the printer or jobs, CUPS creates an RSS feed to alert you. You can read the feed in any RSS reader, such as Safari, the Mac's Mail program, or another RSS-capable web browser in any operating system.

The interface to turn on this feature isn't entirely user friendly. The following steps take the guesswork out of setting up your own feeds:

1. **Open the CUPS web interface by typing one of the URLs (such as `http://localhost:631`) listed in the section "Accessing the CUPS print engine from a browser," earlier in the chapter.**

2. **Select the Administration tab and then click the Add RSS Subscription button.**

   The Add RSS Subscription page opens, as shown in Figure 9-13.

Figure 9-13:
Creating an RSS for print server notifications with CUPS.

3. **In the Name field, type a name for the RSS feed.**

   The CUPS web interface is particular about the format of the name, and it doesn't tell you everything you need to do. If the format is wrong, the interface won't create a feed and won't tell you why. Here's what you need to know:

   • The feed name must end in `.rss`.

   • The feed name must not contain spaces, slashes, question marks, or hash marks.

   • It's best to use simple names.

   Remember this name or write it down. You need it to view your feed.

4. **Select a printer or class (pool) in the Queue field.**

   CUPS won't create an RSS feed if you don't click one.

5. **Select the check boxes next to the types of job, queue, and server events.**

   You may want to leave Job Created and Job Completed blank. Otherwise, your RSS feed could quickly fill with nonurgent RSS articles.

6. **Edit the Maximum Events in Feed field, if desired, and then click the Add RSS Subscription button.**

To view the RSS feed in a web browser, type one of the following URLs in a web browser, replacing the items in italic with your own information:

✔ From the server Mac: `http://localhost:631/rss/`*`feed-name`*`.rss`

✔ From another computer: `http://`*`host-domain-name`*`:631/rss/`*`feed-name`*`.rss`

Figure 9-14 shows a feed in a web browser, logged in from another computer, with an RSS article from CUPS.

Figure 9-14:
An RSS feed generated by CUPS alerts you to a printer problem.

Manage printers

Most printer management options in CUPS appear in two pop-up menus on the page for an individual printer or class. Click the Printers (or Classes) tab to get to the list of printers and then click a printer to get to its management page.

Items in the Maintenance pop-up menu (shown in Figure 9-15) are toggled — that is, when you choose Pause Printer, the item changes to Resume Printer the next time you open the menu. Items in this menu may change, depending on the type of printer and its features.

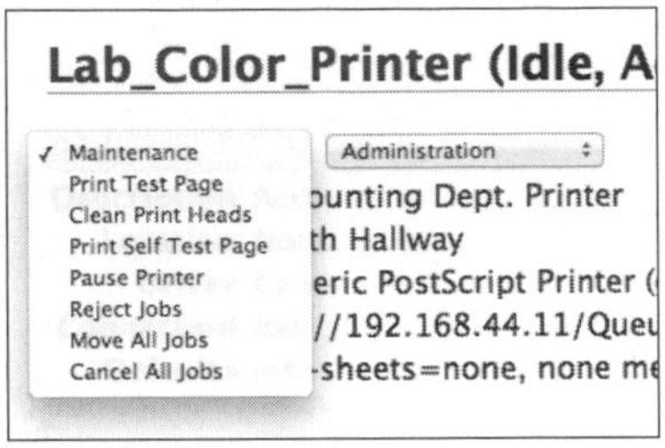

Figure 9-15:
The Main-
tenance
menu on
a printer's
manage-
ment page
in CUPS.

Lab_Color_Printer (Idle, A

✓ Maintenance	Administration ⬦
Print Test Page	ounting Dept. Printer
Clean Print Heads	
Print Self Test Page	th Hallway
Pause Printer	eric PostScript Printer (
Reject Jobs	
Move All Jobs	//192.168.44.11/Queu
Cancel All Jobs	-sheets=none, none me

The Administration pop-up menu contains items that take you to another page with more settings. Here are a few of them:

- ✔ **Modify Printer** is the place to go if you suspect that your printer is set up incorrectly. It takes you to the printer's configuration page, where you set the printer protocol and other items.

- ✔ **Set Default Options** includes a number of options, including print resolution, paper trays, and two-sided printing.

- ✔ **Set Allowed Users** lets you modify the users and groups that can or can't access the printer.

Manage print jobs in the CUPS interface

You can manage print jobs from multiple places. For example, you can move jobs between printers, although not as easily as with System Preferences. You have seen how to move print jobs from a printer's management page (refer to Figure 9-15). You can also perform this task from the Jobs tab.

The Jobs tab lists all printing jobs sent to the queues for your shared printers. You can filter jobs with a search field and a button for completed jobs. The entry for each job displays the status (such as Printer Not Responding or In Process). The Jobs tab also contains buttons to cancel a print job or send it to another printer (Move Job). Clicking one of these buttons brings up another window, where you choose the printer which to move the job.

To see a list of jobs for an individual printer or class only, go to the maintenance page for that printer or class. The jobs in the queue are listed at the bottom.

View logs and edit configuration file

The Administration tab (refer to Figure 9-7) lets you view three logs, including an error log, which is useful for troubleshooting.

The Edit Configuration File option on the Administration tab brings up a field where you can edit lines. It's handy to have because you don't need to go to Terminal to edit the file. But don't even think of touching this field unless you know what you're doing.

A note on the CUPS command line

One of the major features that the CUPS web interface provides is detailed documentation of the Unix commands that you can use in Terminal and how you can manually edit various configuration files. In fact, the Help system (accessible from the Help tab) is geared almost entirely to the text interface.

Some of the text commands, such as printing on both sides of paper, are oriented to the user. But many useful commands are for printer servers. Notably, you use the command line to set a *print quota* (limit on the number of pages a particular user can print to a particular printer each day). This command is described in the help topic called Printer Accounting Basics; you can also search for "quotas" in the CUPS Online Help field.

If you're interested in finding out how to use text commands, the place to start is the Getting Started link, followed by the Command-Line Printing and Options link. The Getting Started tutorial starts at the beginning with the print command lP *filename*.

Don't Forget Your Clients

You probably know how to enable your Mac, Windows, Linux, and iOS clients to print. In this section, I point out a few things that are helpful to know when your clients connect to OS X Server. I also mention some things you might want to remember for Mac and Windows clients.

PPD files

It's helpful for the server and client computers to have the correct PostScript Printer Description (PPD) files for the specific network printer models. The PPD files enable a user to choose special features, such as double-sided printing and the ability to select specific paper trays. OS X Server and Mac and Windows clients come with plenty of PPD files installed.

When adding a print queue to a client computer, you or the user chooses the PPD on the client by selecting the printer model from a list. If you don't see the PPD file on the client, or if the OS X server doesn't have it, check with the printer manufacturer or the software that came with the printer.

If you don't have a PPD file on the clients or the server for a network printer, the user can probably still print to that printer. OS X identifies the printer as Generic PostScript Printer. Users probably won't have access to special features of that particular printer model.

Helping Mac clients print

Since the earliest models, Macs have been good at printing, with easy setup and few printing errors. Today, you connect to network printers in the Print & Scan pane (called Print & Fax in Mac OS X versions before 10.7) of System Preferences. This is the same pane that you configure on the server Mac. You can also add a printer in the Print dialog of any application, in the Printer pop-up menu.

When a Mac client prints to a server's queue that's shared through IPP, the user can monitor the progress of the printing in the Print & Fax pane of System Preferences. The user can also delete a print job from the queue.

On an OS X client, to add a print queue that's shared through LPR and advertised through Bonjour, do the following:

1. **Open the Print & Scan pane (called Print & Fax before OS X 10.7) of System Preferences.**

2. **Click the Add (+) button, and then click the Default icon in the toolbar.**

3. **Click a print queue in the list. Then click the Print Using pop-up menu and select a PPD file for the printer model.**

   Usually, the correct PPD file is chosen for you. If you can't find it or don't know the printer model, choose Generic PostScript Printer.

4. **Click the Add button.**

If Bonjour isn't used with the LPR protocol, choose the protocol from the Protocol pop-up menu. You also need the IP address or the DNS name of the *server* (not the printer). You may also have to know the queue name.

Helping Windows clients print

The best thing you can do for Windows clients accessing your Mac print server is install Bonjour Services for Windows. *Bonjour* is a protocol that Apple created for the advertising and discovery of computers, printers, and other services over a network. Outside of Apple, Bonjour is called ZeroConf or Multicast DNS. (It was also once called Rendezvous.) Mac OS X 10.2 and later clients have Bonjour built in, but Windows doesn't. Apple offers Bonjour for Windows as a free download at `http://support.apple.com/kb/DL999`.

After you install Bonjour in Windows, open the Bonjour Printer Wizard and select a shared printer.

Alternatively, you can use the default (non-Apple) Windows software. Windows XP, Vista, and Windows 7 can send print jobs to the server by using SMB, IPP, and LPR. To connect to print queues on OS X Server, you can use the Add Printer Wizard. To find this wizard, choose Start⇨Printers and Faxes and then click Add a Printer. You can either browse for a discoverable print queue or type a printer address. The latter takes this form: `\\servername\printqueuename`.

Keep in mind that the server name is actually the NetBIOS name or a Windows domain server. You can edit this name on the server Mac, which I describe in the section "Turning on print sharing," earlier in this chapter.

If you have trouble finding a print queue shared with SMB, check the name of the print queue. If it's longer than 15 characters, the name will cause you problems.

Helping Linux and Unix clients print

Linux and Unix systems that use CUPS can print to shared printers in OS X. They need to be configured to send print jobs as PostScript, even if the printer hosted by your server Mac is a non-PostScript printer.

Unix and Linux users need the IP address of the network port of the server Mac. This is the port connected to the client's local subnet. You can find this port in the Server app by selecting your server in the sidebar and then selecting the Network tab. Unix and Linux users also need the queue name, which you can find in the Printers tab of the CUPS web interface.

Printing from iOS devices

iOS devices — iPads, iPhones, and iPod touches — can print directly over Wi-Fi to printers that support Apple's AirPrint. Of course, doing so bypasses the server and all its benefits. To enable iOS devices to print to your Mac OS X Server, you can download AirPrint Activator 2, a free Mac utility from

Netputing (www.netputing.com) that lets iOS devices print to any shared or network printer that is visible on your wireless network, including printers that are not AirPrint-enabled.

In addition, a low-cost commercial utility called Printopia for Mac from Ecamm (www.ecamm.com) works well.

On the device side, the iOS app — including the built-in Safari browser, Apple's iWork suite, and many dozens of third-party apps — must also support AirPrint. To print a document from an iOS device, do the following:

1. **Open the document or page, or select the content to print.**

2. **Tap one of the curved arrow icons (depending on the app) at the bottom of the screen to bring up a screen containing the Print option.**

3. **Tap the Print button.**

4. **Tap Select Printer.**

   The printers will be identified by the names you gave them on your server. You may find other print options here, depending on the app.

5. **Tap Print.**

To cancel a print job from the iPad, iPhone, or iPod touch, double-click the Home button, tap the Print Center icon, tap the print job, and then tap Cancel Printing.

Part IV
Facilitating User Collaboration

The 5th Wave   By Rich Tennant

"I hate when you bring Mountain Lion Server on camping trips."

In this part . . .

In the year 1624, John Donne wrote compellingly that "no man is an island, entire of itself." Of course, Donne was talking about collaboration software, also known as *groupware:* e-mail, group scheduling and calendars, text chat, and user-editable web pages.

But Donne wrote his profound reflection *before* Apple shipped Mountain Lion Server. He didn't know about some of the stuff that other servers don't provide: a wiki-based collaborative environment, already built when you turn on Mountain Lion Server; an interactive contacts manager that users can safely edit without tampering with directory services; and a messaging server that adds video conferencing to instant messaging.

And Donne didn't know that he could access it all from his iPad, iPhone, or iPod touch.

Well, I know it, and I'm sharing it with you in Part IV. It's not profound like *Meditation XVII,* but it does help you serve humankind — or at least your users — with groupware.

Chapter 10

Sharing Contacts with Contacts Server

"**D**o you have the phone number?" That's one question you won't have to ask when sharing contacts on your server. When someone adds an entry to a shared contacts list, everyone with permissions can see it with their Macs, iPads, iPhones, and some Windows PCs. Mountain Lion's Contacts Server also makes contacts available to the built-in contacts, mail, and messaging applications of Macs and iOS devices.

With Contacts Server, users can add or edit contacts without touching the network directory itself. Users can also search the network directory's global address list, which is a list of information that all users can see.

Instead of using Contacts Server, you could share contacts with Apple's iCloud. But hosting contacts on your own server gives you control of what users and devices can do. The larger your network, the more unwieldy iCloud becomes. And iCloud doesn't give you access to your network directory.

This chapter describes everything you need to know about setting up Mountain Lion Server's Contacts Server.

The contacts client and server is called Address Book in Mac OS X 10.6 and 10.7 but is called Contacts in OS X 10.8 Mountain Lion. Both products are basically the same.

> ## Contacts Server and network directories
>
> Contacts Server binds to a network directory, such as Open Directory or Microsoft Active Directory. This binding gives users read-only access to the network directory from the applications that act as clients to Contacts Server. But the key benefit to Contacts Server is that it enables users to modify contacts and add their own contacts to the server without modifying the network directory. Users can also create their own fields for contacts, such as for Twitter names or company-specific information. Such user manipulation is an unheard-of thought with directories based on LDAP (Lightweight Directory Access Protocol), including Open Directory, where changes by users usually aren't permitted or desired. Because Contacts Server acts as a gateway to the directory server, you don't need to give users write permissions to the network directory, and you don't need to modify the LDAP schema.
>
> Mountain Lion Server's Contacts Server stores contacts as standard *vCards,* or electronic business cards. The cards are stored outside the Open Directory or other LDAP directory. Users can e-mail or drag vCards to the desktop for sharing. Contacts clients connected to Contacts Server are authenticated from Open Directory and Kerberos.

Clients for Contacts Server

Apple's Mac and iOS devices have built-in support for Mountain Lion's Contacts Server, which uses an open standard, *CardDAV,* to communicate. Like CalDAV for Calendar Server, CardDAV is based on WebDAV and Hypertext Transfer Protocol (HTTP), both used on the web. Because these are open standards, client software for Windows can connect to Contacts Server.

Mac, iPhone, iPad, and iPod touch support

Mac OS X 10.6 and later come with several applications that support CardDAV and work with contacts service:

- ✔ Address Book in Mac OS X 10.6, Snow Leopard, and Mac OS X 10.7 Lion
- ✔ Contacts in Mountain Lion
- ✔ Mail in Snow Leopard and later
- ✔ iChat in Snow Leopard and Lion
- ✔ Messages in Mountain Lion

For iPad, iPhone, and iPod touch devices running iOS 4.0 and later, the Contacts app can display and add contacts located in Contacts Server.

Windows clients for contacts service

CardDAV Windows clients that support Contacts Server are not common but can be found. Here are two solutions:

- ✔ **eM Client** (www.emclient.com) is an all-in-one mail, contacts, and calendar application for Windows Vista and Windows 7.

- ✔ **SOGo Connector for Thunderbird** (www.sogo.nu) is free, open source software for Windows and Linux. It's a plug-in for Thunderbird, the open source e-mail and news client from Mozilla Foundation. SOGo Connector enables Thunderbird to access CardDAV servers. Although the main piece of software you'll see at the SOGo website is the SOGo groupware server, you don't need the SOGo server to get Thunderbird to work with Contacts Server.

Prerequisites

You don't need to do much to your network to make contacts service available to users. You don't even have to alter the directory. One requirement, though, is that the Mac on which you run Contacts Server must be configured as an Open Directory master. To do so, you use the Open Directory pane of the Server app, as described in Chapter 5. This configuration is necessary because Mac client users are provisioned in Open Directory; in other words, the directory services provide authentication and access privileges.

A DNS entry can be helpful in mid-to-large-sized networks but is unnecessary for home networks. And as with all services, you may need port forwarding if users access the service from the Internet.

Optional DNS

Although it's not a requirement, you can add a *service record* (SRV record) for CardDAV to a DNS server to help clients connect to the contacts service, particularly across the Internet. The service record can be on the DNS service running in OS X Server or on another server. The port number used depends on whether you're using a Secure Sockets Layer (SSL) certificate for contacts service.

If you're using an SSL certificate, the SRV record should map carddavs._ tcp for port 8443 of the server's host name:

```
_carddavs._tcp 86400 IN SRV 0 1 8443 server.company.com
```

If you're not using SSL for contacts service, add a record that maps `_card dav._tcp` for port 8008 to the server host name. For example:

```
_carddavs._tcp 86400 IN SRV 0 1 8008 server.company.com
```

If you're running DNS service in Mountain Lion Server, you can add an SRV record by using the Server app. Follow these steps:

1. **Select DNS from the sidebar, click the Add (+) button, and then select Add Service Record from the menu.**

2. **In the window that appears, select your server's zone, as shown in Figure 10-1.**

   You may only have one choice in the Zone field.

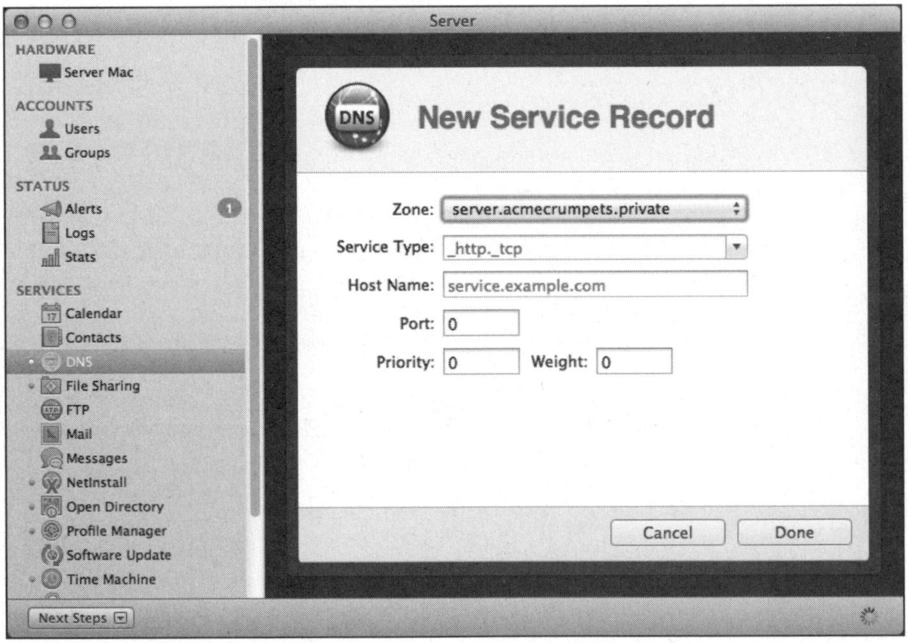

Figure 10-1: Creating a DNS service record for Messages Server.

3. **In the Service Type field, type _ carddavs._tcp**

4. **In the Host Name field, type the server's host name.**

5. **In the Port field, type 8443.**

   Type 8008 if you are not using SSL security with contacts service.

6. **In the Priority field, type 0. In the Weight field, type 1.**

7. **Click Done.**

Internet access through a router

If you want users to access Contacts Server from the Internet through a DSL or cable router or other Internet router, you must configure the router for port forwarding (also called port mapping). Port forwarding protects your network against attacks, while still permitting Address Book or Contacts users on the Internet to access the server.

With *port forwarding,* you set the router to forward traffic from the service port numbers to your server's IP address (shown in the Server app's Hardware pane). For contacts service, the port numbers are SSL 8443 with SSL security or 8008 without SSL. Check your router's instructions on how to configure it.

If you have an Apple router — AirPort Express, AirPort Extreme, or Time Capsule — you can manage it from the Server app. You use AirPort Utility to set the device's Connection Sharing option to Share a Public IP Address. You also need to set the IPv6 mode to Tunnel by choosing Settings⇨Advanced. When you're finished, the Apple router appears in the Server app's sidebar under Hardware. Click it to configure port mapping.

See Chapter 18 for more on using the Server app for port forwarding with Apple routers.

Setting Up the Contacts Server

To start Contacts Server, launch the Server app. Click the Contacts icon and then click the big switch to the On position, as shown in Figure 10-2.

To enable users to search the network directory's global address list, select the Include Directory Contacts in Search check box. If this check box appears dimmed, you haven't configured the Mac to be an Open Directory Master, as described in Chapter 5.

More-advanced settings are not accessible with the Server app but are accessible from the command line. To see all Contacts Server settings using the command line, open the Terminal utility and type the following:

```
sudo serveradmin settings addressbook
```

If you're familiar with configuring with Unix commands, you can change most of these settings by adding a colon followed by the setting and then the configuration value. For example, to set the SSL port number to 8443, type this:

```
sudo serveradmin settings addressbook:SSLPort = 8443
```

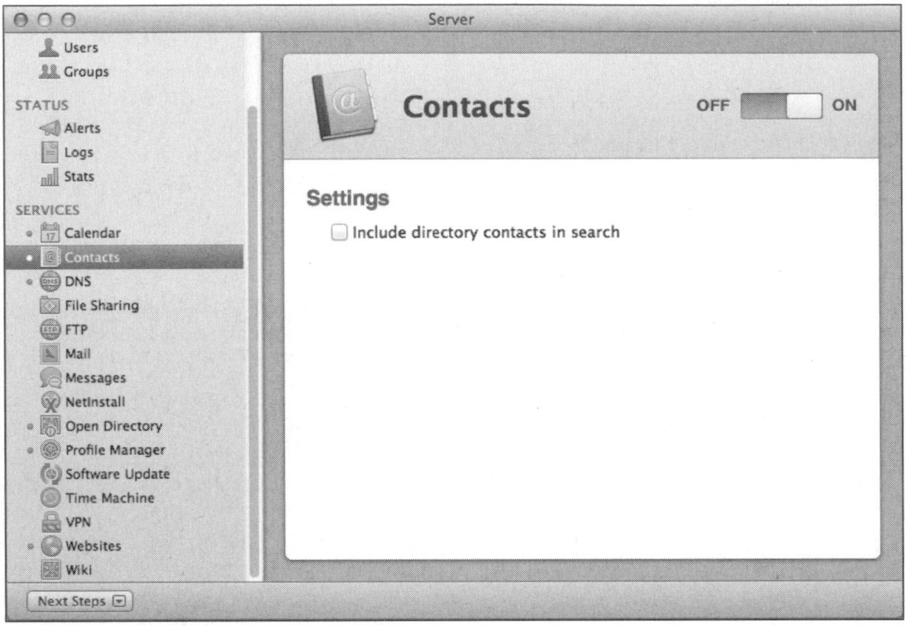

Server

- Users
- Groups

STATUS
- Alerts
- Logs
- Stats

SERVICES
- • Calendar
- • Contacts
- • DNS
- File Sharing
- FTP
- Mail
- Messages
- NetInstall
- • Open Directory
- • Profile Manager
- Software Update
- Time Machine
- VPN
- • Websites
- Wiki

Next Steps ▾

Contacts   OFF ☐ ON

Settings

☐ Include directory contacts in search

Figure 10-2:
Turning on contacts service in the Server app.

Disabling user access

You can disable all users or specific users from having access to Contacts Server. Open the Server app and click Users in the sidebar. Click a username or select multiple users by ⌘-clicking. Now click the Action menu (gear icon) and select Edit Access to Services. In the Server Access dialog that appears, you can select (or deselect) Contacts and other services.

Readers with some experience of Windows, Unix, or Linux servers might recognize this dialog as a graphical representation of the service access control list, or SACL.

Enabling Secure Sockets Layer (SSL) security

You can turn on SSL (Secure Sockets Layer) data encryption for contacts and other services by specifying a digital certificate to use. I recommend always using SSL with contacts to protect sensitive contact data.

Here's how to turn on SSL:

1. **In the Server app, click the name of your server under Hardware in the left column.**

2. **Click the Settings tab.**

3. **Click the Edit button next to SSL Certificate.**

4. **To turn on SSL for all services, click the Certificate pop-up menu and select a certificate.**

   To turn off SSL for all services, select None.

5. **To turn on SSL specifically for contacts, click the arrows next to Calendar and Contacts and select a certificate (see Figure 10-3).**

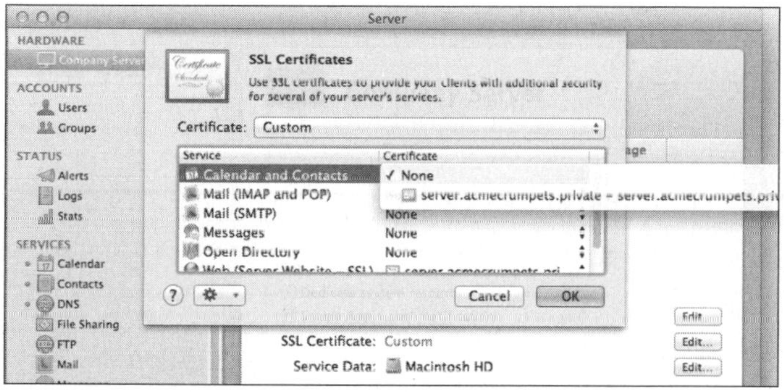

Figure 10-3: Enabling SSL encryption for calendar and contacts services.

Mountain Lion Server comes with a self-assigned SSL certificate that you use for secure services. If you don't see a certificate, open the Next Steps panel at the bottom of the Server application, click the Review Certificates button, and follow the directions. You can use a certificate obtained from a third-party certificate authority or your company's own certificate authority.

You can find more information about SSL and certificates in Chapter 18.

Enabling push notification

You can enable push notification to let Mountain Lion Server notify Macs and iPhone, iPod touch, and iPad devices of changes to data in network contacts. (Calendar and mail service also can use push notification.) Push notification works for clients running Mac OS X 10.6 and later and iOS 3.0 and later. Push notification uses security certificates from Apple, which are automatically obtained during installation. If you don't have a certificate, or have an expired certificate, you can obtain one with the Server app.

To turn on push notifications, do the following:

1. **Open the Server application and select your server under Hardware in the left column.**

2. **Click the Settings tab.**

3. **Select the Enable Apple Push Notifications check box, shown in Figure 10-4, and then click the Edit button to the right.**

   If an Apple certificate has already been created during setup, you'll see it in the Apple Push Notification Service Certificate dialog, along with the expiration date of the certificate.

Figure 10-4:
Turning on push notifications.

4. **Use the Change or Renew buttons to switch to another certificate or renew the current Apple push notification certificate.**

If you don't yet have a push notification certificate, the Apple Push Notification Service Certificate dialog asks you for an Apple ID and password. You can type the ID you use for your iTunes or iCloud account, though Apple recommends that you create a new Apple ID for your organization. (You can follow the instructions in this dialog to create a new Apple ID, if you need it.) If you already have an Apple ID, type it and click Get Certificate.

One more feature in the Apple Push Notification Service Certificate dialog is a link called Manage Your Certificates. Clicking it launches your web browser and takes you to the Apple Push Certificate Portal for your account, which lists your push notification certificates and tells you whether they are active or expired.

Setting Up Users' Client Devices

After your server is set up, you need to configure the client devices to connect to Contacts Server. In this section, I show you how to configure both Macs and iOS devices. Setting up Windows CardDAV clients depends on the third-party software you use, so I'm not discussing that task here. (See the section "Windows clients for contacts service," earlier in the chapter.)

You can also use Profile Manager to set up Mac and iOS devices from the server. I describe how to do so in Chapter 16.

Setting up a user's Contacts or client

The user client for contacts services is called Contacts in Mountain Lion and Address Book in Snow Leopard and Lion. The setup procedure is nearly identical for all three versions.

Enabling the client Address Book or Contacts application to access Contacts Server is referred to as *binding* the client to the server. After you bind, users are authenticated from Open Directory or Kerberos.

To set up the user's Contacts or Address Book (in Mac OS X 10.6 or later) to connect to the server, follow these steps:

1. **Launch Contacts (or Address Book) on the Mac client machine.**

2. **Click the Contacts (or Address Book) menu and select Preferences.**

3. **Click the Accounts icon in the toolbar and then click the Add (+) button.**

   The Add Account dialog slides down, as shown in Figure 10-5.

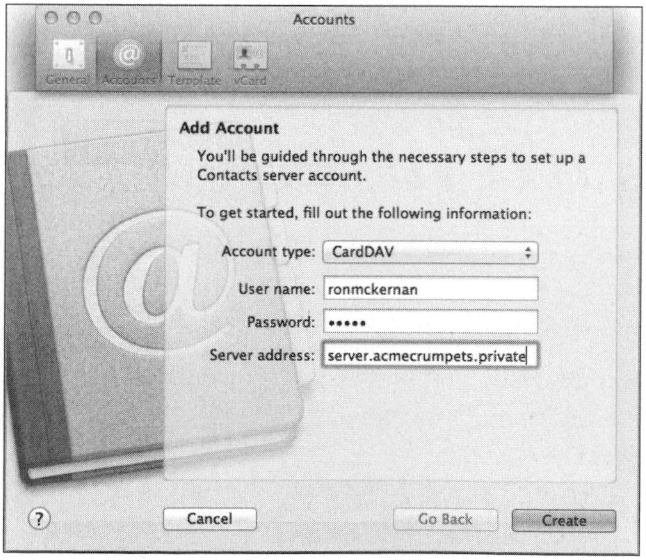

Figure 10-5:
Setting up a
Mac user's
Contacts
(or Address
Book) for
contacts
service.

> **Add Account**
>
> You'll be guided through the necessary steps to set up a Contacts server account.
>
> To get started, fill out the following information:
>
> Account type: CardDAV
> User name: ronmckernan
> Password: •••••
> Server address: server.acmecrumpets.private
>
> Cancel   Go Back   Create

4. **From the Account Type pop-up menu, choose CardDAV.**

5. **Type the username, password, and server host name.**

For example, type a host name like `ourserver.ourhouse.private` in the Server Address field.

6. **Click the Create button.**

The new server account is now in the Accounts list at the left of the Preferences window. When you select the account, the window displays the account information.

The Contacts Preferences window in Mac OS X 10.8 is similar to that of Address Book in OS X 10.6 and 10.7.

If you click the Server Settings tab, you can turn on SSL for this client's connection to Contacts Server. You can also change the port number (use 8843 for SSL).

In the Contacts 6 client in Lion, the server appears in the left page as an entry below the On My Mac area. When you select the server, it turns blue, and the names stored on the server are displayed on the right. The user can search the Contacts Server and Open Directory in the search field. The user can also add a new contact to the server by choosing File⇨New Card.

Address Book 5 in Mac OS X 10.6 looks and works differently. Contacts Server appears as a group with the user's name. The user can select Contacts Server and click the Add (+) button in the Name column. The other users can now see this contact. Additionally, an All Directories group appears, with the new group (on Contacts Server) and the network directory both colored blue. You use these for searching. Click Directory Services, and you can search Open Directory from the search field.

Setting up an iPad, iPhone, or iPod touch

To enable a device running iOS 4.0 and later to access Contacts Server, do the following:

1. **Tap the Settings app.**

2. **Tap Mail, Contacts, Calendars.**

3. **Under Accounts, tap Add Account.**

4. **Tap Other.**

5. **Under Contacts, tap Add CardDAV Account.**

6. **Type the Contacts Server's DNS name and the username and password in the appropriate fields.**

After Contacts Server is connected, it shows up in the iOS device's Contacts app, under Groups.

Chapter 11

Serving Up Calendars

*T*o a large degree, Mountain Lion Server's Calendar Server (formerly known as iCal Server) replicates the calendar of Apple's iCloud service. As with iCloud, when a user adds an item to a calendar, it appears on the user's iPhone, iPad, or iPod touch. Calendar Server enables users to share calendars and to-do lists, invite people to events, and include attachments. When scheduling an event, a user can check whether the people invited are available. Calendar Server allows users to *delegate* calendars to others, which enables users to access Calendar Server's calendar with a web browser. And like iCloud, Calendar Server supplies a web calendar.

So why use Calendar Server rather than iCloud? For control. You *could* use iCloud to share one or more calendars with the people on your network, but you would have little control over it. With Mountain Lion Server, you can specify not only who can use Calendar Server but also which handheld devices can access the calendar. You can use Profile Manager (see Chapter 16) to set up the iOS and Mac clients for use with Calendar Server in the way that best suits your organization.

This chapter describes how to set up Calendar Server and Mac and iOS clients. I tell you a bit about Windows clients as well.

Clients for Calendar Server

Calendar Server is based on the open CalDAV (Calendaring Extensions to WebDAV) standard, which means that client calendaring applications must also be CalDAV-compatible. Not surprising, all Apple calendar clients for Mac and iOS (iPhone, iPad, and iPod touch) use CalDAV.

In addition to CalDAV compatibility, some calendar clients are compatible with Mountain Lion Server's push notification service. These clients include iCal in Mac OS X 10.6 and 10.7 as well as Calendar in OS X 10.8 (Mountain Lion), and iOS 3 and later.

CalDAV clients exist for Windows, Linux, and older versions of Mac OS X that work with Calendar Server to various degrees. The following clients support the CalDAV standard:

- **Mozilla Sunbird and Lightning:** These two open source clients, from the people who brought you the Firefox browser, are available for Mac OS X, Windows, Linux, and Unix. Sunbird is a stand-alone calendar client. Lightning is an extension for the Thunderbird e-mail client.

  ```
  www.mozilla.org/projects/calendar
  ```

- **eM Client:** This commercial messaging client from E&S Software Ltd, is for Windows. In addition to CalDAV and Google Calendar, eM Client supports e-mail, contacts, and tasks.

  ```
  www.emclient.com
  ```

- **Chandler:** From the Open Software Application Foundation, Chandler is an open source calendar and tasks program for Windows, Mac OS X, and Linux.

  ```
  www.chandlerproject.org
  ```

- **GNOME Evolution:** For Linux and Unix, this is an e-mail, calendar, and contact client for users of the GNOME desktop interface. Evolution requires the CalDAV plug-in.

  ```
  http://projects.gnome.org/evolution
  ```

Glaringly missing from this list is Microsoft Outlook. Neither the Windows nor Mac versions support CalDAV, and neither can be used with Calendar Server.

Calendar Server and push notification service are based on open standards. The calendaring functionality uses CalDAV, which is based on WebDAV, which is based on Hypertext Transfer Protocol (HTTP). The push-subscriber technology uses the Extensible Messaging and Presence Protocol (XMPP), which is based on Extensible Markup Language (XML). XMMP sends a small message (like a tweet) to the client, telling it that new data exists. The client then fetches that data.

Prerequisites

Calendar Server requires a few things on your network before you can start using it:

✔ If a firewall is between Calendar Server and your users, it must be configured to allow traffic on TCP port 8008 (or 8443 for Secure Sockets Layer [SSL] encryption).

✔ Calendar Server needs directory service. (See the next section.)

✔ Calendar Server can work better with a DNS system with full reverse lookups running on the network in midsize to large networks.

Here are some more specifics about directory service and optional DNS.

Directory service for Calendar service

Calendar Server must be connected to a directory server of some type on the network. This could be Open Directory running on the same server as Calendar Server, accessible from the Open Directory pane in the Server app. (See Part II for more on directory services.)

Open Directory could be located on the same Mac server or on another server computer (Mac OS X 10.5 Server or later), or the directory could be another non-Apple LDAP server such as Microsoft's Active Directory. You don't need to modify the directory service.

Optional: Setting up DNS for calendar service

Although it's not a requirement, you can add a *service record* (SRV record) for CardDAV to a DNS server to help clients connect to the contacts service, particularly across the Internet. The service record can be on the DNS service running in OS X Server or on another server. The port number used depends on whether or not you're using a Secure Sockets Layer (SSL) certificate.

Setting DNS for calendar service on a non-Mac server

This section provides the SRV setting if you're not running Mountain Lion Server for DNS.

If you're not using an SSL certificate, the SRV record should map `card-davs._tcp` for port 8008 of the server's host name:

```
_caldav._tcp 86400 IN SRV 0 0 8008 calendar.example.com.
```

The _caldav._ term is for a standard connection. If you're using a secure SSL connection, use _caldavs._ instead. Be sure to include the underscores. Use port 8443. It looks like this for

```
_caldavs._tcp 86400 IN SRV 0 0 8443 calendar.example.com.
```

The 0 0 after SRV represent the priority and weight. These are 0 if only one CalDAV server is on the network. If multiple CalDAV servers are on the network, use numbers other than 0.

The 86400 represents the DNS time-to-live number, in seconds. 86400 is one day, but you can use another time period.

Setting DNS for calendar service in Mountain Lion Server

If you're running DNS service in Mountain Lion Server, you can add an SRV record by using the Server app. Follow these steps:

1. **Select DNS from the sidebar, click the Add (+) button, and select Add Service Record from the menu.**

2. **In the window that appears, select your server's zone.**

   You may have only one choice in the Zone field.

3. **In the Service Type field, type _** carddav._tcp **(or _caldavs._tcp if you're using SSL).**

4. **In the Host Name field, type the server's host name.**

5. **In the Port field, type** 8008.

   Type **8443** if you are using SSL security with the calendar service.

6. **In the Priority field, type** 0. **In the Weight field, type** 1.

7. **Click Done.**

Setting Up Calendar Service

You use the Server app to get calendar service up and running. Depending on what you want to do with your calendar service, several configuration tasks are involved, though not necessarily in this order:

✔ Start Calendar Server

✔ Restrict access

✔ Enable e-mail invitations

✔ Enable SSL encryption

✔ Add locations and resources

✔ Turn on push notification

✔ Enable web calendars

I describe how to do these tasks in the following sections.

Starting calendar service and restricting access

After getting your network ready, just a few mouse clicks get Calendar Server running:

1. **In the Server app, click the calendar icon.**

2. **Click the big switch to the On position (see Figure 11-1).**

   You're done.

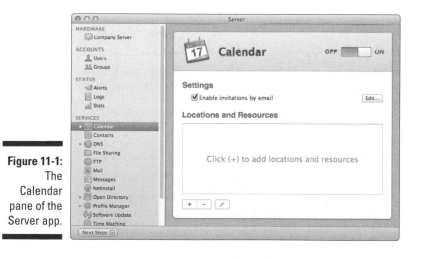

Figure 11-1:
The Calendar pane of the Server app.

As with other services, you can prevent users from accessing calendar service in the Users pane of the Server app. Select a user account, click the gear icon, and then select Edit Access to Services. Deselect the box next to Calendar to prevent the user from accessing shared calendars.

Enabling e-mail invitations

Mountain Lion Server can provide e-mail invitations to users who don't have Calendar-compatible client software — or even to users who don't have calendar accounts. When e-mail invitation is configured, a user invites an external user to an event by adding an e-mail address; Calendar Server checks the host name of the invitee's e-mail address. If the name isn't the same host name as the Calendar Server, Calendar Server can send an e-mail invitation to the invited person. The person can respond by e-mail, and the Server interprets the received e-mail as a response to the calendar invitation.

A prerequisite for running Calendar's e-mail notification feature is having your own e-mail server (either hosted in Mountain Lion Server or elsewhere) or e-mail with your domain, where Calendar Server itself has an e-mail account (such as `CalendarServer@acme.com`). Next, you have to provide Calendar Server with the POP/IMAP and SMTP server information — just as you do when setting up a user's e-mail client software.

Here's how to set up e-mail invitations:

1. **In the Server app's Calendar Server pane, make sure that the check box next to Enable Invitations by Email is selected.**

2. **Click the Edit button.**

   The Configure Server Email Address dialog box appears with a default e-mail address using your server's domain name (for instance, com.app. calendarserver@server.acmecrumpets.com).

3. **Accept this address or type another e-mail address that you'd like the server to use to notify users of invitations. Then click Next.**

4. **In the dialog box shown in Figure 11-2, enter the name of the incoming POP or IMAP mail server and the username and password. Then click Next.**

   The default username is your calendar server's host name. SSL is selected by default. The default port is 993. You can change all these here.

5. **Enter the name of the outgoing SMTP mail server, select an authentication type (Plain, Login, Kerberos, CRAM-MD5, or none), and enter the username and password. Then click Next.**

   A summary screen shows you the configuration you just entered.

6. **Click the Back button to make a correction or click the Finish button.**

   Calendar Server will restart after you click Finish.

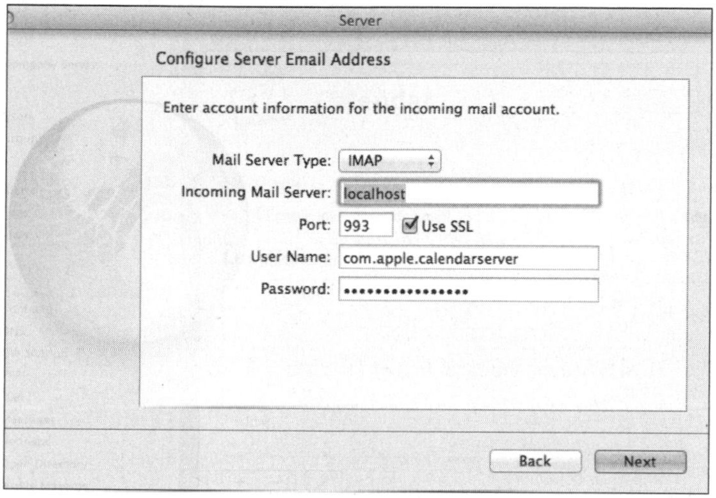

Figure 11-2:
Configuring
e-mail invitations with
an incoming
mail server.

Enabling SSL encryption

To enable SSL encryption with Calendar Server, you simply assign an encryption certificate to the calendar service. You can use the self-signed certificate that Mountain Lion Server's setup process created (which users will have to manually accept) or a signed certificate from a certificate authority. (See Chapter 18 for more on SSL certificates.)

You can use the Server app to assign an SSL certificate to Calendar Server:

1. **In the Server app, under Hardware, select your server and then click the Settings tab.**

2. **Click the Edit button next to SSL Certificate.**

   If your running services have different SSL settings (such as different certificates or some with No SSL assigned), you see a list of services and their SSL settings, as shown in Figure 11-3.

   If all your services have the same setting, the dialog displays only the Certificate menu, with either the word *None* or the name of the certificate. If this is the case, click the menu and select Custom to arrive at the screen in Figure 11-3.

3. **Click the arrows to the right of Calendar and Contacts and select a certificate from the pop-up menu.**

4. **Click OK.**

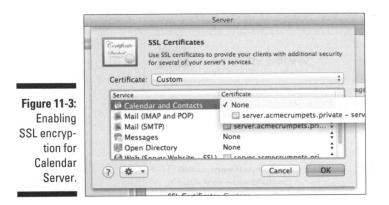

Figure 11-3:
Enabling
SSL encryp-
tion for
Calendar
Server.

Adding locations and resources

In addition to creating events and inviting people to them, users can reserve locations, such as meeting rooms, or resources, such as projectors or other equipment. In Calendar Server, resources and locations share some of the attributes of users and groups, and can accept event invitations. When booking a room, Calendar Server checks whether the time period is free and accepts the booking like an event invitation. Users can include resources and locations in invitations along with people they're inviting.

Resources and locations each get their own calendar. You can have Calendar Server accept invitations if the resource or location is free or mark it as "busy" if it's not. You can also delegate approval of invitations so that a real user approves the use of a resource.

A third option is to have the Calendar Server accept invitations automatically, while assigning a delegate to view and edit the calendar of a resource or location.

You use the Server app to add resources and locations. Follow these steps:

1. **In the Calendar pane of the Server app, click the Add (+) button near the bottom of the window.**

2. **Click the Type menu and select Location or Resource.**

3. **In the Name field, type a name for the item.**

   For a resource, the name might be a piece of equipment.

4. **Click the Accept Invitations menu, and then choose Automatically or With Delegate Approval (see Figure 11-4).**

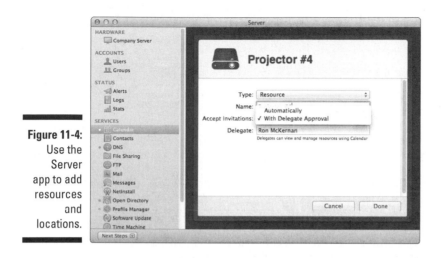

Figure 11-4:
Use the
Server
app to add
resources
and
locations.

5. (Optional) Type the name of a user to be a delegate.

Delegates must be users with accounts in the network directory to which the server is bound (including Open Directory service running on your server Mac). As you type in the Delegate field, a drop-down menu appears with suggestions and a Browse command, giving you a list of all users in the directory.

Note that you can add a delegate and still set Accept Invitations to Automatic.

6. Click Done.

The item you created appears in the Locations and Resources list. You can go back and edit an item in this list by double-clicking.

Turning on push notification

Calendar Server works with Mountain Lion Server's push notification, which lets users (Mac OS X 10.6 and later and iOS 3 and later) instantly know about calendar changes made by other users. As with iCloud, when someone makes a change to a server-hosted calendar, push notification pushes out only the changed part of the information to clients that have subscribed to the update system (and have been authenticated to receive updates). The server contacts clients only when a change is made.

With Calendar Server, multiple users can update an existing event. Event attendees can add private comments to events that only they and the event organizer can see. Calendar Server processes invitations.

Without push notification, calendar clients will frequently ask the server if there are updates. With push notification, the client never contacts the server. The server contacts the client — only when there's a new event invitation or a change. This behavior lightens the load on the server.

Push notification uses an SSL encryption certificate, one where Apple itself is the certificate signing authority. When you turn on push notification in Mountain Lion Server, the Server app contacts Apple's Push Notification Service to get a certificate that will be accepted by clients running Mac OS X Lion or iOS. (For other clients, you have to manually accept the certificates.)

Because Apple is the certificate signer, it requires that you use an Apple ID and password. This ID is the same type of ID that you use to buy songs in iTunes or software from the App Store.

Unless this is a home network, do not use your personal Apple ID for creating a certificate. Your organization should have its own Apple ID.

The Setup Assistant may have set up push notifications for you. If not, follow these steps to turn on push notifications:

1. **In the Server app, under Hardware, select your server.**

2. **Click the Settings tab.**

3. **Click the Select Enable Apple Push Notifications check box.**

4. **Type your organization's Apple ID and password, and then click the Get Certificate button (or Renew Certificate button, as shown in Figure 11-5).**

5. **Click the OK button.**

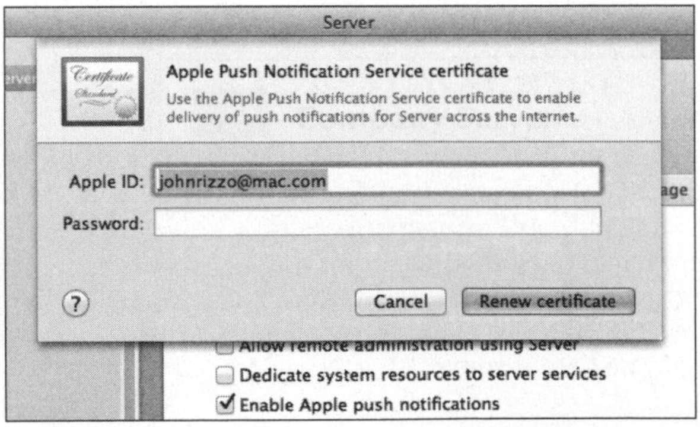

Figure 11-5:
To turn on push notifications, you need to obtain a certificate from Apple.

> Server
>
> **Apple Push Notification Service certificate**
> Use the Apple Push Notification Service certificate to enable delivery of push notifications for Server across the internet.
>
> Apple ID: johnrizzo@mac.com
>
> Password:
>
> ?   Cancel   Renew certificate
>
> Allow remote administration using Server
> ☐ Dedicate system resources to server services
> ☑ Enable Apple push notifications

If you have an existing encryption certificate that has expired, click the Edit button next to Enable Apple Push Notifications. Click the Renew button to redisplay the dialog box (refer to Figure 11-5), and then follow the directions.

Enabling web calendars

The Calendar Server can provide web-based calendars in Mountain Lion Server's built-in wiki-based website. As described in Chapter 12, this site is created automatically when you turn on wiki service in the Server app. You turn on web calendars from within the built-in wiki website itself. (For instructions on how to do this, see the section on enabling calendars and other settings in Chapter 12.)

Setting Up Mac and iOS Clients for Calendar Service

The Server app doesn't have a place to create an actual calendar. Instead, you create a calendar from a Mac or an iOS client and then publish it to a server. Before you can publish a calendar, however, the client must be configured to have an account with Calendar Server.

Adding a Calendar Server account to Mac clients

You can add a Calendar Server account to a Mac client in two ways:

- ✔ **From System Preferences:** This method works with OS X 10.7 and 10.8 clients.

- ✔ **From Contacts (or iCal in Mac OS X 10.7 and earlier) Preferences:** Use this option if you want to create an account for Calendar Server but don't want to alter your Calendar (iCal) or Mail settings. This method is for Mac OS X 10.6 clients.

These two methods are described in the next two sections. You can also use Profile Manager to configure multiple Mac and iOS devices at one time (as described in Chapter 16).

Use System Preferences

In this section, you add a Calendar Server account to a Mac client by using System Preferences. This procedure works for Lion and Mountain Lion clients, and will also add server accounts to the Contacts and Mail applications:

1. **Open System Preferences from the Apple menu.**

2. **If logged in to iCloud, click the iCloud icon and sign off.**

3. **Click the Show All button at the top left and then click the Mail, Contacts & Calendar icon.**

4. **Scroll down to the bottom of the list and click Add Other Account.**

5. **In the dialog box that slides down (shown in Figure 11-6), select Add an OS X Server Account and then click the Create button.**

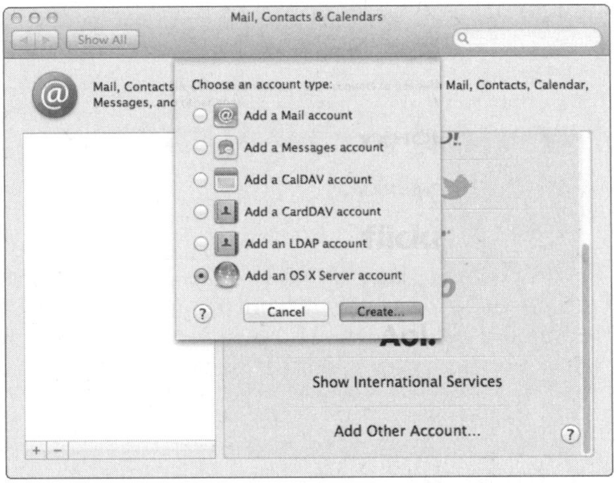

Figure 11-6:
Adding
a server
account to
an OS X
client
by using
System
Preferences.

6. **Select your server from the list or type its host name (such as server. acmecrumpets.private). Then click Continue.**

7. **Type a username, a short username, and a password for the user account on the server. Then click the Set Up button.**

8. **Click Add Account.**

Use the calendar (or iCal) application

To connect the iCal 4 or 5 client (in Mac OS X 10.6 and 10.7) or Calendar 6 (OS X 10.8) to the Calendar Server, you add an account in the calendar client. On the user's Mac, open Calendar (or iCal) and do the following:

1. **Choose Preferences from the Calendar (or iCal) menu, and then click the Accounts icon.**

2. **Click the Add (+) button at the bottom left of the window.**

   The Add an Account dialog slides down.

3. **In the Account Type pop-up menu, choose CalDAV.**

4. **Type a username (use the short name), a password, and the server host name (myserver.domain.edu, for example).**

5. **Click Create.**

You can now change some of the default settings in the main Account Information tab, as shown in Figure 11-7.

The Refresh Calendars pop-up menu sets how the client Mac updates calendar information (including invitations) with the server. The default is Push, which means that the server contacts the client. You can change this to a time interval or manually.

Adding a Calendar Server account to iOS clients

Manually adding a calendar server account to an iPhone, iPad, or iPod touch is similar to using System Preferences in Lion or Mountain Lion clients:

1. **From the home screen, tap Settings.**

2. **If logged into iCloud, tap the iCloud icon and sign off and then tap the Settings button at the top left.**

   If you are not logged in to iCloud, skip this step.

3. **Tap the Mail, Contacts & Calendar icon.**

4. **Tap Add Account. Scroll down to the bottom of the list and tap Other.**

5. **Tap Add CalDav Account.**

6. **Type your server's host name (such as server.acmecrumpets.private), and then tap Next.**

7. **Type a username and password for the user account on the server.**

8. **Tap Save.**

You can also create these settings in Profile Manager and apply them to multiple devices at once (as described in Chapter 16).

Creating a calendar on the server by using the Calendar client

Calendars shared by using the server are created from a client, such as the Calendar client application in Mountain Lion or iOS. After a calendar is created, a user can publish it to the server for sharing. Simply do this:

1. **Choose File➪New Calendar➪OS X Server.**

2. **Enter a name for your calendar, and then press the Return key.**

Setting a delegate by using the Calendar client

You can set another user to be a *delegate,* or proxy, for one of your calendars. Delegates can be read-only delegates or read/write delegates. A *read-only delegate* can see everything that the main user can. Delegates for resources or locations can see everything about them, not just whether they're available. A *read/write delegate* can also make changes to another user's calendar.

To create a delegate, follow these steps:

1. **In the Calendar (or iCal) client, choose Preferences from the Calendar (or iCal) menu and then click the Accounts icon.**

2. **Click an account to select it. Then on the Delegation tab, click the Edit button.**

3. **Click the Add (+) button in the dialog box that appears.**

4. **Type the account name of the user who will be the delegate.**

5. **(Optional) Select the Allow Write check box if you want the delegate to be able to edit your calendar.**

6. **Click Done.**

Delegates must have user accounts in the same authentication directory as the user.

Note that any resources or locations for which you are a delegate will show up in the Delegation tab.

Chapter 12

Hosting Websites and Wikis

- -

In This Chapter

▶ Using and managing the built-in wikis, blogs, and calendars

▶ Editing the wiki pages and enhancing navigation

▶ Hosting your websites

- -

A ny server can host a website, but Mountain Lion Server creates a complete, dynamic site for you to help your group collaborate. By merely turning on web and wiki services, every user gets an automatically updated web portal called *My Page*. Users get access to a collaborative environment that includes wikis, blogs, web calendars, and mailing lists. The site uses *wiki* technology, which enables group editing of content with a web browser. With a few mouse clicks or finger taps, users can edit files with Macs, PCs, and iOS devices.

With OS X Server, you can also host your own websites for use in your organization and for publishing to the Internet. Under the hood are the powerful, industry-standard, open source Apache Web server and the PostgreSQL database. But you don't need to know anything about Apache or SQL.

Prerequisites

Before hosting a website, you need to do a few things:

▸ If you want your website to be visible on the Internet, you must own your domain name and register it with a domain name service, such as Network Solutions. (You can find a complete list of domain name registration services at `http://internic.net`.)

If you just want your users to access your site from the Internet but don't need others to see your site, you don't need a registered domain name. Instead, you can have a private domain name (in the form `server.example.private`), as described in Chapters 3 and 4, configured with virtual private networking (VPN). Your users then access your site through a secure (private) connection.

✔ You may want to have domain name service (DNS) configured so that users can type your server host name (such as `www.acme.com` or `server.acme.private`). DNS will have your domain name *resolve* (or point to) the IP address of the web server. This DNS setting could be on a DNS server on your network or on the Mac server itself, if it's acting as the network's DNS server.

If Mountain Lion is your only server on the network and you've created a `.private` host name, the installer will set up DNS for you in Mountain Lion Server.

If DNS isn't set up, users will have to enter the IP address of the server in their web browsers. (You can find some information on DNS throughout this chapter and in Chapter 4.)

✔ If you're serving content to the Internet, check your firewall. The automatically created website uses port 80, or port 443 if you're using Secure Sockets Layer (SSL) security.

The Automatically Created Collaboration Website

Mountain Lion Server can set up a sophisticated wiki-based website containing collaboration tools for your user accounts. No HTML coding or design layout is required. The built-in website is dynamically created and updated and is user-configurable.

You can limit users' access to features or give them access to everything. Users of Macs, Windows, Linux, and Unix can create their own pages, wikis (editable by all or some users), and blogs, and upload pictures, movies, and audio — all from a web browser. The website can display shared calendars for groups of people to use. And if users want to add some HTML code, they can — again, from the web browser.

There are a variety of ways to use the site. Teachers can create a wiki where students can upload homework assignments from home. Managers can create blogs to update others on the progress of projects. User-created content is automatically indexed and searchable, and links between articles can be made automatically. And a project team can use a shared calendar to keep track of progress.

Turning on and setting up a wiki-based site

To use Mountain Lion Server's built-in website, first open the Server app and click Wiki in the sidebar. Then click the big switch to turn on wiki services, as shown in Figure 12-1.

If you want iPad, iPhone, and iPod touch devices to be able to edit the wiki, select the Enable WebDAV Access to Wiki Files option.

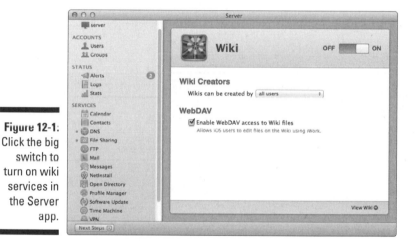

Figure 12-1: Click the big switch to turn on wiki services in the Server app.

The Wikis Can Be Created By pop-up menu gives you a choice of All Users, which allows anyone to create a wiki article, and Some Users, which limits who can create a wiki article.

To see the automatically created site, click View Wiki, in the lower right. This brings up the site's home page (shown in Figure 12-2). Users can get to the home page by typing your server's host name in the form `http://server.example.net` or `http://server.acmecrumpets.private` in a web browser. Users can also type the server's IP address.

The home page has four links:

- **My Page** is a personal web page for each user account, created when a user first clicks the My Page link. Users can edit their My Page, add a blog, more pages, and files. If a user wants to let others edit content, he or she can create a wiki. To see other users' My Page pages, click a link on the People page.

- **All Activity** is a list of changes everywhere on the site, such as new entries in anyone's blog or changes to any wiki or page.

✔ **Wikis** lists all wikis belonging to users and groups.

✔ **People** lists other users' My Page pages. A user's My Page doesn't show up in People until the user makes changes to the default page.

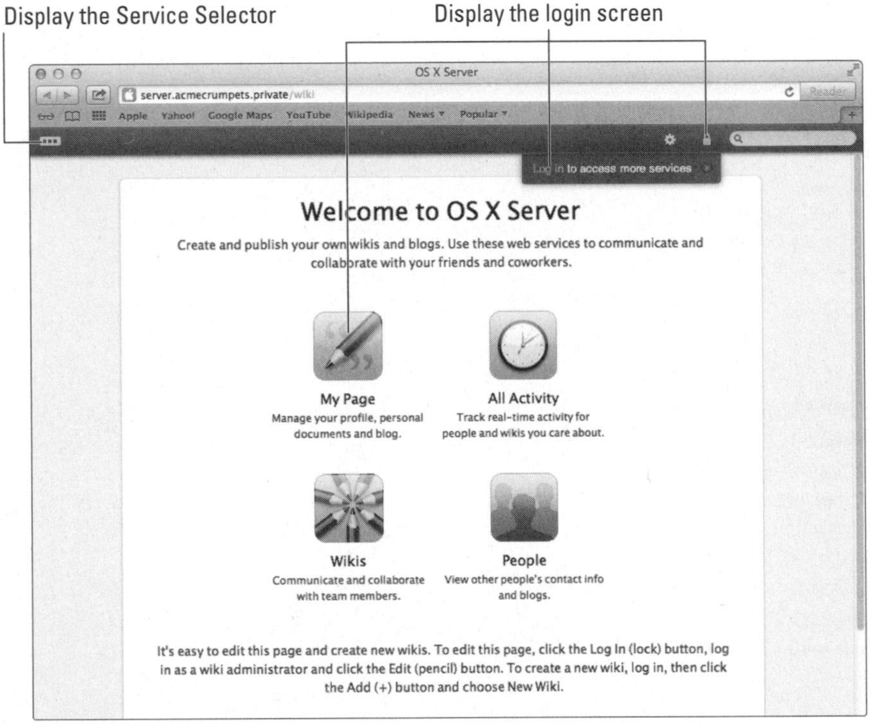

Display the Service Selector   Display the login screen

Figure 12-2:
The default web home page of the built-in website.

Navigating the built-in website

Before you create any content, take a look around the site. You can display the login screen by clicking Log In to Access More Services, which appears at the top right of the home page (refer to Figure 12-2). You can also log in by clicking the lock icon in the upper right of the page or by clicking the My Page icon.

The best way to navigate through the site is by using the pop-up navigation bar called the Service Selector, as shown in Figure 12-3. Click the Service Selector icon in the upper left of any page (refer to Figure 12-2). The Service Selector includes the same links to the home page, My Page, All Activity, Wikis, and People as described in the preceding section.

Mountain Lion Server's built-in website has a useful help system. You get to it by selecting Help from the gear icon at the top right of any page.

Figure 12-3:
The Service
Selector.

Some pages have their own navigation items in the upper right. These links refer to items *within* the scope of that page, not the entire site. For instance, the Home button (shown in Figure 12-4), takes you to the home page of the particular wiki you are in — not the home page of the entire site (refer to Figure 12-2). The Activity button displays a list of items that have been changed in this particular wiki. The Other button (not shown) is where you access a calendar if enabled.

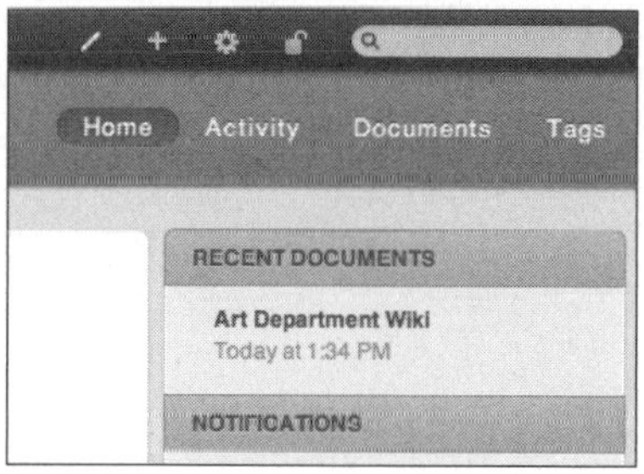

Figure 12-4:
The naviga-
tion links
for a wiki.
Different
types of
pages have
different
links.

My Page pages have a different navigation bar. Where a wiki has a Home button, My Pages has a Profile button, which takes you to a user's page. A Blog button is displayed if the user has blogs enabled.

Creating a new wiki and setting access

A wiki is a place where multiple users can make changes. In Mountain Lion Server's collaboration website, a wiki can also be a destination page containing a host of other features. A wiki you create can contain blogs, as well as other wikis, pages, and uploaded documents and multimedia.

If you or a user has write permissions, you can create a wiki from any page, including the home page, My Page, a document page, or another wiki. Both administrators and users can create a wiki. Just follow these steps:

1. **From any page of the built-in website, click the Add (+) button in the upper right and choose New Wiki, as shown in Figure 12-5.**

Figure 12-5:
You can
create a
new wiki
from any
page in the
server's
built-in site.

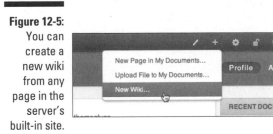

2. **In the Create a New Wiki dialog shown in Figure 12-6, type a name and description for the wiki and then click Continue.**

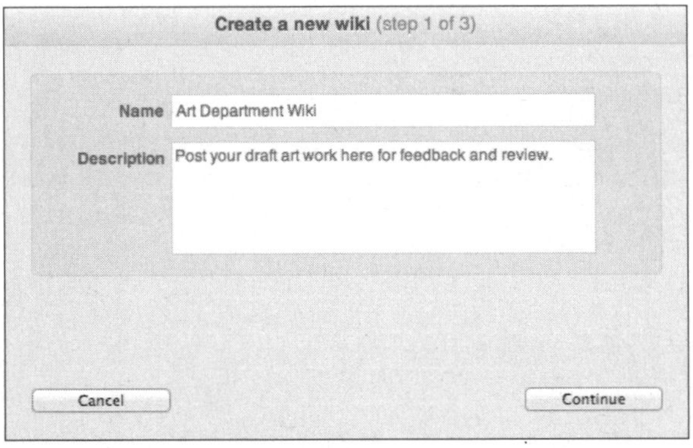

Figure 12-6:
Enter a
name and
description
for the wiki.

3. **In the Set Permissions dialog, choose an access permission for each type of user.**

   By default, three items appear: you (the owner), All Logged In Users, and All Guests. For each, you have the following choices from the pop-up menus: Owner (can change settings), Read and Write, Read Only, and No Access. (With these settings, you're creating a type of access control list used in file sharing, as described in Chapter 8.)

   It's convenient to add a group of users and set permissions on the group rather than on individual users.

4. **To add a user or group, type a name in the empty field at the top, press Return, and then choose a type of permission.**

   In Figure 12-7, I added the name of a group account, Art Department, and gave it read and write permissions. I also set the permissions for everyone not in the group to No Access.

5. **Click the Continue button to display the Set Appearance dialog.**

Figure 12-7:
Add users
and groups
and set
access
permissions
for the new
wiki.

6. **(Optional) Click the Upload button to add a photo or an image for the wiki's icon.**

   A 48-x-48-pixel image is optimal, but any image will work. You can also choose a color scheme here.

7. **Click the Create button and then click the Go to Wiki button.**

   The home page for the new wiki appears.

You can edit the wiki name and description, the user and group permissions, the appearance, and the icon at any time while you're in the wiki. Just go to the gear icon and select Wiki Settings.

You can now create a new page for the wiki by choosing the Add (+) button in the upper right and selecting New Page from the pop-up menu. Users who don't have write permissions for the wiki won't see the New Page option in the menu.

Creating blogs

You can use blogs to disperse information to others, such as homework assignments to students, status updates to co-workers, or messages to your family. Unlike wikis, blogs are not meant to be edited by other users.

Users can create blogs in their My Page profile pages. A wiki owner can also create a blog in a wiki. But first, blogs need to be enabled. Here's how to enable blogging for your personal area and for a wiki:

1. **Navigate to one of your personal pages or to a wiki you created.**

2. **Click the Action menu (gear icon) and select either My User Settings (from My Page or a subpage) or Wiki Settings (from a wiki you created).**

   3. In the Settings window that appears, select the Blog check box next to Services and then click Save.

With blogging enabled, you can start creating blog entries. Simply click the Add (+) button at the top menu bar and select New Blog Post. Type a title for the post in the dialog that appears and then click Add. The new post appears in editing mode, which is described in the next section.

You can access blog entries by clicking the Blog link in the upper right of a My Page (or People page). If you're in a wiki, click the More link and select Blog.

Adding content and editing wikis, blogs, and pages

Users can add content to and edit wikis, pages, and blogs for which they have write permissions, including the site's home page, your My Page, and other pages. You actually can edit from a web browser if you enter edit mode while on a page. Just follow these steps:

   1. Navigate to the page you want to edit.

   For a blog, click the blog post title to display an individual post. You can't edit blog posts while viewing the entire blog.

   2. If the page is not in edit mode, click the pencil icon in the toolbar.

   A new editing toolbar replaces the standard toolbar, as shown in Figure 12-8. Hovering over a toolbar icon displays a description of the icon's function. Here's what's in the toolbar:

   • Edit text on the page by simply placing the cursor on the page or selecting text and typing.

   • Format and arrange text with the standard text manipulation tools.

   • Create a link for selected text by using the curved arrow icon. Figure 12-8 shows the menu that appears when you click the Link icon.

   • Attach a file to the page with the paper clip icon.

   • Insert movies or audio with the musical notes icon.

   • Insert a table with the square icon.

   • The box icon lets you add a bit of HTML to the page's content. You can use standard HTML tags.

   3. Click the Save button on the editing toolbar when finished.

Figure 12-8:
The editing
toolbar lets
you edit
text, add
links and
photos, and
more.

Using comments, tags, and notifications

Some pages containing content have a Document Info sidebar on the right. This sidebar contains several collaboration and navigation tools, as shown in Figure 12-9. (Some pages display a truncated version.) You can expand a set of topic headings by clicking the triangles to the left. Under each topic heading, you can also add content by clicking the Add (+) button to the right of each item. Click the check mark to save your addition.

If you're viewing the site from an iPad, you need to be holding it in landscape mode to display the Document Info sidebar.

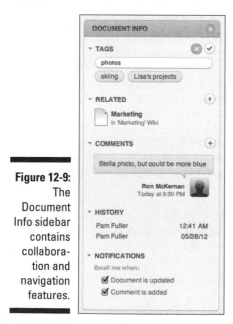

Figure 12-9:
The
Document
Info sidebar
contains
collabora-
tion and
navigation
features.

Tags section

Expand the Tags section to view and add tags that help identify the page content and link the page to related pages. Clicking a tag displays a list of pages, blogs posts, and files that are marked with that tag. If you don't see a tag you want, you can also search for a tag to find pages containing that tag.

Users can tag pages that are related for easy location and then filter pages by a tag. You might tag pages with a project or person name, a topic, or another common identifier.

To add a tag to the current page, click the Add (+) button and start typing. The browser will fill in the word if the tag already exists. When you finish typing, click the check mark.

Tags you add here are visible in other places on the site. For example, they appear in the Tags item in the toolbar, which is available on different types of pages throughout the site. The Tags toolbar item displays a list of *all* tags in the site, not just those on the viewed page.

Related section

Expanding the Related heading displays a list of pages that have been marked as related to the current page. Click a page to go to it. To add a page to the list, click the Add (+) button and select an existing page from the pop-up menu.

Comments section

Although Figure 12-9 shows one comment, this expanded heading can display a number of comments about the current page, which behaves like a mini discussion forum. To add a comment, click the Add (+) button, type your comment in the thought balloon, and then click the check mark to save the comment. Shorter comments tend to work better in this format, so bone up on your Twitter skills.

History and Notifications sections

The History heading displays a list of older versions of the page, who made each change, and when the person made it. Click an old version in a list to bring up that version.

Notifications are check box settings that tell the server to send you an e-mail when a change, a comment, or both are added to the page.

Enabling calendars and other settings

Users can administer wikis that they create as well as group wikis from a web browser within the wiki. They can turn on a group calendar, edit the wiki's name, change user access permissions, change the appearance, and perform other tasks.

All these tasks are accomplished from the main wiki page of the user or group site. Click the Action menu (gear icon) in the toolbar and choose Wiki Settings. (If you don't have write permissions for the wiki, the Wiki Settings item won't appear.)

The Settings page appears and displays the General settings, as shown in Figure 12-10. In the left sidebar are links to different types of settings. The following sections describe what these settings pages do.

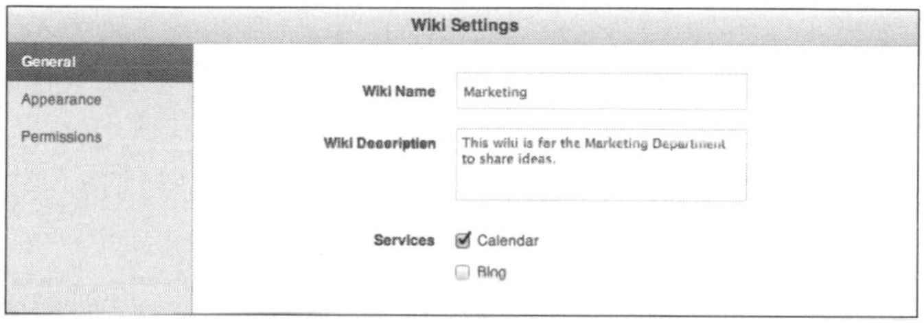

Figure 12-10:
The Settings page for a wiki opens with the General settings.

Wiki Settings	
General	
Appearance	**Wiki Name** Marketing
Permissions	**Wiki Description** This wiki is for the Marketing Department to share ideas.
	Services ☑ Calendar
	☐ Blog

Turning on calendars for a wiki

A wiki can have its own web calendar. First, however, you must have Calendar service turned on in the Server app and you must have write permissions for a wiki. You also have to be using a computer or an iPad; you can't turn on a web calendar with an iPhone or iPod touch.

To create a calendar for a wiki, go to the wiki, click the Action menu (gear icon) in the toolbar, choose Wiki Settings, and click the Calendars check box. (If the check box appears dimmed, Calendar Server probably isn't running.) Then click the Save button. You can also enable a blog for this wiki by clicking the Blogs check box. (See "Creating Blogs," previously in this chapter, for more on blogs.)

To get to the wiki calendar, go to the More link in the upper right and select Calendar from the menu; you use the command to view the shared wiki calendar and add events to it. The web calendar is also available at this URL: `http://your-domain/webcal`.

One reason to use a wiki-based web calendar is that it grants access to Windows and Linux users as well as Mac and iOS device users. If you use the Calendar Server (described in Chapter 11), you will have to find compatible clients for your Windows users.

Changing the wiki name, icon, and appearance

The General pane of the Wiki Settings dialog shown in Figure 12-10 lets you change the wiki name and description.

To change how a wiki looks, click Appearance to the left to display the window shown in Figure 12-11. You can replace the color banner at the top of the page with your own art by clicking the Upload button next to Color Banner. You can similarly replace the solid color background with a piece of art, and replace the default wiki icon with your own, as I did in Figure 12-11. To simply change the color of the default banner, click a new color in the Color Scheme area.

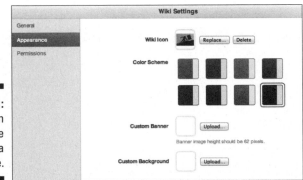

Figure 12-11:
You can customize the look of a wiki here.

When you finish, click the Save button in the lower right of the screen.

Although you make these changes from the main wiki page, they apply to all the pages related to a wiki, including blogs, calendars, and other wiki pages.

Editing user permissions

The Permissions pane of the Wiki Settings dialog, shown in Figure 12-12, is where you change user access settings. You can limit the access of users and groups and define access to wiki comments (described in the "Using comments, tags, and notifications" section, presented previously).

In the top half of the Permissions pane, you have the same choices you have when you create a new wiki, and you can add new users and groups to give them access to the wiki. In Figure 12-12, I've created several owners (who are able to change these settings) and am in the process of adding a group.

At the bottom of the page, you can use the Comments pop-up menu to specify who can leave comments — only authenticated users or anyone — or to ban comments by selecting the Nobody option. The Comment Moderation pop-up menu lets you require comments to be moderated for all commenters or just anonymous commenters. The default is no moderation.

Click the Save button in the lower right when you finish.

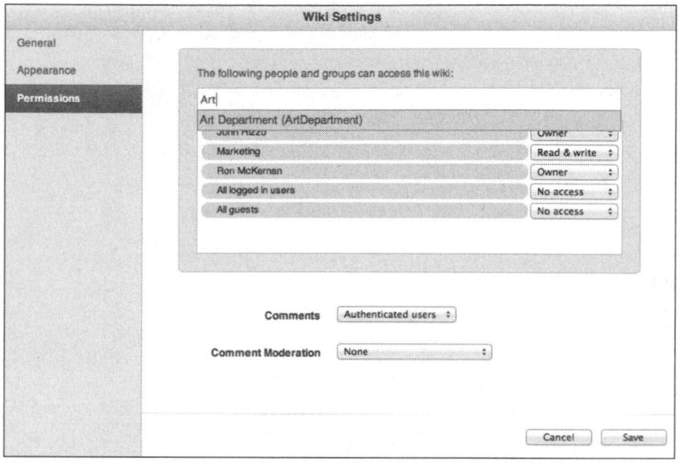

Figure 12-12:
Setting user
and group
access to a
wiki.

Hosting Your Own Websites

With wiki services turned on, your server's fully qualified domain name
(`server.example.net` or `server.example.private`) will take users
to the OS X Server's built-in wiki-based site. If you want to host your own
website, the following possibilities are available:

- ✔ Replace the built-in wiki-based site with your own.
- ✔ Run the built-in wiki-based site in addition to your own.
- ✔ Run multiple websites, with or without the built-in wiki site.

If you want to host a website that is visible to the Internet, you must own a
domain name (such as `mydomain.com`) purchased from a registrar such as
Network Solutions or GoDaddy. These companies can often host the required
DNS records if you don't want to host them on OS X Server.

As with other services in Mountain Lion Server, you use the Server app to
configure and manage your websites. To turn on web services, open the
Server app and click Websites in the sidebar. The window shown in Figure 12-13
appears. As with other services, you turn web services on and off with the
big switch.

In the Websites area are two entries: Server Website and Server Website
(SSL). These settings are for the default website, whether that's the built-in
wiki-based site or your own. The first entry is for standard access, and the
second is for secure, certificated access.

Figure 12-13:
The Server app's Websites pane.

With these two default entries, you can't change the IP address or the port numbers, which are 80 for standard web and 443 for secure (SSL) access. You can add new domains, and use redirects and aliases, as described in "Virtual hosting, aliases, and redirects," later in the chapter.

In the lower-right corner is the View Server Website link. Clicking this link takes you to the website set to use your server's fully qualified domain name. This link is a quick way to see whether your website is correctly configured. Clicking it will take you to the built-in wiki site, your own site, or a placeholder site, whichever is configured with your server's fully qualified domain name.

With Mountain Lion Server, Apple restored the ability to configure several features that were removed from the graphical interface of Lion Server. These features include redirects, URL aliases, and enabling CGI execution. The full Apache command-line set is still available by using the Terminal application in the Applications⇨Utilities folder.

Replacing the built-in wiki-based site with your own site

If you want to use your own website rather than the built-in wiki site, simply turn off wiki services (with web services turned on in the Server app). With wiki services turned off, your site's domain name takes you to a placeholder index page, shown in Figure 12-14, rather than the home page (refer to Figure 12-2). Clicking View Server Website in the Websites pane of the Server App also takes you to the placeholder index page.

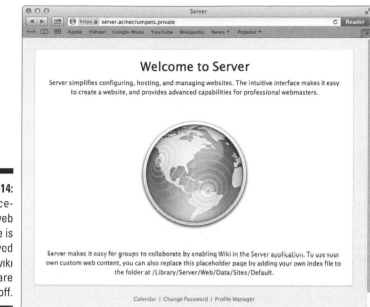

Figure 12-14:
This place-
holder web
page is
displayed
when wiki
services are
turned off.

The placeholder index page actually has some functionality. The Calendar link takes you to a personal web calendar, if you have calendar services enabled in the Server app. (The URL is `server.example.net/webcal`.) The Profile Manager link takes you to Profile Manager, if you have that service turned on in the Server app. The third link lets you change your password.

You can replace the placeholder page with your own index page (and entire custom site) by placing your index page in the default location, `/Library/Server/Web/Data/Sites/Default`. When you do, the server's domain name will take users to your site.

Note that the default website location is on your server's startup drive or partition. To change the location of the website files, do the following:

1. **Double-click one of the Websites entries to display the configuration page for the site.**

2. **In the Store Site Files In pop-up menu, select Other.**

3. **Navigate to a location on another directory or drive and then click the Choose button.**

4. **Click the Done button at the bottom right of the configuration page.**

5. **Move your website files to the new location.**

For more on other configuration options, see the section "Virtual hosting, aliases, and redirects," later in the chapter.

Running your own website and the built-in wiki-based site together

To host your own website while retaining Apple's wiki-based website, you'll need three things:

- ✓ Wiki services turned on in the Server app
- ✓ A new website entry in the Websites pane of the Server app
- ✓ A domain name for the new site, and DNS entry for each domain name

If you don't want to use the built-in wiki, and want to use your server's host name for your custom site, you don't need to change DNS settings. Just turn off wiki service and use the Websites pane's default Server Website entry, as described in the preceding section.

If you do host multiple sites, you need to set up DNS with a zone and a record for the site. If you are using the Server app for a DNS server on your Mac, go to the DNS pane, click the Add (+) button, and type the domain name and IP address for the site. In the Aliases field, add any aliases you are using.

You can host multiple websites on one server, each with a different domain name, in several ways. If the multiple sites share an IP address, they're called *virtual hosts.* To set up virtual hosts, create a new entry in the Websites entry in the Server app for each domain name and set them to the same IP address.

If you set the sites to have different IP addresses, the process is sometimes called *multihoming virtual hosting* or simply *multihoming.* (You can find more about virtual hosting in the next section.)

To publish a custom website in addition the default site, do the following:

1. **Launch the Server app and select Websites from the sidebar.**

2. **Click the Add (+) button to display the dialog for a new website, as shown Figure 12-15.**

3. **In the Domain Name field, type the site's fully qualified DNS name.**

    The *fully qualified DNS name* is a unique identifier for the website. For example, two different fully qualified DNS names might be www.abc.edu and teachers.abc.edu. You might use these two names to host both the built-in default site and a new site.

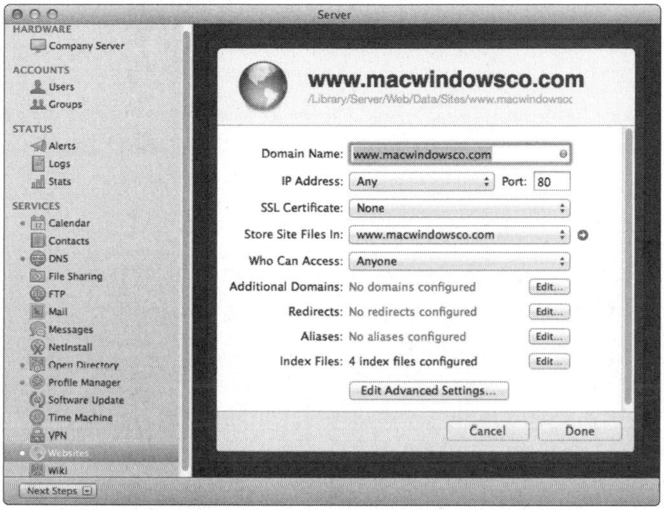

Figure 12-15:
The configuration pane for your new site.

4. **To specify a custom location to store your website files, use the Store Site Files In pop-up menu to choose the folder where your website files are located.**

   If you accept the Default Location setting, the Server App creates a folder for you at this location: /Library/Server/Web/Data/Sites/ www.*domain*.com. It's safer to store web data on a hard drive or storage device other than the boot drive. To view the folder contents, click the View Document Root Contents link in the dialog.

5. **From the IP Address pop-up menu, choose an IP address that clients use to connect to the website, or choose the Any setting to have the site accessible from any IP address available to the server hardware.**

6. **(Optional) In the Port field, change the port number.**

   The default port setting is 80. If you're using SSL, port 443 is the default. You can have multiple websites using the same port if you want, or you can choose a port number that isn't being used by another service. You may be able to use port 8080, which is another port that the server uses as a default. Port numbers 81–87 are generally safe to use for websites. Chapter 18 lists ports used by services.

7. **(Optional) Add Secure Sockets Layer (SSL) security to the website by choosing a certificate from the SSL Certificate pop-up menu.**

   The Server app doesn't allow you to use SSL without a certificate. You can use the self-signed SSL certificate that was created during server installation or use one from a certificate authority. (See Chapter 18 for more on SSL certificates.)

8. **(Optional) In the Who Can Access pop-up menu, select a group account to allow only those registered users to visit the site, or select Customize to restrict access to subfolders of the website.**

The default selection is Anyone, which is the typical setting for a website. Selecting a group can be useful if your website is not visible to the Internet.

Using Customize lets you add a *realm,* a collection of files or directories on the website. You can create a realm that includes a portion of a website that only a group can access. You can also create multiple realms. Realms are often used with WebDAV.

9. **Click the Done button.**

Your new site appears in the Websites list of the Web pane of the Server app, along with the location of its files (refer to Figure 12-13). If you want to make changes, you can edit the configuration by double-clicking it in the Websites list. You delete a configuration by selecting it from the Websites list and clicking the Delete (–) button.

You can do even more with your hosted websites. The additional settings in the configuration pane for a website are described in the next two sections.

Virtual hosting, aliases, and redirects

I mention in the preceding section that you can host multiple websites that use the same IP address — a process called virtual hosting. But the site configuration pane in Figure 12-15 contains several other options that you can use separately or together to determine how URLs point to servers or directories:

- ✔ **Additional domains:** You can add additional domain names that will take users to the website. This gives you multiple domains for one site.

- ✔ **Redirects:** When a user types the URL for your site, a *redirect* sends the web browser to a new location, either on your server or elsewhere. One common use of a redirect is to have multiple similar domains (such as example.org and example.net) go to the same website.

  You can enter a *redirect path,* which specifies a directory to redirect, rather than the domain name. This feature lets you send users to another folder on your site when they enter the specified folder in the URL. You also enter the destination URL.

- ✔ **Aliases:** An *alias,* which is similar to a redirect but works within the site, enables a user to type one URL to get to another folder. For instance, an alias can enable a user to type a short URL (example.com/documents) to get to a folder with a longer path (example.com/123/abc/documents/public).

✔ **Index files:** You can specify multiple types of index files. By default, this option includes index.html, index.php, /wiki/, and default.html, which cover most situations. The files are ordered by preference, but you can change the order.

Dynamic generation, CGI scripting, and other advanced settings

The Edit Advanced Settings button of a site's configuration pane (refer to Figure 12-15) brings up another dialog that deals with dynamically generating web content, as shown in Figure 12-16. CGI scripting is the most commonly used feature listed here. If your website uses any of the features shown in this dialog, you can turn then on here. If not, don't worry about it.

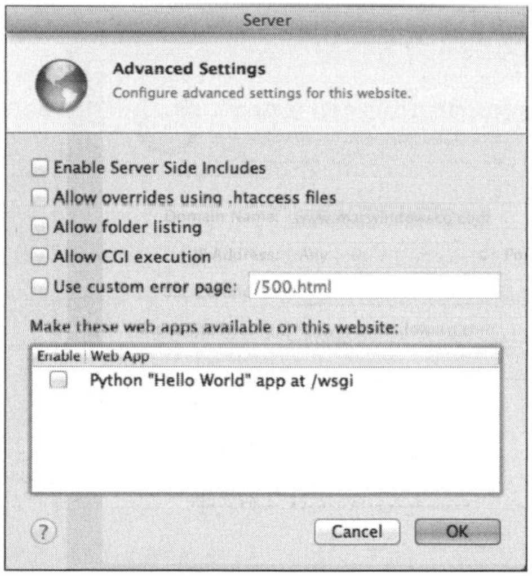

Figure 12-16: Use the Advanced Settings dialog to turn on CGI scripting and other features.

Here are the options:

✔ **Enable Server Side Includes:** This turns on SSI, a scripting language that can be used to post content from different files onto a web page.

✔ **Allow Overrides Using .htaccess Files:** Enables you to use a .htaccess file to make changes to a specific directory.

✔ **Allow Folder Listing:** Lets the web page list the contents of a directory.

✔ **Allow CGI Execution:** Turns on the capability to run Common Gateway Interface (CGI), which delegates the generation of web pages to executable files called *CGI scripts.* Basically, CGI is another scripting language for generating web pages.

✔ **Use Custom Error Page:** Turns on and sets the path of a custom error 500 page you've placed on your website. Error 500 occurs when the server can't find a requested page due to a problem with a CGI or an SSI script or some other cause.

Troubleshooting website access problems

If the dot next to the domain name is red (refer to Figure 12-15), you have a problem: The Server app can't resolve the DNS name to your server's IP address. To fix this problem, try the following:

✔ **Change the domain name to something that will resolve.** Compare the spelling and form of the fully qualified domain name that you entered in the Websites pane of the Server app with what's in your DNS server. For instance, `server.example.com` and `www.example.com` are not the same, unless they are both set up to point to the same IP address. The same is true for `www.example.com` and `example.com`.

✔ **For multiple sites, check your virtual host settings in the Websites pane of the Server app.** You can't have two virtual hosts with the same domain name.

✔ **Assign another available IP address.** You can assign another IP address if you're using multiple Ethernet cards in a Mac Pro or a USB Ethernet adapter on any Mac. To do so, double-click the site in the Websites list of the Server app and choose an IP address from the pop-up menu.

✔ **Check your port number to see whether another service is using it.** Chapter 18 has a list of port numbers used by services.

✔ **Check your alias and redirect settings for conflicts or missing entries.** If you have both aliases and redirects, keep in mind that Apache processes all redirects before processing aliases.

Chapter 13

Running an E-Mail Server

*H*osting your own e-mail server has advantages over using an outside provider. With the ability to customize e-mail options whenever you need to, you gain flexibility. If you have confidential data in your e-mail, storing your messages on your own server will give you peace of mind. When using an outside e-mail server, such as an Internet service provider or an offsite host, users in your building who e-mail one another send traffic out through your Internet connection and back. This traffic can slow the Internet connection in organizations with limited Internet bandwidth. Using your own e-mail server keeps internal e-mail traffic off your Internet connection.

Setting up your own e-mail service isn't rocket science, but you do need to know some things. In Mountain Lion Server, setting up e-mail is easier than it's ever been in OS X Server. This chapter describes setting up e-mail service with all the trimmings, including spam and virus blocking and domain name service (DNS). I also show you how to change the location of the data store — an important task if you don't want to run out of space on your boot drive.

Understanding Mail Protocols

Mountain Lion Server uses three standard protocols to send and receive mail:

 ✔ Users send e-mail with the *Simple Mail Transfer Protocol (SMTP)*.

 ✔ Users receive e-mail with either the *Post Office Protocol (POP)* or the *Internet Message Access Protocol (IMAP)*.

You can choose to use IMAP, POP, or both. Different client computers may use one or the other to communicate with the server. You can specify which to use when you create an account on the client (including Mac, iOS, Windows, and Linux). The differences between IMAP and POP follow:

- **Use POP for a slower server Mac with limited storage.** POP downloads e-mail to the client computer and deletes the e-mail from the mail server. The client disconnects from the server as soon as the last message is downloaded. Because clients are connected to the server for only short periods, there is little use of the server's processor and RAM by a client, and large numbers of users can access the server with minimal impact. And because e-mails are deleted from the server, POP has the advantage of using less server storage space than IMAP. All this makes POP an attractive alternative for a slower server Mac with limited RAM and hard drive space.

- **Use IMAP for a better user experience.** IMAP requires more server resources but can provide more benefits for the user. An IMAP connection to the server can last as long as the user needs, allowing the user to download content on demand. This feature can result in faster response times, and users can read one large message at a time without waiting for a whole batch to download. IMAP retains messages on the server after they're read unless the user deletes them. This requires a lot more hard drive space than POP. (You can put a cap on the total amount of e-mail a user stores on the server.) A benefit is that IMAP permits users to have a mail folder structure on the server, which appears the same from any computers they use.

Mountain Lion Server uses both POP and IMAP when you turn on mail service with the Server app. You can turn off one or the other by using the command line. Open Terminal (in Applications⇨Utilities). To turn off POP, type the following exactly, including spaces:

```
sudo serveradmin settings mail:imap:enable_pop = no
sudo serveradmin stop mail
sudo serveradmin start mail
sudo serveradmin status mail
```

To turn on POP, change no to yes. To turn off IMAP, replace the first line with the following:

```
sudo serveradmin settings mail:imap:enable_imap = no
```

Mountain Lion Server's e-mail service uses the open source Postfix as the *mail transfer agent (MTA)* to send SMTP e-mail to the Internet. Mountain Lion Server uses the open source Dovecot for POP and IMAP e-mail.

Where Mountain Lion Server stores mail

Mountain Lion Server temporarily stores mail going to the Internet in this location: `/Library/Server/Mail/Data/spool`. You might need to include that location for backups.

Incoming IMAP e-mail is stored in directories for each user, with each message stored as a separate file. The message resides in the folder `/Library/Server/Mail/Data/mail`.

Messages stay here until the user deletes them from the client e-mail application (or the e-mail application is set to automatically delete). You can change this location if you want to move it off the boot drive. In the Server app, select your server in the sidebar, click the Settings tab, and click the Edit button next to Service Data. You can now select another hard drive to store data for all services.

Mail Service and the Internet: DNS

If you want your e-mail server to send and receive mail over the Internet, you will need an Internet domain name (which ends in .com, .org, .net, or others) and DNS service.

You can buy a domain name at a domain name registrar such as `www.networksolutions.com` or `www.godaddy.com`. If you own a domain name for a website, you can use it for e-mail as well. If you set up your server with a `.local` or `.private` domain name, you'll need to reconfigure it with an Internet domain. You change the host name in the Network tab of the Server app's server pane. If you change the host name, you must change any DNS settings that you may have for the server.

DNS service can run on your Mountain Lion Server Mac, on another server in your organization, or elsewhere, such as at your ISP or at the Internet registrar where you obtained your domain name.

How MX records help send e-mail

An SMTP server sending a message looks at the domain name of the e-mail message and asks a DNS server for the corresponding IP address of an e-mail server — either the final destination server or an intermediate e-mail server on the Internet. The DNS server looks up the domain name in an MX record and then sends the IP address back to the SMTP server. The SMTP server can then send on the e-mail message. MX records can list multiple IP addresses for a given domain name, ranked in order for the SMTP server to try.

Regardless of where you host your DNS service, you will need to create a mail exchanger (MX) record on the DNS server. You also need to make sure that DNS has a *machine record,* a DNS entry that identifies your mail server on the network. Typically, if DNS is set up, it will have a machine record.

DNS service set up with mail exchanger (MX) records allows mail to be sent to the correct host on your network. Even if you are running e-mail service on Mountain Lion Server, where you create the MX record depends on the location of your DNS service:

- ✔ **Your Internet service provider or domain registrar supplies the DNS service for your network.** Sometimes the ISP or registrar can set up and host MX records for you, and sometimes they offer a web interface for entering your mail server's IP address and domain name.

- ✔ **Your network has DNS service running on a non-Mac server.** In this case, the server administrator creates an MX record for your mail server that's hosted on the DNS server.

- ✔ **The DNS service is running on one of your OS X servers.** Use the Server app to access any of these servers to create an MX record.

- ✔ **You're running DNS service on Mountain Lion Server.** In this case, use the Server app to create an MX record. This process is described in the next section.

The one situation where you would *not* use an MX record is when you are using a relay server.

Creating an MX record in OS X Server

If the Mountain Lion Server installer could not find a DNS server on the network for the host name you entered, it configures basic DNS for you during installation. The installer creates a zone and a reverse lookup zone. In this case, you can add an MX record to the DNS zone created for you.

To create an MX record in Mountain Lion Server, do the following:

1. **Launch the Server app, and then select DNS in the sidebar at the left.**

   The DNS pane appears in basic view, as shown in Figure 13-1. The Host Names field displays the host name and associated IP address. We want to see a more detailed structure.

2. **Click the Action menu (gear icon) and select Show All Records.**

   The Host Names field turns into a Records field, as shown in Figure 13-2. This field displays all zones, including the primary and reverse lookup zones, and all DNS records contained in each zone.

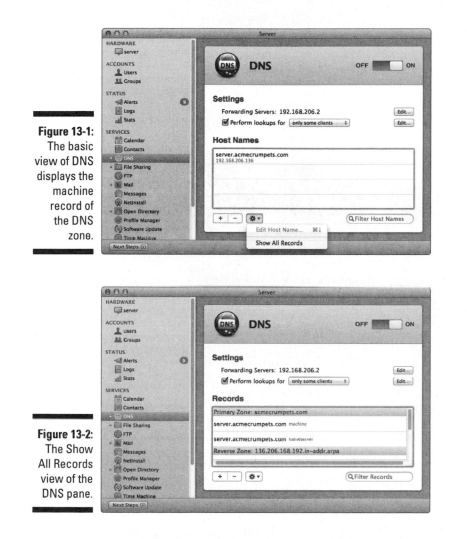

Figure 13-1:
The basic view of DNS displays the machine record of the DNS zone.

Figure 13-2:
The Show All Records view of the DNS pane.

3. **Click the Add (+) button and select Add Mail Exchanger Record from the pop-up menu.**

4. **In the pane that appears, type the domain name of your mail server (see Figure 13-3).**

   Typically, your mail server domain name is in the form mail.*yourdomain.com.*

5. **If you have more than one primary zone, select one from the Zone menu.**

6. **In the Priority field, type a priority number.**

   If this is your only Mail server, type 10. If this is a backup Mail server, the priority number should be higher than that of your primary Mail server. Typically, the priority numbers are in multiples of 10 (10, 20, 30) to enable you to add other servers later between those numbers.

Figure 13-3:
The window
for creat-
ing an MX
record.

Priority numbers tell the DNS server to which Mail server to route incoming mail. The highest priority has the lowest number, which is 10 in this example. If that server is out of commission, the mail is routed to the next priority number, 20.

7. Click Done.

Your new MX record appears in the Records field, as shown in Figure 13-4.

If you have other Mail servers for redundancy, you can add more MX records by clicking the Add (+) button.

Figure 13-4:
A newly
created MX
record listed
in your pri-
mary DNS
zone.

Relay servers

You may also need to connect your e-mail server to the Internet by specifying a *relay server,* which is another mail server to which you forward outgoing mail. Your Internet service provider may require that you relay e-mail to one of their servers. Or you may need to relay e-mail to another server in your organization if you have a server designated to send outgoing mail through a firewall. If you designate a relay server, you won't be using MX records on your server.

The next section includes a description of designating a relay server in Mountain Lion Server.

Don't specify a relay server without telling the operator of the server. You may look like a spammer, which could get your server blacklisted.

Setting Up E-Mail Service

With DNS correctly configured (on your server or somewhere else), you can set up your e-mail server. Here's what you do:

1. **Launch the Server app from the Dock and select Mail in the sidebar.**

2. **Check the host name next to Provide Mail For. If you want to change it, click the Edit button and type a new DNS name.**

   The new name must be a valid, fully qualified domain name that is properly configured in DNS with your Internet service provider, a DNS hosting service, or your own network. The mail server host name must be resolvable to an IP address with both forward and reverse DNS entries. If you change this host name, you may have to update the DNS MX record (described in the preceding section).

3. **In the Mail pane (shown in Figure 13-5), click the switch to the On position.**

4. **If you're using an Internet service provider to relay mail to the Internet, do the following:**

   a. *Select the Relay Outgoing Mail through ISP check box.*

   The relay server could be a server in your own organization. A new dialog appears, as shown in Figure 13-6.

   b. *Enter an IP address or a DNS name for the relay server.*

   c. *If your ISP requires authentication for its SMTP relay, enter a username and password.*

   d. *Click OK.*

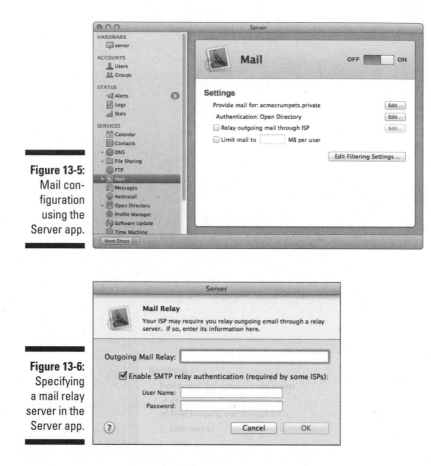

Figure 13-5:
Mail con-
figuration
using the
Server app.

Figure 13-6:
Specifying
a mail relay
server in the
Server app.

The Mail pane (refer to Figure 13-5) has two more elements:

- **Limit Mail to *[blank]* MB per User:** This option lets you set a quota, the maximum amount of storage space that you want to allow for each user. The default is 200MB, which is not a lot of space for IMAP mail.

- **Edit Filtering Settings:** This button is used to block spam and viruses. I describe how to set up this option in the section "Blocking Spam and Other Nasty Bits," later in this chapter.

Authenticating and Encrypting Mail

Mountain Lion Server lets you select the method to authenticate clients and encrypt passwords when they sign in to the e-mail server; it can also encrypt e-mail messages with the Secure Sockets Layer (SSL) standard. OS X Server offers different methods of authentication for different mail clients and for different sources of user accounts.

Securing mail authentication

The Server app gives you options for password encryption for SMTP and IMAP/POP. Which you choose depends on what your e-mail clients support and where the user accounts are housed: in Open Directory, Active Directory, local accounts on the Mac, or a mix. Mountain Lion Server will choose an authentication method based on how those accounts are usually authenticated, but you can change the authentication methods.

To choose an authentication method, go to the Mail pane in the Server app (refer to Figure 13-5) and click the Edit button next to Authentication. In the Authentication dialog, click the Authentication menu to display the choices shown in Figure 13-7.

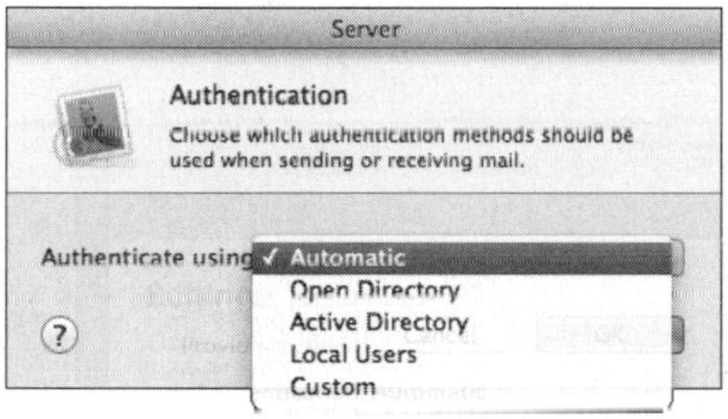

Figure 13-7:
The first level of mail authentication settings.

Here you see choices for Open Directory, Active Directory, and Local Users:

- ✔ **Open Directory:** Kerberos and Digest (CRAM-MD5)
- ✔ **Active Directory:** Kerberos and cleartext
- ✔ **Local User:** Digest (CRAM-MD5)

If your user accounts are in two or three of these categories, Mountain Lion Server defaults to Automatic. You can change any of these settings by selecting Custom. For instance, if all your users were from Active Directory, you might want to disable Cleartext authentication. When you select Custom, the dialog expands to the one shown in Figure 13-8.

Here's the lowdown on your choices:

- ✔ **Kerberos** is the most secure authentication method used by the mail server. To use Kerberos for mail, you need Kerberos authentication in Open Directory or on another server. When you create an Open Directory master, Kerberos is automatically enabled. Apple recommends Kerberos over Digest.
- ✔ **Digest (CRAM-MD5)** is almost as secure as Kerberos but is not used in large organizations.

✔ **APOP** is a login encryption type similar to Digest but used only for POP clients.

✔ **Cleartext** is an unsecure authentication method that sends passwords unencrypted. If you choose cleartext in addition to the more secure authentication methods, clients that don't have the more secure methods set up can log in without encryption. If you deselect the cleartext option, clients can't log in until they're configured for encryption.

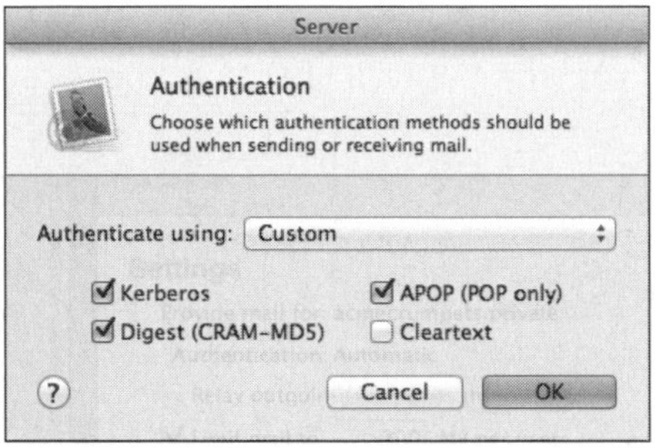

Figure 13-8:
The selection of mail authentication methods.

You can choose multiple authentication methods to support multiple e-mail clients. It's a good idea to disable any authentication method that your clients aren't using. If you use only one type of authentication, it will require your clients to use it.

Securing e-mail messages with SSL

The preceding methods encrypt only passwords and usernames. You can also encrypt e-mail itself with the Secure Sockets Layer (SSL). For POP and IMAP, SSL encryption is between your server and your clients. For SMTP, SSL encryption is between your server and other e-mail servers.

To use SSL, do the following:

1. **In the Server app, select your server in the sidebar under Hardware.**

2. **Click the Settings tab and then click the Edit button next to SSL Certificate.**

   The SSL Certificates dialog appears, as shown in Figure 13-9.

3. **In the pop-up menus to the right, choose a certificate or choose None for SMTP and for POP/IMAP.**

4. **Click OK.**

The Mail Server uses SSL encryption if a POP or an IMAP client asks for it. If a client isn't set up to request an SSL connection, the mail service can still deliver mail to that client. For mail servers that don't request SSL, Mountain Lion Server's mail service sends mail unencrypted.

Figure 13-9:
Selecting
an SSL
certificate
for e-mail
service.

Blocking Spam and Other Nasty Bits

Mountain Lion Server is integrated with several types of filtering software to keep spam and viruses from reaching users. It uses the open source spam-blocking software called SpamAssassin, which does a statistical analysis of incoming e-mail to determine whether it's probable spam. It also supports the blacklisting of certain e-mail servers, rejecting e-mail from known spammers. For this, Mountain Lion Server communicates with servers of the Spamhaus Project, an international not-for-profit organization that collects spam blacklist data. Mountain Lion Server also includes software that scans incoming messages for viruses.

To access the filtering settings from the Server app, click Mail in the sidebar and then click the Edit Filtering Settings button. Three settings are available, as shown in Figure 13-10:

✔ **Enable Virus Filtering:** This option is either on or off. Virus filtering uses the open source ClamAV (www.clamav.net) software to keep track of known malicious e-mail viruses, worms, and other malware and is automatically updated regularly. When ClamAV detects malware in an e-mail message, it stores it in a folder instead of delivering the message to the user. It then sends an e-mail notification to the administrator.

Although fewer viruses are written for Macs than for Windows PCs, your Mac e-mail server can just as easily pass malware to your Windows clients as any other server. Don't put your Mac clients at risk for getting infected with the malware that does exist.

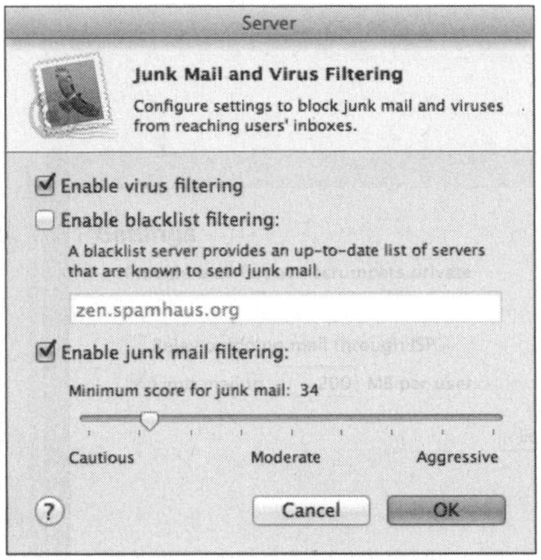

Server

Junk Mail and Virus Filtering
Configure settings to block junk mail and viruses from reaching users' inboxes.

☑ Enable virus filtering
☐ Enable blacklist filtering:
   A blacklist server provides an up-to-date list of servers that are known to send junk mail.

   zen.spamhaus.org

☑ Enable junk mail filtering:
   Minimum score for junk mail: 34

   Cautious   Moderate   Aggressive

   ⑦   Cancel   OK

Figure 13-10:
Filtering set-
tings in the
Server app.

✔ **Enable Blacklist Filtering:** This check box specifies a blacklist server to prevent spam from known spam servers from reaching you. Any mail coming from a server on the blacklist will be rejected.

If you select this option, the default blacklist server is zen.spamhaus. org. You can change this setting to another blacklist reporting site, if you like. A blacklist isn't 100 percent foolproof, however; you may find that it rejects legitimate mail.

✔ **Enable Junk Mail Filtering:** This check box activates the slider that you can use to set the severity of filtering. The higher you set the slider, the higher the chance that junk e-mail will be detected. Any messages deemed to be spam are marked JUNK and forwarded to the user. How you set the slider is really a matter of philosophy. Setting the slider toward the left (Cautious) lets more spam get through to users, where their own spam filters deal with it. Setting it toward the right (Aggressive) sends fewer junk mail messages to users but could trap more legitimate e-mail (false positives). If the server filters legitimate e-mail, users don't know about it. I tend to be conservative in setting server-based spam filtering, but it may be more secure to accept more false positives and prevent phishing e-mail from getting to users.

Mountain Lion Server's junk-mail filtering uses a statistical method known as *Bayesian filtering.* For example, instead of stopping every message with the word *loan,* it takes into consideration the context of the message and the frequency of the word used in known spam. Bayesian filtering assigns a probability calculated on history based on a mathematical formula, which results in a high degree of accuracy of detection and few false-positive IDs.

Creating User E-Mail Addresses

When you create a user account after mail service has been set up and started, Mountain Lion Server automatically creates an e-mail address based on the short name followed by the domain name. For example, if you create a user account called Ron McKernan, the automatically created address would be ronmckernan@acmecrumpets.com. In the Users pane of the Server app, click the Add (+) button to display the New User dialog. Type a new user's name in the Full Name field and press the Tab key. A short name and e-mail address will be created for you, as shown in Figure 13-11.

Figure 13-11:
With mail service turned on, an e-mail address is created automatically for a new user account.

New User

Full Name:	Bob Benito
Account Name:	bobbenito
Email Address:	bobbenito@acmecrumpets.com
Password:	
Verify:	
	☐ Allow user to administer this server
Home Folder:	Local Only
Disk Quota:	☐ Limit usage to _____ MB

Cancel   Done

For user accounts that you've already created, you'll have to manually create an e-mail address for each user. In the Server app, double-click a user in the Users pane and add an e-mail to the Email Address field (refer to Figure 13-11).

You can also create multiple e-mail addresses for any user. For example, you might assign info@acme.com to a user who's responsible for a public website.

To create an alternative e-mail address for a user, you must use Workgroup Manager (available at http://support.apple.com/kb/DL1567) to create a second short name for the user. Here's how:

1. **In Workgroup Manager, click the Accounts icon in the toolbar.**

2. **Click the globe icon below the toolbar on the left, and then select the account's directory domain.**

   Log in if prompted.

3. **Select the user from the list on the left.**

4. **Click the Basic tab.**

5. **Double-click the empty space in the Short Names list box, as shown in Figure 13-12, and then type a short name that you want to use in the e-mail address for the selected user.**

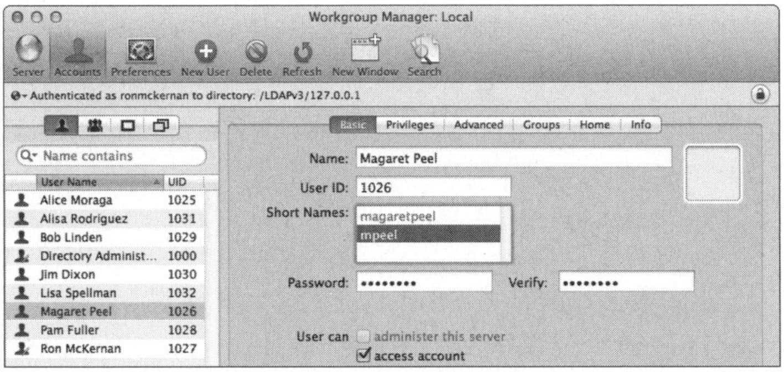

Figure 13-12: To create a new e-mail address for a user, create an additional short name.

If a virtual host is enabled, type the full e-mail address (for example, info@acme.com).

6. **Click the Info tab and type the email address using the new short name and your domain name.**

   If mpeel is the new short name, it would be mpeel@*yourdomain*.com

7. **Click the Save button.**

Setting Up a Mailing List

Mailing lists, or *listservs,* are good ways to enable group discussions via e-mail. When a member of the listserv sends a message to the list address, the message is delivered to all the members. Mountain Lion Server does not have Lion Server's capability to host a listserv that anyone can join but does let you create a mailing list of which everyone in a group is a member. That is, members must have user accounts on your server.

To create a listserv, go to the Groups pane under Accounts and double-click the name of a group. Next, select the Enable Group Mailing List check box. Now, when a group member sends mail to *groupname.domain*.com (or .net, .org, and so on), all group members will receive it, provided their e-mail addresses are entered in their user accounts, as described in the preceding section.

Chapter 14

More Collaboration with Messages

Some of Mountain Lion Server's built-in goodies may not be central to everyone's mission but can be of great value to groups that can use them. If you take a look at this chapter, you may find yourself in the latter group as I explore Messages Server.

Messages Server is a collaborative tool for brainstorming sessions, virtual meetings, video conferencing, and file sharing. One way to think of Messages Server is as a live version of the wiki tools I describe in Chapter 12, plus video and audio. Messages Server works for Mac, Windows, and Linux computers, and for iPhone, iPad, and iPod touch devices.

Instant Messaging, Conferencing, and More

Messages Server provides instant messaging, audio and video conferencing, and file transferring; it supports Mac, Windows, and Linux clients, as well as mobile phones. Messages works on a person-to-person basis and in multiuser situations.

Messages Server can also create *persistent chat rooms,* which let participants leave or log off. When they return, they can see everything that happened in their absence. Users can send chat messages to other users who are offline. Messages also acts as a kind of automatic note-taking service because users can generate chat transcripts. On the server, you can log chat text so that the administrator can read it or forward it to a group that needs it.

Chats aren't just text, however. The server and clients support audio and video conferencing, using the built-in mics and video cameras of most Macs and iOS devices. You can also use Messages Server to broadcast a presentation or movie to Macs running the Messages application (OS X 10.8 and later).

Messages service is private and secure, using Secure Sockets Layer (SSL) encryption. Users must have accounts in (and be authenticated by) the Open Directory domain, which means that they can use Messages services from any computer and still see their buddy lists, groups, and other information.

Mountain Lion Server's Messages service is compatible with a number of instant-messaging servers and clients. Messages service is based on the open standard Extensible Messaging and Presence Protocol (XMPP), also called Jabber, which is used in the Jabber and Google Talk servers. This compatibility enables Messages Server to communicate (or federate) with other XMPP servers or domains, including Google Talk, to enable users of both to interact. XMPP support also means that the server supports Jabber clients on any platform.

Clients for Messages Server

For Macs, the Messages client application (in OS X 10.8 and later) is the best to use and most trouble free, seamlessly accessing all features in Messages. Messages Server works with older versions of the Mac iChat client, as well as the latest and greatest version. There are also a number of other Jabber clients for Macs as well.

For Windows, Linux, Unix, mobile phones, and iPad and iPod touch devices, you can use any instant-messaging client that supports XMPP or is Jabber-compatible. Instant-messaging clients often support multiple protocols. A lot of XMPP clients are available, and more are popping up all the time. If you're looking for an open source client for OS X, Windows, and Linux, try Pidgen (www.pidgin.im). Trillian (http://www.ceruleanstudios.com) is a Windows commercial product with a free version and a $25 pro version.

For iOS, you need to install a Jabber-compatible client app. If you search the App Store, you'll find many dozens, including several that are free. Monal from Anurodh Pokharel is a good free app. The $9.99 BeeJive IM with Push (from BeeJive, Inc., www.beejive.com) is a popular iOS app that supports multiple chat protocols, including XMPP. Separate versions are available for iPhone, iPad, and iPod touch devices. Another option is Agile Messenger HD Pro ($7.99 from Agilemobile.com.). Agile Messenger also supports full Facebook support from within the app. Both apps work with text only, not video, and are available from the App Store.

For a list of XMPP-compatible clients for various platforms, check out http://xmpp.org/software/clients.shtml.

Reality check: Not all XMPP clients and servers communicate smoothly with Messages service. You may find versions of XMPP software that have some issues, and you may find some that work better than others. Do a little testing before distributing a chat client to all your users.

Prerequisites

Before you set up Messages service, you need to take care of several network items. Quite likely, your network already has some of these things.

Open Directory configuration

To authenticate users, Messages uses Open Directory, or another LDAP (Lightweight Directory Access Protocol) server bound to Messages Server. Messages Server doesn't directly access the LDAP server. Messages users must have directory accounts in a directory domain. (See Chapter 5 for information on Open Directory.)

You also need an Open Directory master if you want to enable authentication with Kerberos or to use a Kerberos domain controller on another server. If you use the latter, the Kerberos realms of the controller and Messages Server must match.

Firewall ports

If your Messages users are crossing a firewall to get to the server, you have to open some firewall ports. This is true for any service, but Messages requires a relatively large number of firewall ports to be open. (See Chapter 18 for more on firewalls.)

Internet routers

If you want Internet users to access Messages service on your server and you have a DSL, cable router, or other Internet router, you need to configure it for port forwarding.

DNS configuration for some situations

You may not need to do anything to your DNS server to support Messages service. But you could optionally add DNS records in two cases:

✔ You're enabling server-to-server communications so that your server talks to other chat servers. DNS can help users on different servers discover each other.

✔ You want to provide your users with a shorter Messages address.

In either case, you'd add a Service (SRV) locator record for Messages to your DNS server.

To have DNS control connections between your Messages Server and other XMPP servers, you add an SRV record that maps the XMPP's TCP port 5269 to your server host name. The SRV record takes the form

```
_xmpp-server._tcp 86400 IN SRV 0 1 5269 server.mycompany.com
```

where *server.mycompany.com* is your server's full domain name.

The other SRV records enable users to have a shorter Messages address (such as bobsmith@mycompany.com) instead of using the server's full host name (such as bobsmith@server.mycompany.com). The DNS record looks like this, specifying port 5222:

```
_xmpp-client._tcp 86400 IN SRV 0 1 5222 server.mycompany.com
```

If you're using Mountain Lion Server for your DNS service, you can create a new SRV record with the Server app by following these steps:

1. **Select DNS from the sidebar, click the Add (+) button, and select Add Service Record from the menu.**

2. **In the window that appears (shown in Figure 14-1), select your server's zone (there may only be one choice).**

3. **In the Service Type field, type** _xmpp-client._tcp.

4. **In the Host Name field, type the server's host name.**

5. **In the Port field, type** 5269.

6. **In the Priority field, type** 0. **In the Weight field, type** 1.

7. **Click Done.**

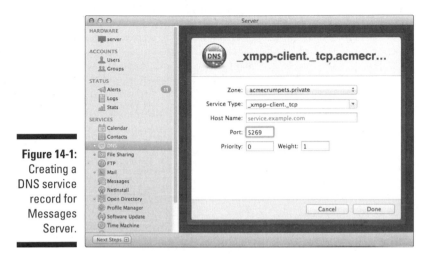

Figure 14-1:
Creating a
DNS service
record for
Messages
Server.

Configuring Messages Service

To turn on Messages service, just click the Messages icon in the Server
app's sidebar and then click the big switch to the On position, as shown in
Figure 14-2.

Figure 14-2:
The
Messages
pane of the
Server app.

At this point, if you have an Apple wireless router (AirPort or Time Capsule) on the network and listed in the Server app's sidebar, you may see a dialog box asking whether you want to allow Internet access to Messages service. Clicking the Allow button makes Messages Server available to users on the network; clicking Don't Allow makes it unavailable. To change this setting later, select the Apple router from the Server app's sidebar. For non-Apple routers, you need to configure the router for port mapping (see Chapter 18).

Assigning screen names for users

User chat names are called Messages screen names and are equivalent to Jabber IDs used by other chat services. Mountain Lion Server creates the Message screen name (also called a Jabber name) when you create user accounts in Open Directory.

Screen names consist of a user name and an associated Messages server, and look similar to e-mail addresses. They come in the form of *user-short-name@ Messages-domain-name*. For instance, a Messages screen name might look like this: ronmckernan@messages.acmecrumpets.com. The short name for the user is created when you create an Open Directory account (as described in Chapter 16). The *Messages-domain-name* part of the screen name identifies the Messages server.

You can add or view the Jabber names in Workgroup Manager, which you can download from `http://support.apple.com/kb/DL1567`. Here's how:

1. **In Workgroup Manager, if you see Not Authenticated, click the lock icon at top right and log in with your Open Directory credentials.**

2. **Click the Accounts icon in the toolbar, and then select the Users icon on the left side.**

3. **Select a user from the list at the left, and then click the Info tab.**

4. **Click the Add (+) button next to the Chat field.**

   The user's short name appears in the Chat field.

5. **Click the arrows to the left of the user's short name and select Jabber, as shown in Figure 14-3.**

   The full Jabber name appears in the Chat field.

6. **(Optional) Edit the name, if desired, and click Save when you're finished.**

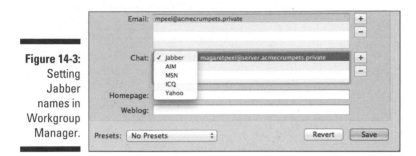

Figure 14-3:
Setting
Jabber
names in
Workgroup
Manager.

Saving and archiving chat messages

When you click Archive All Chat Messages in the Server app, Mountain Lion Server begins saving all Messages messages that users create. It stores this information in `/Library/Server/Messages/Data/message_archives`.

If you want to store this chat archive in a different location, you need to use the command line. Open Terminal in the `/Applications/Utilities` folder and type the following on one line:

```
sudo serveradmin settings jabber:savedChatsLocation = "/path/message_archives"
```

where *path* is the new location you'd like to use. (If the path was on another drive, it would look something like `/Volumes/MyOther HardDrive/ myfolder`.)

If you've lost track of where you set the archive, you can find it (and all Messages Server's settings) by typing **sudo serveradmin settings jabber**. Note that these commands are case-sensitive.

Enabling server-to-server federation

Server-to-server (S2S) communication, known as *S2S federation,* enables communications with other XMPP servers, including Google Talk, Jabber, and other Messages Servers, as long as the servers are visible to the Internet. Users of each federated server can communicate with each other.

Selecting the Enable Server-to-Server Federation check box turns on S2S. Click the Edit button to get access to further S2S settings. In the dialog box that appears (see Figure 14-4), you have a choice of Allow Federation with All Domains, which lets your users connect to a user on any XMPP server, or Restrict Federation to the Following Domains. The latter choice restricts access to domains or complete server host names that you add with the Add (+) button. (You can have both domains and server names in this list.)

Figure 14-4:
Server-
to-server
settings for
Messages
Server.

You can require S2S sessions to use encryption by selecting the Require Secure Server-to-Server Federation check box and choosing an SSL certificate. With this setting, Messages Server blocks a user from connecting to a user in another domain if the latter doesn't support encryption. The other server must also be using a public key certificate.

If the Require Secure Server-to-Server Federation check box appears dimmed, you probably don't have a certificate assigned to Messages service. You can add or change the certificate in the Server app by selecting your server in the left column and clicking the Settings tab. Next to SSL Certificate, click the Edit button and then select a certificate for Messages. (See Chapter 18 for more about certificate management.)

Finally, if you're configuring server-to-server federation, you may need to add an SRV record to your DNS server, as described in the section "Prerequisites," earlier in this chapter.

Advanced configuration

Messages server also has some advanced settings that you can change with the Unix command-line interface by using Terminal.

The Server app doesn't enable you to make these changes and doesn't let you see the current settings for these items. To see all Messages settings, including the hidden ones, type this in Terminal:

```
sudo serveradmin settings jabber
```

You must set up Open Directory before configuring Messages service. (See Chapter 5 for more on Open Directory.)

The next few sections describe the settings that you can make with the command line.

Turning autobuddy support on and off

The autobuddy feature is turned off by default. When autobuddy is turned on, however, all Messages Servers in a particular group are added automatically to everyone else's buddy list. The upside is that users don't have to add buddies manually. The downside is that if users remove buddies from their list, autobuddy adds them back.

Apple removed the autobuddy setting from the graphical interface tools in Lion Server. To turn it on using Terminal, type the following:

```
sudo serveradmin settings jabber:enableAutoBuddy = yes
```

If you start autobuddy while Messages users are logged in, they can't communicate with the added buddies until the user first logs out and in again.

Adding host domains

Mountain Lion Server can host Messages service on multiple domains. The default is a single domain, the server host. You add other host names for use by Messages, as long as DNS is configured to resolve the names to the Messages Server IP address.

Unlike some previous versions, however, Mountain Lion Server no longer provides a way to add multiple domains by using the server tool applications. You can still do this with the command-line interface. Open Terminal and type the following, all on a single line:

```
Sudo serveradmin settings jabber:hostsCommaDelimitedString="domain1.com,domain2.com,domain3.com"
```

Note that there is no space after the commas. Substitute your real domains for *domain1.com* and so on. Include the server host in the list if it is one of the Jabber domains.

Part V
Managing Clients

The 5th Wave   By Rich Tennant

"They can predict earthquakes and seizures, why _not_ server failures?"

In this part . . .

Ask not what your computer users can do for you. Ask what you can do for your users.

That's been the theme of most of this book so far. But now I switch gears and describe how the server can help *you*, whether the server is managing hundreds of computers and handheld devices in the enterprise or your handful of home devices.

It's not about authoritarian control and being the big network boss. Well, okay, there is some of that. But client management also has user benefits. It keeps computers up-to-date and safe from malware, all without you having to visit every device.

Client management is based on directory services, which I describe in Part II. You may want to review those chapters if you haven't yet set up your directory.

In this part, I cover the concepts for managing desktop accounts and take you through the steps needed to make it all work. I start at the beginning, creating users and groups, divulging some useful tricks along the way about managing accounts. I tell you how to service client computers with new copies of software and software updates, all from Mountain Lion Server. I also suggest that you use Apple's tools to keep an eye on the server itself so that it remains healthy.

In Chapter 18, I switch gears a bit, moving on to secure remote client access to the network and other security issues. These topics constitute client management in the sense of keeping control of security, which protects the client computers as well as the server. Kind of like your own airport security, but without having to take off your shoes.

Chapter 15

Mass Deployment of OS X

· ·

· ·

*W*alking around your office installing OS X on computers can easily consume your day — or week. And having multiple Macs all downloading 4GB copies of OS X over the Internet can quickly eat up your network bandwidth.

No problem. Have Mountain Lion Server deploy the operating system for you. Using System Image Utility, you can implement three features of OS X Server — NetBoot, NetInstall, and NetRestore — to move the operating system over the network to the client Macs. Each tool automatically deploys the OS in a different way and for a different purpose. All three tools start with using System Image Utility to create a *system image* — a prototype installation that will be used across your network. You can even customize the image with your own settings.

NetBoot, NetInstall, NetRestore

In Chapter 4, I recommend installing Mountain Lion Server by creating a recovery drive on a USB flash drive. The Mac then boots from the USB stick, downloads Mountain Lion from Apple, and installs the operating system on the Mac's internal drive.

This process is similar to how NetBoot works with NetInstall and NetRestore. Instead of using a USB flash drive, NetBoot enables the client Macs to boot from your server from a disk image. Every time the Mac starts, it boots from a clean copy of the startup drive image, regardless of any changes made by users. Booting from a known clean configuration is a useful way to deploy public Macs, such as those in a school computer lab.

But you can also use NetBoot as a mechanism to deploy the operating system remotely. Boot the client Macs from the server with NetBoot while using NetInstall or NetRestore to install OS X on the Macs' internal hard drives. The two deployment techniques both result in a remotely installed OS, but work a little differently.

NetInstall installs a disk image at a distance. Think of it as running an installer from the server to install the OS on the client. This installer-at-a-distance can then set up some customized settings. NetRestore sends the entire disk image out to the client, erasing the client drive and restoring the disk image on the blank drive. NetRestore is a quick way to restore a Mac's hard drive to a predetermined state. A NetRestore image is like a clone of a user's volume that is used to restore the user's boot volume via NetBoot.

Note that updating the system image will update the disk image installed on the client computers.

In Mountain Lion Server, Apple refers to the NetBoot, NetInstall, and NetRestore features as part of the *NetInstall service,* which you can turn on and manage in the Server app.

Creating a System Image

System Image Utility is easy to use. When you launch it, it lists volumes or installers from which it can create images. (It can't create an image of the drive from which you booted.) The first screen lists the OS X 10.8 Mountain Lion installer that you downloaded from the App Store, if you have it in your Applications folder. (You may remember that when you download the installer from the App Store, you can keep the file by quitting the installer after it automatically launches.) System Image Utility recognizes that the file is there. But you can also create a disk image that includes applications that you want to run on the client Macs.

You can also create images from a Mac that you set up with specific applications.

You access System Image Utility from the Server app's Tools menu at the top of the screen. When you select System Image Utility, the window shown in Figure 15-1 opens. You can choose whether to create a NetBoot, NetInstall, or NetRestore image. From within System Image Utility, you can save the image to the NetBoot share in /Library/NetBoot.

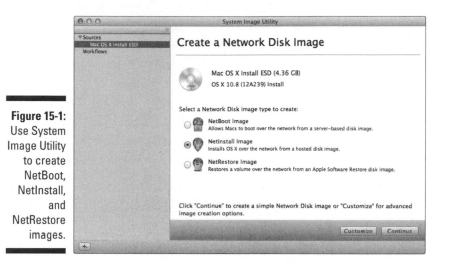

Figure 15-1:
Use System
Image Utility
to create
NetBoot,
NetInstall,
and
NetRestore
images.

Creating a NetBoot set

You may first want to create a NetBoot set that you will use to remotely boot the client Macs while you are installing via NetInstall or NetRestore. Typically, you configure a Mac with the operating system version that you use, connect the Mac to the server with a FireWire cable, and boot that system in target disk mode (by holding down the T key).

Follow these steps to create a NetBoot image:

1. **Open System Image Utility.**

2. **In the Sources list in the upper-left corner, select the Mac in target disk mode.**

3. **Select the NetBoot Image radio button and then click Continue.**

   The Image Settings dialog appears, as shown in Figure 15-2.

4. **Enter a name and description for the image, and create an administrator account for the image.**

5. **Click the Create button.**

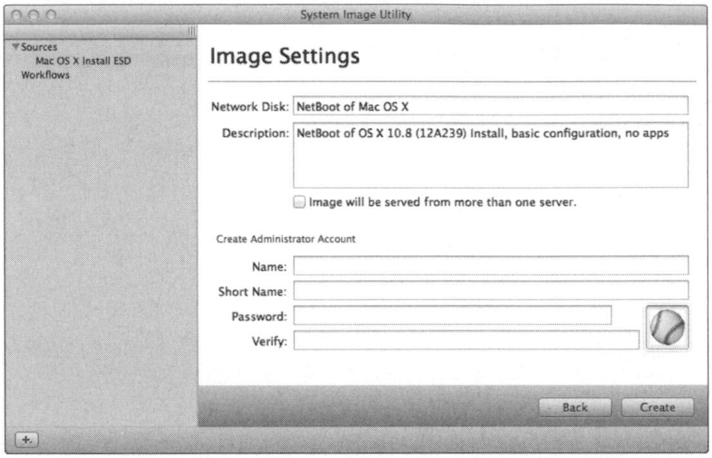

Figure 15-2:
Saving a
NetBoot
image.

Creating a Custom NetInstall image

With a NetInstall image, you have the chance to customize and tailor an installation by including applications that aren't part of the standard OS X package. You can configure network settings and assign new computer names to the Macs, as well as run scripts for various topics. And you can add configuration profiles to the image.

When Mountain Lion installer is located in the server's Application menu, it forms the basis of the NetInstall image and appears as a CD icon (refer to the top of Figure 15-1). Select the NetInstall radio button and then select Continue if you want to run the Mountain Lion installer on your client Macs.

To add to the base OS, do the following:

1. **Click the Customize button.**

   Two windows appear. One is the Automator Library, shown in Figure 15-3, which contains scripts that define different types of actions to occur during the installation. These actions are combined to create *workflows*.

   The other window that opens is the custom view of System Image Utility, as shown in Figure 15-4. Mountain Lion installer is the base image (listed as the Source in the Define Image Source action at top) to which you can add workflow actions. Two workflow items are defined for you at the start. The first box is Define Image Source, which defines the Mountain Lion installer as the image source. The second workflow item in the figure is Create Image, which will create the disk image.

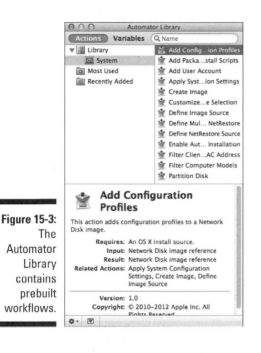

Figure 15-3:
The
Automator
Library
contains
prebuilt
workflows.

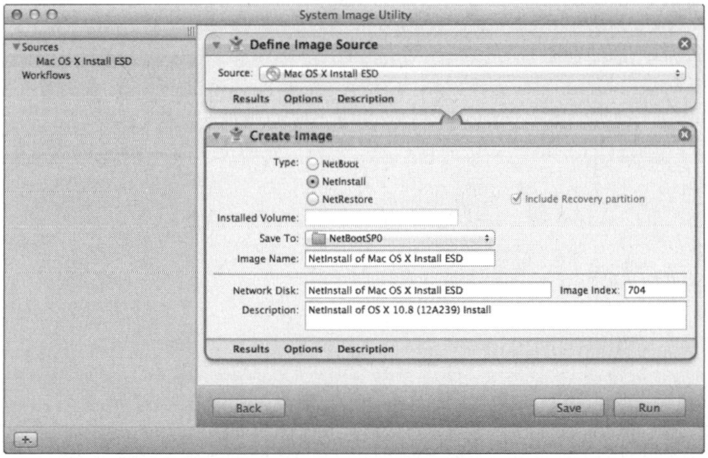

Figure 15-4:
The custom
view of the
System
Image
Utility.

2. **Drag the Add User Account item from the Automator Library to the main System Image Utility window, between the top and bottom boxes.**

   Add User Account appears as a new action in the workflow with data fields, as shown in Figure 15-5.

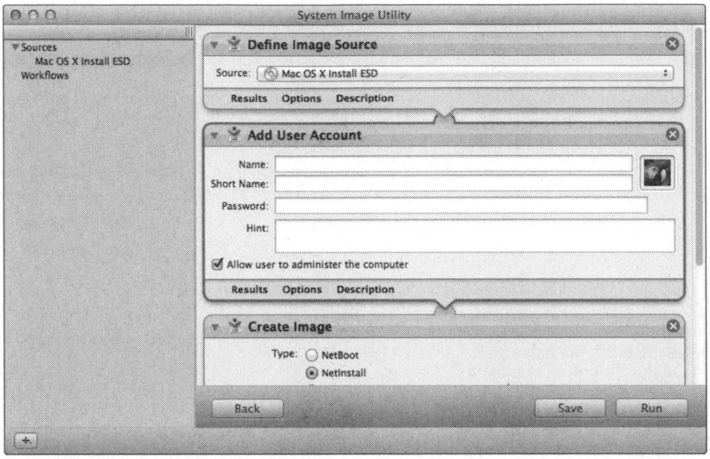

Figure 15-5:
A work-
flow item,
Add User
Account,
has been
added.

3. **Click Description, at the bottom of the new box, to see what the workflow item does.**

   In this case, the item sets up the destination Mac with a new user account. Workflow actions can perform a variety of tasks, such as binding to directory servers. You simply enter the information (such as host names) in the box in System Image Utility.

4. **When you finish adding workflow items and filling in the required information, click the Run button to create the image.**

Setting Up and Starting the NetInstall Service

The NetInstall service in the Server app is where you enable NetBoot for NetInstall and NetRestore. But you won't be able to turn on NetInstall service until you make at least one image available to all Macs on the network. Follow these steps to first set up NetInstall with an image and then turn on NetInstall:

1. **Create a NetBoot or NetInstall image with System Image Utility, as described in the preceding section.**

2. **Make sure that the image (.nbi folder) is placed in this location:**
   `/Library/NetBoot/NetBootSP0`.

3. **Open the Server App and click the Images tab, as shown in Figure 15-6.**

Figure 15-6:
The Images
tab of the
Server app's
NetInstall
pane.

4. **Select the disk image in the list, click the Action menu (gear icon), and select Edit Image Settings.**

   The window in Figure 15-7 appears.

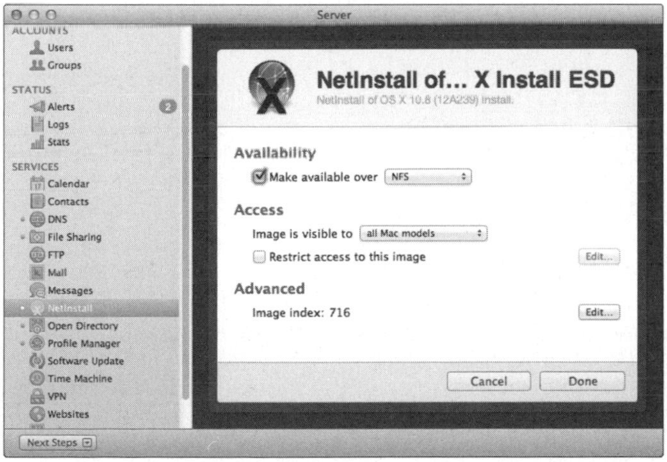

Figure 15-7:
Editing an
image's set-
tings in the
Server app's
NetInstall
pane.

5. **Select the Make Available Over check box, and choose either NFS or HTTP from the pop-up menu.**

6. **(Optional) To prevent some Mac models from seeing the image in System Preferences⇨Startup Disk:**

   a. In the Image Is Visible To pop-up menu, select Only Some Mac Models.

   A list of every Intel-based Mac ever made appears.

b. Select Mac models that will be able to see the image.

    This feature is useful if you're installing a newer version of OS X that your older Macs don't support, or if you're creating an image for notebooks or another subset for special use.

7. **(Optional) To further restrict access to the image to the Macs of one or more specific users, select the Restrict Access to This Image check box and type the MAC address of one or more Macs in the dialog that appears.**

    The MAC address of a computer is a unique identifier for its Ethernet port. To find the MAC address for a Mac computer, open System Preferences and click the Network icon to open the Network System Preferences pane. Click the Advanced button and select the Ethernet tab. The MAC address is referred to as the Ethernet ID.

8. **Click the Done button.**

9. **Click the big switch to the On position.**

    Client Macs will now be able to see the image.

Designating a default image

If you have more than one boot image on your server, you can use the Server app to set the default image. Go to the NetInstall pane, click the Images tab, and select an image from the list. Then select Use as Default Boot Image from the Action menu (gear icon). The word *Default* appears to the right of the image in the list.

NetBoot's share points

With the NetInstall service turned on, the two folders storing images and client data become share points, shared with NFS. If you go to the File Sharing pane of the Server app, you'll see NetBootSP0 and NetBootClients0 in the Share Points list. Double-click one of these, and you'll see that both SMB and AFP are turned off. Do not change any of these settings.

Starting a Client Mac from NetBoot or NetInstall

Using NetBoot to start a Mac is sometimes called *diskless booting* because the client Mac doesn't actually need a hard disk.

You can start a client Mac from a NetBoot or NetInstall image by holding down the N key while restarting the client Mac. This action forces the Mac to look for a server with the NetBoot/NetInstall image. Release the N key when a globe icon appears onscreen. If you have a NetInstall or NetRestore image, the Mac starts from the image on the server and begins the installation process.

If you want the Mac to always boot in diskless mode from NetBoot, select it as the default startup drive in System Preferences as follows:

1. **Boot the Mac from the NetBoot image by restarting while holding down the N key.**

2. **Open System Preferences from the Apple menu and click the Startup Disk icon.**

3. **Select the network volume that appears in the list.**

4. **Click the Restart button.**

You need to have file service turned on, because NetBoot uses file sharing to set up share points that the client Macs can boot from.

Chapter 16

Managing iOS and Mac Accounts

· ·

In This Chapter

▶ Managing accounts with the Server app

▶ Using Profile Manager to configure iPhones, iPads, and Mac clients

▶ Administering accounts with Workgroup Manager

▶ Employing Workgroup Manager and Managed Preferences to manage Mac clients

▶ Controlling client configurations with Software Update Server

· ·

*O*ne of the more useful features of a server is to be able to manage
client devices so that you don't have to go around to each device
individually to set them up the way you want. In addition, Server-based
device management gives you control of what's on the devices. In the case of
Mountain Lion Server, the devices to manage are Apple devices: Macs, iPads,
iPhones, and iPod touches.

There's a quick look at the Users and Groups account settings in Chapters 3
and 4. In this chapter, I dig into more advanced features in managing user and
group accounts, as well as managing clients.

In the first half of this chapter, you look at using the Server app to manage
user and group accounts, discover some of the new things that Mountain
Lion adds, and find out how to use Profile Manager to remotely configure
computers and iOS devices and to set policies on how they're used. The
second half of this chapter is more advanced, describing using Workgroup
Manager to manage user and group accounts and to set group policies.

I end this chapter by describing Software Update Server, which enables you
to control what Apple software updates get installed on the client devices
under your charge.

User, group, and computer accounts

Mountain Lion Server has four types of accounts: user, group, computer, and computer group accounts. *User accounts* aren't necessarily individual people; more than one person may have access to a particular user account, such as a shared administrator account. A long name, a short name, and a mostly hidden user ID (UID) number define a user account. System processes, which are considered to be users but aren't actually people (at least, not yet), can also have user accounts.

In the local directory of the Mac client, the first UID is 501. In a network Open Directory domain, the first UID is 1025. System-level users, such as root (UID 0) or the directory administrator default (UID 1000), generally have lower level numbers.

When you combine a number of individual user accounts, you create a *group account.* Group accounts have group IDs (GID). Groups make it possible to better manage access to resources on a larger scale. In Mountain Lion Server, many collaboration services, including wikis, blogs, and shared folders, can be accessed with group accounts.

The third type of account, a *computer account,* is created for computers bound to the shared directory. Combine computer accounts, and you get a *computer group.* Workgroup Manager and Profile Manager can handle computer accounts; the Server app does not. Profile Manager refers to computer accounts and computer group accounts as *device accounts* and *device group accounts*, respectively.

The Server App and Profile Manager versus Workgroup Manager

For managing user and group accounts, you can use either the Server app or Workgroup manager. The Server app provides a simple, well-designed interface that hides details that you may not need to bother with, but also has some hidden management features that some people may need.

Workgroup Manager provides access to settings that aren't available in the Server app. It allows for editing the raw data in the Lightweight Directory Access Protocol (LDAP) database (see Chapter 5). In addition to managing user and group accounts, Workgroup Manager lets you create computer accounts and computer group accounts.

Apple hasn't upgraded Workgroup Manager for several releases of Mac OS X Server, and the user interface reflects this. It doesn't use standard Apple interface elements such as the gear-icon pop-up menus, making it difficult to browse around and figure things out. For managing user and group accounts, I recommend using the Server app when possible because it requires fewer actions to accomplish some of the same tasks.

Another aspect to both these tools is managing the configuration of Macs and iOS devices. The Server app lets you turn on Profile Manager, which you then access from a web browser. Workgroup Manager uses a feature called Managed Preferences. Profile Manager is clearly the more powerful tool, and easier to use. You can use Profile Manager to push settings to Mac and iOS devices, and to set restrictions (or *group policies*) on what users can do with the devices. Whether you're keeping track of your devices at home in the enterprise, Profile Manager is a very useful tool.

One problem with Profile Manager is that it doesn't support Macs running OS X older than version 10.7 (Lion). Workgroup Manager's Managed Preferences features do support the older Macs. You can set preferences settings for Mac clients in the shared directory domain. You can define which applications users are permitted to launch.

Managing Accounts with the Server App

This section describes everything you can do with the Server app to manage user and group accounts, including a hidden feature and a few tricks. For instance, the Server app lets you create a global password policy for all users, to view and edit UID and GID numbers, and create server-based home folders.

Setting up and managing user accounts with the Server app

The Server app lets you manage user accounts alone; Profile Manager lets you manage devices. Mountain Lion Server doesn't care which device a user works on — Mac, PC, iPad. The user accounts are attached to the person, not the computer or device. Multiple users could share a client computer, but each could still have his or her own user account. Similarly, a single user with a single account can operate multiple devices on the network.

Profile Manager, on the other hand, can do mobile device management through the use of computer accounts.

Creating new user accounts

To create and manage user accounts in the Server app, click Users in the sidebar to the left. For group accounts, click Groups. You see the window shown in Figure 16-1, which includes user accounts already created.

Whether you're using accounts stored locally on the Mac or on a shared network directory, the procedure for creating new accounts is the same. However, you do want to make sure that you know what you have. If you create a bunch of local accounts when what you really want are Open Directory accounts, you'll have to create all the accounts again.

Figure 16-1:
The list
of user
accounts in
the Server
app.

The user list in Figure 16-1 includes accounts on the local computer (identified by the words *Local User* under the name) and accounts in a shared network directory (identified by the words *Local Network User*). The pop-up menu near the top lets you view all users, or local users, or network directory accounts. If you add new accounts and they don't become network users, you haven't yet set up an Open Directory master. If you want to set up an Open Directory master, do it now. See Chapter 5 for instructions.

When you're ready to add a user account, do the following:

1. **In the Server app, click Users in the sidebar.**

2. **Click the Add (+) button in the lower-left corner of the user list.**

3. **Enter the new user's name, as shown in Figure 16-2.**

   A short name is generated automatically, but you can edit it. Short names don't contain spaces, although they can contain punctuation, including periods, underscores, and hyphens. They're usually lowercase.

4. **Type an e-mail address with your own server's domain or another domain.**

   If you have Mail Server running while you're creating new user accounts, the Server app automatically creates an e-mail address for the account and enters it for you in this dialog. For this reason, set up your e-mail service first if you're going to create a lot of accounts.

5. **Enter a password.**

   You can click the key icon next to the Password field to open the Password Assistant, which generates random passwords and tests password strength.

Figure 16-2:
Adding a
new user
account in
the Server
app.

6. **(Optional) Select the Allow User to Administer This Server check box if you want to grant the user full administrative privileges to control services, modify accounts, change passwords, and install software on the server.**

   If you don't want to give someone *full* admin rights, you can create limited administrators with Workgroup Manager, as I detail in the section "Creating user accounts with Workgroup Manager," later in this chapter.

7. **(Optional) Change the icon for a user by clicking the user icon and selecting Edit Picture.**

   You can import a photo, take one with the Mac's camera, or use another icon.

8. **Set the Home folder menu to None — Services Only, or leave it set to the default Local Only.**

   The default enables you to create a server-based home folder for the user.

9. **Click the Done button.**

Deleting user accounts

To delete a user, just click the user in the Users list on the left and then click the Delete (–) button. The Server app asks you to confirm the action. To delete multiple users at the same time, hold down the ⌘ key while clicking usernames.

Unlike in OS X's System Preferences, deleting a user account in the Server app doesn't delete the user's home folder or any files the user created on the server.

Editing user accounts and joining groups

The Server app presents a different user account pane for editing some of the information you originally entered. You can also add new information and add the user to groups. In the Users pane (refer to Figure 16-1), double-click a user to bring up the account's window, as shown in Figure 16-3. Note that the account window differs from the New User setup window.

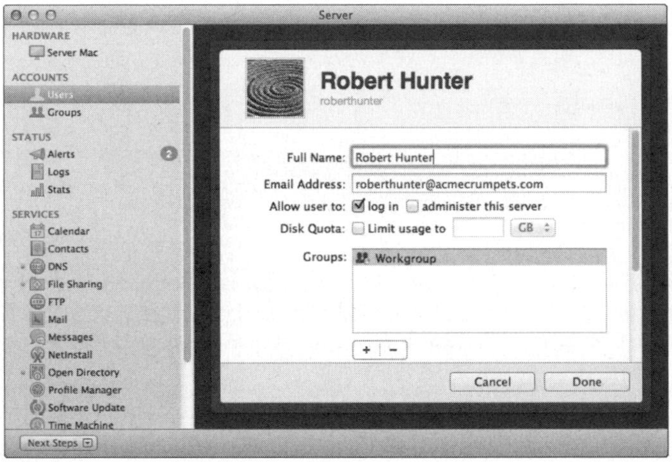

Figure 16-3:
The Server app's basic user account pane.

You can do several things in the account window. You can edit the e-mail address or add one, if you haven't already. You can make the user an administrator or remove that privilege and prevent the user from logging in by deselecting Allow User to Log In.

You can also edit the user's full name, but you can't change the short name here. So, if I change the user's name in Figure 16-3 from Robert Hunter to John Barlow, the short name would still be `roberthunter`. Apple makes it more difficult to change short names because this change can create problems if you've already configured a lot of services. But the Server app does allow you to change the short name in another location, which I describe in the next section.

There is no way to add any contact information aside from the e-mail address. The Open Directory database can store the user's chat address(es), street address, phone numbers, and other information. To add this information, you have to use Workgroup Manager.

Another thing you can do in this pane is designate a user as a member of multiple groups. (When you edit a group account, you can designate multiple users to be a member of one group.) In Figure 16-3, note that a group called Workgroup is already in the field. The server makes all Open Directory user accounts members of the Workgroup group.

Here's how to add one or more groups to a user from the user's account window (refer Figure 16-3):

1. **Click the Add (+) button below the Groups field.**

   An empty field containing the cursor appears in the Groups list box. When you start typing the name of a group, a drop-down menu appears, listing groups that begin with (or are close to) the letters you've typed. But included in the list is the word *Browse*. Selecting Browse brings up a list of *all* groups.

2. **Start typing the word** browse **and then press the Return key.**

   A window lists all existing groups — easier than typing group names one at a time.

3. **In the window that lists groups, select a group or ⌘-click to select multiple groups, and then drag them to the main window's Groups box, as shown in Figure 16-4.**

Figure 16-4: Editing group membership for a user in the Server app.

4. **Close the small window containing the groups list, and then click the Done button in the main window.**

Editing the short name, UID, user alias, and other advanced options

The Server app includes an advanced settings dialog for user accounts. Apple took such great pains to hide this dialog from users that you can't get to it from any menu or button. To see this dialog, do the following:

1. **In the Server app, click Users in the sidebar.**

2. **Control-click (or right-click) a user from the Users list to bring up a contextual menu.**

You can use the gear icon to access all items in this contextual menu — *except* for the Advanced item, which is available only here.

3. Select Advanced Options from the contextual menu.

The dialog shown in Figure 16-5 appears.

Figure 16-5:
The advanced user account dialog in the Server app.

Edit advanced settings for Ron McKernan
Changing these settings might prevent this user from logging in.

User ID:	1031
Group:	staff
Account Name:	ronmckernan
Aliases:	info

List aliases separated by commas

Login shell:	/bin/bash
Home Directory:	/Users/ronmckernan

Cancel   OK

Local Network User
Ron McKernan
Local Network User

Apple hides this dialog because it contains items that should not be changed carelessly. The safest way to edit them is when you're first setting up your server and need to make a correction. Later changes may prevent a user from logging in or from getting access to shared folders. Here's what you can edit in this dialog:

- **User ID (UID):** The unique Unix number for an account.

- **Group:** A Unix group that all users belong to, typically called staff. This name doesn't appear in too many places. Change it at your own risk.

- **Account Name:** The short name that you can't edit in the main user window.

- **Aliases:** Additional short names you can add with which a user can log in, using the same password. Aliases can be useful for a shared account, or for administrators in some cases. This field is not all that dangerous to edit. You can type multiple aliases separated by a comma and a space.

- **Login Shell:** The Unix shell that the user can work in if he or she has access to the command line.

- **Home Directory:** The same home directory setting defined in the main user editing pane, but spelled out as a path here.

Changing passwords and setting password policy

The Server app's Users pane provides two types of password management. First, you can manually change a password for a user account. To do this, select a user from the Users list, click the gear icon, and select Reset Password from the pop-up menu. Type a new password, verify, and click the Change Password button.

The other thing you can do is create a password *policy* that applies to all local user accounts or all network users. To set password policy, do the following:

1. **Select Local Users or Local Network Users from the pop-up menu at the top.**

   The All Users setting does not work for setting global password policy.

2. **Click the Action menu (gear icon) under the Users list and select Edit Global Password Policy.**

   A dialog appears, shown in Figure 16-6, presenting a dozen policy settings, all of which are turned off by default. You can create requirements for passwords, such as the minimum number of characters. You can require that new passwords be different from previous passwords or that they be different from the account name. You can disable login after so many failed attempts or a period of inactivity, or have login expire on a certain date. Remember, though, that these policies apply to all users.

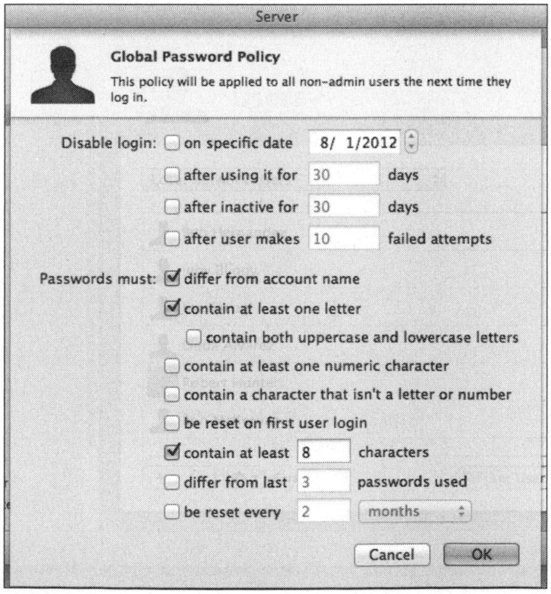

Figure 16-6: Setting global password policy for users.

3. **Select the check boxes for options you want to enable and change any numbers as necessary.**

4. **Click the OK button when finished.**

Restricting access to services (SACLs)

The capability to restrict user access to services is another useful item in the Users pane of the Server app. Select a user or ⌘-click to select multiple users. Click the Action (gear) menu, and choose Edit Access to Services.

A new dialog displays the user services that the Server app manages, such as File Sharing, Calendar, and Contacts (see Figure 16-7). Wiki and Web are not listed here because access to these services cannot be restricted. Selecting or deselecting these check boxes grants or denies (respectively) a user's ability to access a service.

Figure 16-7:
Restrict
access to
services by
deselect-
ing check
boxes.

Server

Service Access
Select which services these users can access.

☑ 📅 Calendar
☑ 📇 Contacts
☑ 🔷 File Sharing
☑ 🔵 FTP
☑ 📧 Mail
☑ 💬 Messages
☑ ⚙️ Profile Manager
☑ 🔘 Time Machine
☑ 🔒 VPN

[Cancel] [OK]

Note that it might be easier to apply these restrictions to a group. To do that, select a group in the Groups pane and choose Edit Access to Services in the Action menu (gear icon) there.

The list of services that a user can and can't access is called a *service access control list* (SACL). The term comes from the ACLs used to restrict access to file share points, described in Chapter 8.

Setting up and managing group accounts

In the Server app, managing groups is similar to managing user accounts, although you have fewer options to choose among for groups.

Creating new group accounts

Follow these steps to create a group:

1. **In the Server app, click Groups in the sidebar.**

   Figure 16-8 illustrates the Groups pane in the Server app with group accounts already created.

Figure 16-8:
The Groups
pane in the
Server app.

2. **Click the Add (+) button in the lower-left corner under the Groups list and then enter a group name in the dialog.**

   The short name for groups is created automatically.

3. **Click the Done button.**

Adding members to a group

The group you just created has no members. To add some, do the following:

1. **In the Server app, click Groups in the sidebar and double-click the name of a group in the list.**

   The pane for that group appears, similar to that for a user. The bottom half is a list of users (members) belonging to the group.

2. **Click the Add (+) button below the Members field.**

   An empty field containing the cursor appears below the last username. When you start typing the name of a user, a drop-down menu appears, listing members whose names begin with (or are close to) the letters you typed. Included in the list is Browse. Selecting Browse brings up a list of *all* users.

3. **Start typing the word** browse **and then press the Return key.**

   A window lists all existing users — easier than typing usernames one at a time.

4. **In the window that lists users, select a user or ⌘-click to select multiple users, and drag them to the main window's Members list, as shown in Figure 16-9.**

   The small window with all users also includes all groups. You can add other groups as members of a group.

Figure 16-9:
Drag users to add them to a group in the Server app.

5. **Close the small window with the groups list, and then click the Done button in the main window.**

To remove a member from a group, select the user and click the Delete (–) button.

Adding collaboration tools for a group

In the editing window for a group (refer to Figure 16-9), you can also direct Mountain Lion Server to set up collaboration tools for members of the group. In the section called Group Services, selecting the items in the following list will create them automatically:

✔ Selecting Give This Group a Shared Folder enables a shared server folder with access privileges for members of the group. File-sharing services must be already running.

✔ Selecting Make Group Members Messages Buddies makes all group members buddies in Messages. Messages services must be already running.

✔ Selecting Enable Group Mailing List signs up the group members to a listserv. E-mail services must be running.

✔ Clicking the Create Group Wiki button sets up a collaboration wiki for the group.

Deleting a group

Deleting a group is the same process as deleting a user. Select the group from the Groups list and then click the Delete (–) button. Deleting a group removes the ability for users to connect to common collaboration resources associated with that group, including shared folders, wikis, blogs, and group calendars.

Configuring Clients with Profile Manager

Profile Manager provides an automated way to configure account settings on Macs running OS X 10.7 and later, as well as iPad, iPhone, and iPod touch devices. It gives administrators fine control of devices and can be useful at home, as well as in business and education.

Profile Manager sets up the client devices for services running on Mountain Lion Server, adding configuration information about e-mail, virtual private networks (VPNs), and other services, including non-Apple technologies such as Microsoft Exchange Server. You can also set Profile Manager to configure settings limiting access to features such as the App Store. You can even set up parental controls for your kid's devices. You can create profiles for all users, as well for specific users, for groups, or for certain devices.

Mountain Lion Server provides three places where you interact with Profile Manager:

✔ **The Server app,** where you turn on Profile Manager service. The Server app automatically pulls together basic user configuration information for client access to the services.

✔ **The Profile Manager web app** is where you edit the default configuration profile and create others for specific users, groups, or devices. The Profile Manager web app also pushes settings and invitations to enroll to users.

> ✔ **The My Devices user web portal** is a web interface that is unique to each user with accounts in the shared network directory. Users can go to the web portal to download settings profiles to their Lion and Mountain Lion Macs and iOS devices.
>
> The web portal also lets users enroll their devices in the Profile Manager service. After devices are enrolled, the server will automatically push configurations and changes to configuration to the devices. Users get another benefit as well: From the web portal, a user can remotely lock or even wipe the data from a lost Mac, iPhone, iPad, or iPod touch.

Profile Manager has a few prerequisites. You must have users' accounts in a shared directory, such as Open Directory. It's also best to have services (such as calendar and file service) turned on before running Profile Manager so that it can gather the data from the services.

The next few sections describe using the Profile Manager service on the server end and on the user device.

What you can do with configuration profiles

A *configuration profile* is a small XML file that Profile Manager sends to Lion and Mountain Lion clients and to iOS devices. When a Mac or iPod, iPhone, or iPod touch receives a configuration profile, software on the device recognizes the configuration profile file and imports the settings. A configuration profile can create dozens of settings in a client device. Here are a few:

✔ Basic account info in a directory service (Open Directory, Active Directory, or LDAP)

✔ E-mail, calendar, contacts, and messages (settings that install user address, passwords, and server info, such as POP and SMTP servers)

✔ Microsoft Exchange Server settings for connecting to Windows servers

✔ VPN and network settings

✔ Printing preferences and restrictions

✔ Enforcement of password policies, which you can set in the Server app

✔ Restrictions, such as preventing Mac and iOS applications from launching, blocking users from making changes to System Preferences, turning on parental controls, blocking Macs from accessing external storage devices or optical discs, and preventing iOS users from watching YouTube

✔ Certificates (a configuration profile can install security certificates in a device)

✔ Custom preferences for other applications

Configuring Profile Manager on the server

Little typing is involved with using Profile Manager. It takes information that is already in the system, such as account names, e-mail addresses, mail server configuration data, and your server's domain name for the various services.

You perform two tasks on the server. The first is to turn on Profile Manager service with the Server app to create the first profile (see the next section). The second task, if desired, is to use Profile Manager to create further configuration profiles.

Using the Server app to turn on and set up Profile Manager

If you have your services running before you turn on and set up Profile Manager, the Server app automatically creates a profile with the settings of the running services.

To turn on the Profile Manager service and have it create the first configuration profile, do the following.

1. **Click Profile Manager in the sidebar, click the On switch, and wait for the service to start, as shown in Figure 16-10.**

   Next to Include Configuration for Services are icons for services that are already turned on. Profile Manager will create a profile for all Mac and iOS users that will configure these client devices for these services.

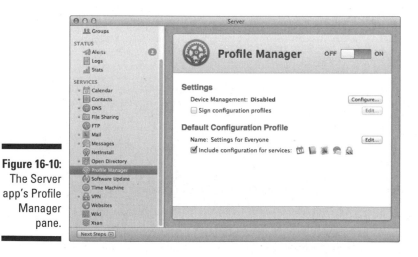

Figure 16-10: The Server app's Profile Manager pane.

2. **Select the Include Configuration for Services check box.**

3. **(Optional) Change the name of the default configuration profile, which is Settings for Everyone.**

4. **Make sure that the Include Configuration for Services check box is selected.**

5. **If Device Management indicates Disabled, click the Configure button and follow the directions in the assistant that appears.**

   This step enables a mobile device management (MDM) server that will enable remote lock, remote wipe, and other services.

6. **(Optional) Select the Sign Configuration Profiles check box for secure transmission of profiles.**

7. **(Optional) Select a security certificate in the dialog that appears, and click the OK button.**

   Should you choose to change this later, you can click the Edit button next to Sign Configuration Profiles.

The Server app has now collected information from the accounts and the running services and has created a configuration profile for all users. It gives a default name called Settings for Everyone. You can change this name with the Edit button.

If you'd like to edit the configuration profile or create new ones for individual users, groups, or devices, go to the Profile Manager web app, described in the next section.

Creating additional profiles with the Profile Manager web app

You can access the Profile Manager web app from a web browser by using a URL in this form: `http://server.example.com/profilemanager`. Or, in the Server app's Profile Manager pane, click the arrow next to Open Profile Manager in the lower right. Your web browser launches and asks you to log in.

The Profile Manager web app opens, shown in Figure 16-11, and displays the configuration profile created by the Server app, which applies to everyone, and lists the services that have settings in the profile. The web app also lists your Open Directory group accounts under Everyone. You can create a different configuration profile for each group.

You can now create a profile for a subset of users that configures more items. Follow these steps:

1. **Select a user or group from the left two columns.**

   If you added devices or created groups of devices (described in the next section), you can select them as well.

2. **Under the Group name on the right side of the window, click the Edit button.**

   The Settings page appears.

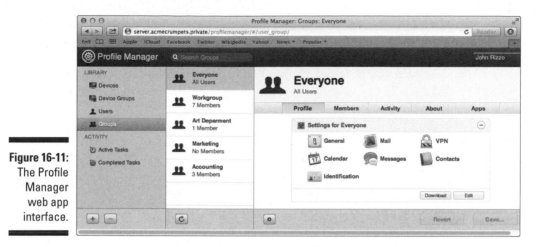

Figure 16-11:
The Profile
Manager
web app
interface.

3. **Select a setting type from the scrolling list on the left.**

   Settings types are organized into three areas: OS X and iOS, iOS only, and OS X only.

4. **Select an item and then click the Configure button.**

5. **Select settings options in the configuration window, like the one shown in Figure 16-12.**

   As you can see, I chose iOS restrictions, which lets me prevent users from purchasing apps, installing apps, or syncing while roaming. (See "What you can do with configuration profiles," earlier in the chapter, for more on what's possible.)

Figure 16-12:
A configu-
ration profile
settings
window
showing
iOS device
restrictions.

Settings for Art Department
3 Payloads Configured – Created 07/02/12 at 9:13 PM

iOS	
Restrictions 1 Payload Configured	
Subscribed Calendars Not Configured	
APN Not Configured	
OS X	
Identification	

Allow Photo Stream (disallowing can cause data loss)

☑ Allow screen capture

☐ Allow installing apps

☐ Allow In-App Purchase

☑ Require iTunes password for all purchases

☐ Allow multiplayer gaming

☑ Allow adding Game Center friends

☐ Allow iCloud backup

☐ Allow iCloud document syncing

☐ Allow automatic sync while roaming

[Cancel] [OK]

6. **When you finish with the settings in the window, click another item in the list on the left.**

If you don't want to use anything in this settings window, *don't* click the Cancel button. Clicking Cancel will undo all the settings you made during the current session. Instead, use the Delete (–) button at the top right.

7. When you finish, click the OK and Save buttons.

The profile for this group now shows the areas that you configured, displayed on the right side, as shown in Figure 16-13.

Figure 16-13: A new, customized configuration profile for a group.

A note on mail, contacts, and calendar profiles

As mentioned, if services such as mail, contacts, and calendar are turned on, Profile Manager will create profiles for these settings. If you look at these profiles in the web app, as described in the preceding section, you'll see that the username and password fields are blank. Each user will be prompted to enter a username and password when he or she installs the profile.

Creating profiles for devices

When more than one person works on a device, as in a school computer lab or workstations in an art department, managing configuration profiles for the device rather than for users is more convenient. The same is true for a user who has more than one Mac but needs different settings on each.

To create profiles for devices, just use the procedure in the preceding section, but select Devices or Device Groups in the left column (refer to Figure 16-13). If you don't have any devices listed, you can create a placeholder until a user connects with the device. Follow these steps:

1. Click Devices in the left column.

2. Click the Add (+) button and select Add Placeholder from the pop-up menu.

3. **Enter a name and serial number (or UDID, IMEI, or MEID) and then click the Add button.**

   iPhone, iPad, and iPod touch devices have a Unique Device ID (UDID), which you can find in iTunes with the device plugged in to the computer. Select the device from the sidebar and then click the serial number. It will change to a UDID. iPads with 3G also have an International Mobile Equipment Identity (IMEI) engraved on the back. Verizon iPhones also have a Mobile Equipment ID (MEID).

   The device now appears in the middle column. If you select it and click the About box, you find more information about it.

For the serial number for Macs running Lion and Mountain Lion, choose Apple menu⇨About This Mac, and click the More Info button. For iOS devices, go to Settings, click the General item, and then click About.

Configuring profiles on clients

After you have a configuration profile, either the one created by the Server app or your own, users can access it from a web browser. They'll have a choice of downloading a configuration profile or enrolling the device in the mobile device management (MDM) service provided by Profile Manager. First, here's how to download a profile to have Profile Manager configure the client device:

1. **From the Lion or Mountain Lion Mac or iOS device, log in with a web browser at *yourdomain.com*/mydevices.**

   The My Devices page appears. Figure 16-14 shows the page on an iPhone, but the page looks almost identical on a Mac.

2. **Click the Profiles tab.**

   Clicking the Show Contents link displays what settings are in the profile.

3. **Click the Install button.**

   This step downloads a file with a filename in the form `name-of-profile`.mobileconfig. A new window opens, describing what's in the profile and asking you to approve.

4. **Inspect the window that appears for accuracy.**

   In OS X 10.7 or 10.8, the downloaded configuration profile launches System Preferences, which displays a dialog. Click Show Profile to expand the list to get profile details, as shown in Figure 16-15.

5. **Click Continue, and then click the Install button.**

   On a Mac running Lion or Mountain Lion, System Preferences displays a new Profiles pane.

Figure 16-14:
The My Devices page, where iOS and Mac users download a configuration profile.

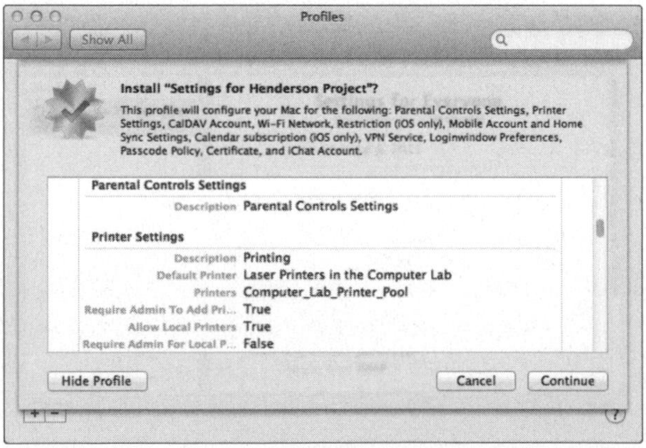

Figure 16-15:
System Preferences displaying a configuration profile request.

Installing an enrollment request is similar to downloading a profile. When a device is enrolled, the MDM service pushes configuration changes to the device, so the user no longer needs to access the web portal. (An enrollment is actually a type of configuration profile.) Enrollment also enables a user to lock or wipe the Mac or iOS device from the web portal. Here's how to enroll:

1. **After logging in to the web portal, click the Devices tab, as shown in Figure 16-16.**

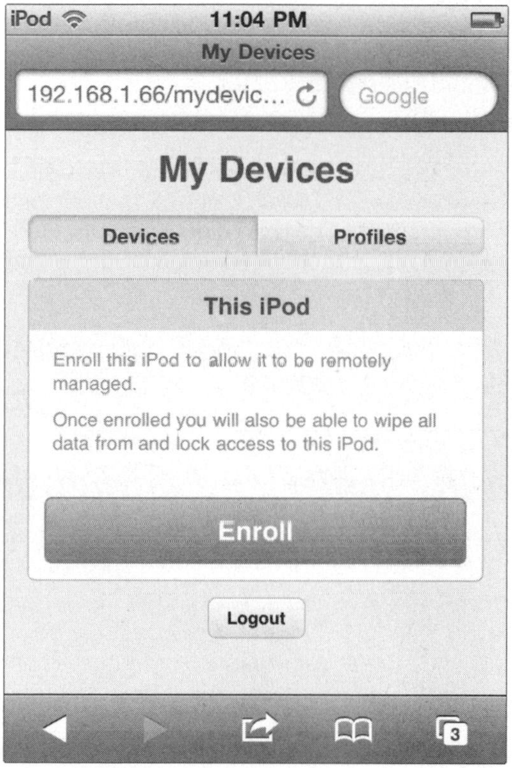

Figure 16-16: An enrollment request, which looks the same in iOS or Mac Lion.

2. Click the Enroll button.

3. After the configuration profile file downloads and you're warned that settings will be changed, click the Install button.

You're asked for a password if the profile contains an e-mail configuration.

To remotely lock or wipe a device from the admin's Profile Manager web page, choose either command from the gear icon. Users can find the commands in their My Devices page under the Devices tab.

Managing Accounts with Workgroup Manager

As Uncle Ben Parker reminds fans of *Spider-Man,* "With great power comes great responsibility." Workgroup Manager has great power for modifying the directory databases in Mountain Lion Server, so care in understanding the capability of this server tool is critical to healthy account management.

Workgroup Manager is not installed with Mountain Lion Server. You must download it separately from `http://support.apple.com/kb/DL1567`.

You can open Workgroup Manager installed on any Mac OS X 10.8 computer connected to the same network as the Open Directory master (see Chapter 5). For the most consistent results in Workgroup Manager, connect directly to the Open Directory master. Don't connect to replica servers or any server bound to the directory. Replica servers contain read-only copies of the directory databases that are periodically synchronized from the master, so editing accounts on replicas forces directory updates on the master from the replica; instead, the master needs to update the replicas.

Connecting to the server and authenticating to the directory

Workgroup Manager is preconfigured to connect to the server on which it's installed. In the Workgroup Manager Connect screen, enter the address, username, and password of the local administrator created when you installed Mountain Lion Server.

If you're running Workgroup Manager from another system or you've changed the host name of the server postinstallation, do the following:

1. **Choose Server⇨Connect and type the host name of the server in the Server field.**

2. **Enter the administrator's username and password in the corresponding fields.**

3. **Click the Connect button.**

You could also click the Browse button to locate available servers on the network, but for the most consistent results, enter the server's fully qualified host name, such as *server.example.com*, in the Address field.

Workgroup Manager loads the default screen, shown in Figure 16-17. In this example, a number of users have already been created.

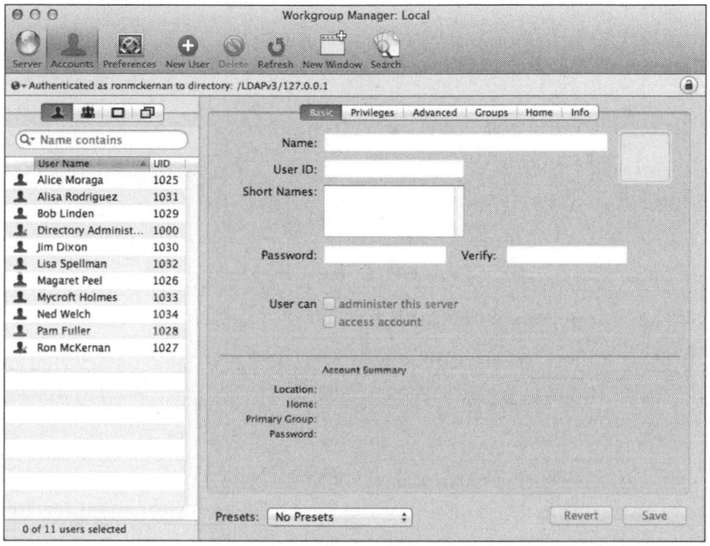

Figure 16-17:
Workgroup
Manager's
default
screen after
connecting
to a server.

Just below the toolbar is a small globe icon followed by text indicating the status of the directory you're browsing. The first time you connect to an Open Directory master, the status bar displays `Viewing directory: /LDAPv3/127.0.0.1. Not authenticated`. This message indicates that you're browsing the shared directory on the server itself but haven't yet authenticated to modify the directory.

Clicking the globe icon allows you to change the directory you're browsing. A lock icon on the right side of this bar is used to authenticate to the directory, as I describe in the following section.

After you launch Workgroup Manager and connect, you need to authenticate to modify the directory:

1. **In Workgroup Manager, click the lock icon on the right side of the window to authenticate as the directory administrator (which you create in Chapter 6).**

2. **Enter the username and password of the directory administrator in the dialog, and then click the Authenticate button.**

   The status next to the globe icon changes to `Authenticated as Directory Administrator to directory: /LDAPv3/127.0.0.1`, and the lock icon changes to an open lock.

Creating user accounts with Workgroup Manager

After you're connected and authenticated to the directory, you can add, remove, and modify accounts. Follow these steps to create a new user:

1. **Click the Accounts icon.**

2. **Select the Users tab just below the globe icon, and then click the New User icon in the toolbar.**

   A new user is created, named Untitled 1. If Untitled 1 already exists, the new user is Untitled 2, and so on.

3. **In the Basic tab (refer to Figure 16-17), enter the username in the Name field.**

   A short name is generated automatically, based on the name.

4. **Enter a password.**

   The user ID (UID) is automatically generated based on the first available number higher than 1025 — the first UID used for regular directory accounts.

5. **Click the Save button.**

Changing default account settings

With Workgroup Manager's Accounts icon selected in the toolbar, you can select any account from the list of users and modify its settings.

The initial short name is the only user attribute that can't be changed with Workgroup Manager. You can change it with the Server app, as described in the section "Editing short name, UID, user alias, and other advanced options," earlier in the chapter. Additional short names, or *aliases,* can be added by clicking the field below the existing short names on the Basic tab of Workgroup Manager, but some services require the user to enter the original short name.

After a user account is created and its UID is set, don't change the number for it. Permissions and access to various services are tied to the particular UID for the user; changing the UID could have unintended consequences and make it impossible for a user to access server data.

Setting server administrators and directory administrators

By default, new user accounts aren't administrators. You can enable users to be server administrators or directory administrators or both. Server administrators can use the Server app to modify services and settings of Mountain Lion Server. Directory administrators have privileges to change user and group settings.

To enable a user to be a server administrator:

1. **Log in to Workgroup Manager.**
2. **Click the Accounts icon in the toolbar, and then click the Basic tab.**
3. **Select a user, and then select the User Can Administer This Server check box to allow users to administer this server.**

To enable a user to be a directory administrator, select the user name in the list on the left, click the Privileges tab and choose None or Full from the Administration Capabilities pop-up menu.

Editing group membership

Continuing with the Users (head icon) tab selected on the left, you can set group membership for the selected user in the Groups tab on the right. Near the top are fields for primary group ID and short name. By default, all new users created in Workgroup Manager are members of the primary group called Open Directory Users, which has a short name of staff and a group ID (GID) of 20.

When you click the Add (+) button, a drawer slides out of the Workgroup Manager window, displaying the current group accounts, as shown in Figure 16-18.

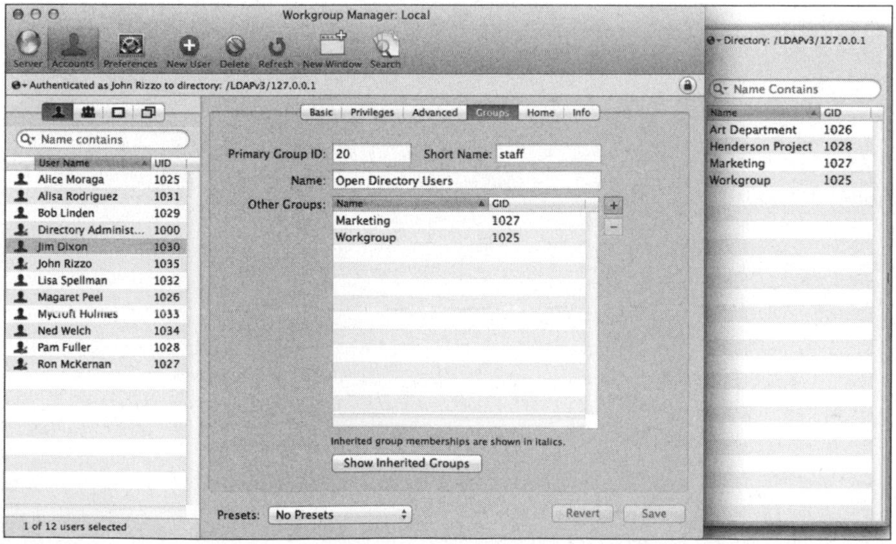

Figure 16-18: User account group membership in Workgroup Manager.

You can change the primary group by dragging a group from the slide-out list over one of the three fields: Primary Group ID, Short Name, or Name.

Additional group membership can be added by dragging groups to the Other Groups list.

Because groups can be members of other groups (called *nested groups*), click the Show Inherited Groups button to see additional groups that the user is a member of via nested groups.

Setting the location of a user's home folder

With the user icon selected on the left, the Home tab, shown in Figure 16-19, gives you various options for setting the location of a home folder:

✔ Select None (the default) if the user shouldn't have a home folder on the server. This option is handy if the user doesn't need to log in to a home folder — useful for an account that accesses only sharing or collaboration resources.

Figure 16-19: Setting the home folder for a user account in Workgroup Manager.

✔ Select a directory (identified as a path) if you want the user to have a server-based home folder. The default is /Users, but you can specify another location. Folders that appear here are shared folders that you previously configured as automounted home folders on this server with the Server app or on another server bound to the directory. Note that Figure 16-19 shows a folder shared with AFP.

✔ The Disk Quota field allows you to specify an upper limit on the amount of disk space that the folder can use. This limit applies to all data created by a user on the volume where the home folder exists, not just on the share point where the home folder is stored.

You won't use the other buttons on this page much, but here's what they do:

✔ Click the Add (+) button to add a new location for user home folders. In the dialog that appears, enter the OS X Server/share point URL (the URL may point to another server besides Mountain Lion Server), the path to the home folder, and the full path the Mac OS X client will use to access the home folder. The new location will be available to all users in the directory.

✔ If users store only their home folders on the local Mac OS X computer, set the home folder to /Users. By doing so, regardless of where the user logs in, his or her home folder is in the local Users folder.

If you don't see a /Users folder in the list, and you want one, click the Add (+) button and then enter **/Users/*short name*** in the Full Path field. Leave the Mac OS X Server/Share Point URL and Path to Home Folder fields blank.

✔ Next to the Add (+) button, three additional buttons exist for managing home-folder locations. The double-window button duplicates a home-folder location. The Minus (–) button deletes a home-folder location for all users in the directory but leaves the data intact in the home folders. The pencil button allows you to edit home-folder locations.

✔ The Create Home Now button generates a new home folder at the specified location. This process doesn't overwrite an existing home folder with the same short name. The home folder is created automatically the first time a user logs in if this button isn't clicked, so creating a home folder from Workgroup Manager isn't required.

Editing other user account settings

Workgroup Manager's User Accounts pane has a few more areas you can edit.

The Info tab

The Info tab lets you add contact information, including street address, phone numbers, e-mail and chat addresses, and other information about a user. Details entered in this tab become part of the account record in the user database. Users can see data you enter here in the Contacts client in Mountain Lion or the Address Book client in OS X Lion if Contacts Server (see Chapter 10) is running.

The Advanced tab

You can find several unrelated settings on the Advanced tab:

✔ Deselecting Allow Simultaneous Login prevents a user from logging into the server from more than one computer at the same time.

✔ The Comment and Keyword fields can help you quickly locate accounts based on similar comments or keywords that you add here.

✔ The User Password Type pop-up menu allows you to assign the user to a different password database. When managing directories other than Open Directory, such as the unshared local directory of users, another choice is Shadow Password, the standard password type for local accounts in OS X.

✔ Login Shell selects which Unix shell environment the user has when connecting to the server from Terminal. To disallow Terminal access on the server, choose None from the pop-up menu.

Disabling and deleting user accounts with Workgroup Manager

An alternative to immediately deleting a user account is to disable access to the account by deselecting the Access Account check box in the Basic tab of a user account. (This check box is visible in Figure 16-17.) Disabled accounts are shown in the Users list with a red X through their icons.

The more disabled accounts you have, however, the more difficult it becomes to manage a large group of users. After a while, deleting a defunct user is the best option to keep your directory tidy. To delete an account, click the Users tab just below the globe icon. Click to select a user and then click the Delete (–) button.

Files in shared and home folders created by deleted users remain on the server. However, data in Mail, Messages, Contacts, and blogs is removed from the server when the user account is deleted.

Creating group accounts with Workgroup Manager

Creating a group account with Workgroup Manager is much the same as creating a user account. Group accounts contain one or more user or group accounts. Group accounts that are members of another group are *nested accounts*.

To create a new group account with Workgroup Manager, follow these steps:

1. **If you're not logged in, click the lock icon on the right side of the Workgroup Manager window, and then enter the username and password of the directory administrator in the dialog; click the Authenticate button.**

2. **Select the Groups tab just below the globe icon, and then click the New Group icon in the toolbar.**

   A new group is created, named Untitled 1, as shown in Figure 16-20. If Untitled 1 already exists, the new group is Untitled 2, and so on.

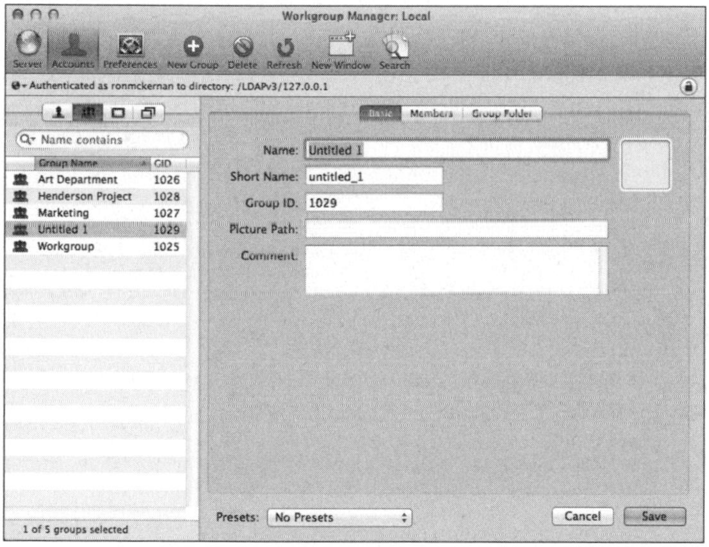

Figure 16-20: A new Untitled 1 group created in Workgroup Manager.

3. **In the Basic tab, enter the group's name in the Name field.**

   A short name is generated automatically.

   The group ID (GID) is generated automatically based on the first available number higher than 1025 — the first GID used for regular directory accounts.

   The Basic tab includes a field to enter a picture path, used to set a custom picture to identify this group. You can use the Comment field for human-readable comments regarding this group account.

4. **Add users and groups to the group membership by clicking the Members tab at right (see Figure 16-21) and then the Add (+) button.**

A users and groups drawer slides out the side of the Workgroup Manager window. Users are shown under a User icon (a single silhouetted figure) and groups under a Group icon (three silhouetted figures).

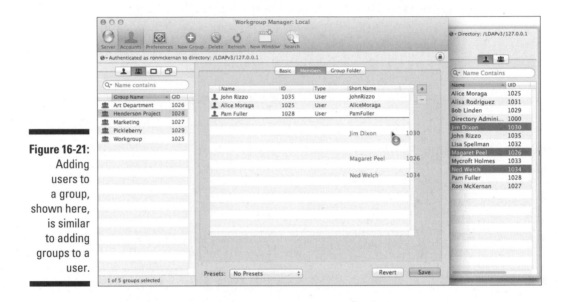

Figure 16-21:
Adding users to a group, shown here, is similar to adding groups to a user.

5. **Drag user and group accounts (shown in Figure 16-21) to the Members tab to add them to the new group.**

    ⌘-click to select multiple users. To remove a user or group, click the account name in the Members tab and then click the Delete (–) button.

6. **Click the Save button.**

Like a user account, a group can have its own automounting folder on a share point. The process is like assigning a home folder to a user (shown in Figure 16-19), except that you select Groups on the left. Where the users screen has a Home Folder tab on the right, the groups screen has a Group Folder tab. When you set the share point and folder, group members can access the shared folder as well as save and edit content, subject to permissions set for the shared folder. (See Chapter 8 for details on setting file-sharing permissions.)

When you select a share point for a group folder, you must specify an owner of the folder. Click the ellipsis (. . .) button next to the short name to select a user to be the group folder's owner. This can be a member of the group or an administrator. The owner can create, edit, or delete any file or folder in the group folder.

Editing and deleting group accounts with Workgroup Manager

Although you can't change the short names of user accounts, you can modify any aspect of a group account within Workgroup Manager. Simply access an existing group account in the same way that you would for a new account. (See "Creating group accounts with Workgroup Manager," earlier in this section.)

The group ID (GID) shouldn't be changed after a group is created. The GID is tied to file permissions and resources in Mountain Lion Server; changing it may have unintended consequences, making data and resources unavailable to users.

Group accounts, unlike user accounts, can't be disabled; however, removing all members of a group effectively disables anyone from accessing the group resources. To permanently remove a group, do the following:

1. **Click the Groups tab just below the globe icon, and then select the group to be deleted in the list of accounts.**

2. **Click the Delete icon in the toolbar, and then confirm the deletion of the group account by clicking Delete in the dialog that appears.**

Files in shared folders created by deleted groups remain on the server. However, data such as blogs, wikis, and group calendars in other services is removed from the server when the group account is deleted.

Importing and exporting accounts

You can use Workgroup Manager to import and export account records. Periodically exporting accounts can help you restore your Open Directory domain if the worst should happen and your archive won't restore the databases.

When you export user accounts from the archive process, user passwords aren't ever exported from Workgroup Manager. In addition, the Kerberos Key Distribution Center (KDC), which controls single sign-on, can't be exported.

Importing accounts can make a large influx of new users easier to manage. For example, a school may have a list of new students each fall taken from the registrar's database, manipulated, and imported into Workgroup Manager. Third-party utilities, such as Passenger from MacinMind Software (www. macinmind.com/Passenger), can help massage the raw data into a format compatible with an Open Directory domain.

To import users in Workgroup Manager, choose Server⇨Import; then select a file and click the Import button. Chapter 6 describes how to import users and groups from another directory server by using the Server app.

Exporting accounts in Workgroup Manager is straightforward. Follow these steps to export a list of accounts:

1. **If you're not logged in, click the lock icon on the right side of the Workgroup Manager window, and then enter the username and password of the directory administrator in the dialog; click the Authenticate button.**

2. **Depending on the type of account you plan to export, click the Users, Groups, Computers, or Computer Groups tab below the globe icon.**

3. **Select the accounts from the list you plan to export.**

   Hold down the ⌘ key to select more than one account.

4. **Choose Server⇨Export.**

   A Save As dialog appears, allowing you to enter a name for the exported list of accounts and to select the location to save the file.

5. **Click the Export button.**

   Repeat this process for each type of account — users, groups, computers, and computer groups — you're exporting.

If you need to delete a number of accounts, you could also export the account lists before they're deleted. This saves you time if any account is deleted in error or needs to be added again later.

Configuring OS X Clients with Managed Preferences

Managed Preferences for Mac OS X (MCX) is a powerful feature that allows Mountain Lion Server to manage system, user, and applications preferences on Macs connected, or bound, to an Open Directory domain. With MCX, a Mac client can automatically load predefined settings from the central server. You can also define which applications can run. If you don't want users buying items from the App Store, you can prevent the App Store from launching. If you don't want users to change preferences, you can prevent them from launching System Preferences.

You can make a lot of these same settings with Profile Manager, but only with Macs running OS X 10.7 and later. With MCX, you can do this with any version of OS X.

MCX can manage any preference by storing a *manifest,* one or more preference files, on the Mac. Managed preferences can be set for almost any system, user, or application preference that uses Apple's standard preference list (.plist) files. Many system and user settings are preconfigured for easy management in Workgroup Manager under the Preferences icon.

Before I get to setting up managed preferences, the next section describes how to create computer group accounts, which are very useful for applying managed preferences.

Creating computer and computer group accounts

Managed preferences make apparent the importance of computer and computer group accounts. Specific computer and computer group preferences streamline management of Energy Saver settings, mobile accounts, and hardware-specific preferences, for example.

 You don't need to create computer or computer group accounts in Workgroup Manager unless you plan on using managed preferences. You could use the list of computer and computer group accounts to help you organize and manage large deployments of OS X systems, but Workgroup Manager isn't a great replacement for a simple spreadsheet or database of systems.

You could create a new computer account by selecting the Computer tab (square icon) in Workgroup Manager and then clicking the New Computer icon in the toolbar. However, you then need to type the Ethernet ID to identify the computer. It's easier to first create a computer group and then browse the list of bound computers to add the computer to the list, creating a computer account by default.

Here's how to create a computer group and add computer accounts:

1. **If you aren't logged into Workgroup Manager, click the lock icon to authenticate as the directory administrator and enter the username and password of the directory administrator in the dialog; click the Authenticate button.**

2. **Click the Computer Groups tab (two overlapping squares) below the globe icon, and then click the New Computer Group icon in the toolbar.**

   A new computer group named Untitled 1 is created. If Untitled 1 already exists, the new group is named Untitled 2, and so on. Figure 16-22 shows an example of a new computer group. Much like a group of user accounts, a computer group has Name, Short Name, Group ID (GID), and Comment fields in the Basic tab of Workgroup Manager.

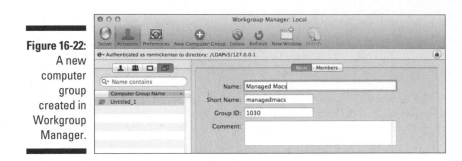

Figure 16-22:
A new
computer
group
created in
Workgroup
Manager.

3. **Enter a name for the computer group.**

   The short name is generated automatically based on the Name field. The Group ID (GID) will be created for you.

4. **Click the Members tab to add computers to the group.**

   Click the Add (+) button in the Members tab to add computers or existing computer groups to the new group or click the ellipsis (. . .) button to select computers already bound to the directory to add to the computer group.

5. **Click the Add button.**

You now have members in a computer group. Click the Computer Accounts tab (a single square) in Workgroup Manager and note that the computer you added now has a computer account as well.

Configuring managed preferences

In Workgroup Manager, click the Preferences icon in the toolbar to manage preferences for accounts connected to the Open Directory domain. The left side of the Preferences pane uses the same tabs (users, groups, computers, and computer groups) as the Accounts pane. Figure 16-23 shows Workgroup Manager with the Preferences icon on the toolbar selected and a computer group selected.

Note the icons on the right side of the Workgroup Manager window under the Overview tab, such as Applications, System Preferences, and Dock. These icons represent preferences manifests that you can preset in Workgroup Manager. The Macs in the selected computer group will become configured with the settings that you create within each icon. (Some of the preset preferences icons don't apply to different types of accounts and therefore aren't displayed.)

Although the Overview tab has many commonly managed preferences, nearly any preferences list in OS X can be managed. Other preferences manifests can be added in the Details tab.

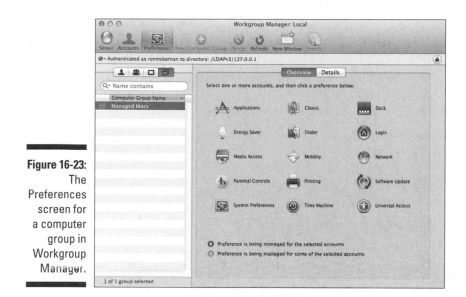

Figure 16-23: The Preferences screen for a computer group in Workgroup Manager.

As an example of how to set up managed preferences, here are directions on configuring a list of applications that can be launched on Macs that belong to a computer group. Users of these Macs are prevented from launching applications not on your list. This restriction can be useful for Macs in a public place, such as a school computer lab.

Note that you can designate individual applications, or applications that reside in folders, such as Microsoft Office. You select those in two places. Here's how to set allowed applications:

1. **Click the Preferences icon in the toolbar, and then select the Computer Group tab (two overlapping squares) above the list of accounts.**

2. **Select a computer group at the left side and then click the Applications icon under the Overview tab.**

   For applications the reside in folders (such as Microsoft Office), click the Folders tab instead.

3. **From the Manage options, select Always, and then select the Restrict Which Applications Are Allowed to Launch check box.**

4. **Click the Add (+) button and select applications from the list that appears; click the Add button in the dialog.**

   You can ⌘-click individual applications to select multiple items in the list.

   The list of applications that appears includes those that are installed on your server Mac. Any application you want to permit users to launch must be also installed on the server.

If you are in the Folders tab, when you allow an application residing in a folder to be launched (such as Office), you also allow helper applications to run. You can manually deselect the helper apps to disallow them.

5. **Click the Apply Now button to save your settings.**

If you get a message asking you to digitally sign applications, click the Sign button if you want to enable the server to identify apps on the Macs.

Figure 16-24 shows the result of these steps so far: a list of applications that users are allowed to launch if their Macs are in the Managed Computers computer group.

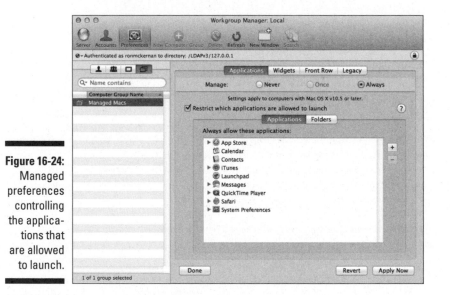

Figure 16-24:
Managed preferences controlling the applications that are allowed to launch.

6. **Click the Done button to return to the Overview tab.**

You can also manage other preferences from the Overview tab. Referring to Figure 16-23, you can click the icons for Dock, Finder, Media Access, Network or the others to configure settings or restrict access as managed preferences. For instance, if you click the Dock icon, you can select applications that will appear in the Dock of the managed Macs.

If you now click the Details tab, shown in Figure 16-25, you can view precise information about each preferences manifest.

The Details tab allows you to edit the preferences manifests by double-clicking an item in the. A sheet slides down to show the details of the preferences.

With the Details tab, you can import preferences from other applications or sources. Click the Add (+) button to add those preferences files (in the `.plist` format) to Workgroup Manager.

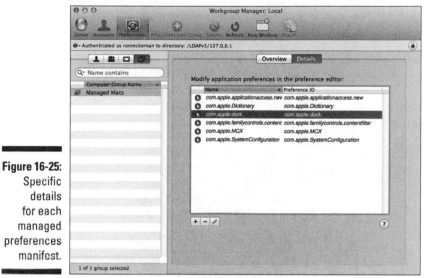

Figure 16-25:
Specific
details
for each
managed
preferences
manifest.

You can also set managed preferences for user, group, or computer accounts from their respective tabs above the list of accounts.

Inheriting, combining, and overriding preferences

You can set managed preferences for all types of accounts in an Open Directory domain: users, groups, computers, and computer groups. A group with managed preferences is referred to as a *workgroup*. Managed preferences can't be controlled for computers that aren't bound to the domain, but users in the domain also can't log in at those computers with directory accounts until they're bound.

Because managed preferences can be applied to all types of accounts, you have a specific hierarchy for inheritance, combining, and overriding preferences. Some settings, such as controlling which items are opened at login, are cumulative because no one particular setting overrides another — any number of items can be opened at login.

Some settings are inherited from workgroups to the user level or from within nested workgroups. Settings with only one ultimate outcome — such as the position of the Dock onscreen — use an order of priority to override the same setting for different account levels. The prioritization of conflicting preferences to override the same setting also applies for inheritance. The order of inheritance and overriding preferences is

- Workgroup (the least specific level)
- Computer group
- Computer
- User (the most specific level)

For example, a preference set at the workgroup level can't override the same preference set for the computer group, computer, or user level. In this sense, a preference set for the user always wins when overriding other levels.

However, setting preferences at the user level can be time-consuming and complicated to manage. Managing at the workgroup or computer-group level saves time and energy, and making your life a little easier is one of the reasons you bought this book.

Enforcing managed preferences

You can set managed preferences with four restrictions:

- **Always:** The preference is enforced continuously. Users can't change the preference.
- **Once:** The directory sets the preference one time. The user is then free to change the setting.
- **Often:** The Often setting isn't present in Workgroup Manager's Overview tab for preferences management, but it can be set within the raw preferences manifests with the Details tab.

  Often sets the preference when the user logs in. During the user session, the preference can be changed, but it's reset on subsequent logins to the managed setting.

- **Never:** Effectively, Never means preferences management for that setting is disabled, and the user can set whatever preferences are desired.

These settings appear when you select the Preferences icon, select an account, select the Overview tab, and then select a preferences icon. This is described in the "Configuring managed preferences" section, earlier in this chapter.

Using Software Update Server to Control Updates from the Server

Mac users are accustomed to getting notices from Software Update telling them that Apple has a software update ready for them — that is, unless they've turned off Software Update. Some users may choose to install the updates and some may not, so if you're managing your organization's Macs, you may not know exactly what configuration your users have. In addition, Apple sends updates to OS X, Safari, iTunes, AirPort Utility, and other items. Your organization may not need or want them all.

Mountain Lion Server's Software Update Server ends the uncertainty. It downloads Apple's software updates to your server, providing them to users all at once over your local network. This feature lets you control the software versions on users' Macs and prevents them from installing updates for which your organization may not be ready.

Software Update is a service listed in the Server app's sidebar. Here's how to use it:

1. **Select Software Update in the sidebar and then click the big switch to the On position.**

   The Software Update pane defaults to the Settings tab, as shown in Figure 16-26.

Figure 16-26: The Settings pane of Software Update.

2. **Select one of the two options:**

   - *Automatic:* Downloads all updates from Apple and enables them for installation on clients

   - *Manual:* Lets you select which updates to download and send to users.

3. **View the available updates by clicking the Updates tab (shown in Figure 16-27).**

   If you don't see the list of updates, select Check for Updates in the Action (gear) menu.

   If you selected Automatic in Step 2, the server will install any updates that are applicable to the clients' accounts listed in Open Directory.

Figure 16-27: The Updates tab of Software Update shows the available Apple updates for Macs.

4. **If you selected Manual in Step 2, select one or more updates to enable by ⌘-clicking them in the list, click the Action (gear) menu, and then select Enable from the pop-up menu.**

   To find out more about a particular update, select it from the list and choose View update from the Action (gear) menu.

As with Profile Manager, Software Update Server requires the Mac clients to be bound to a network directory such as Open Directory.

Chapter 17

Creating Mobile Accounts for Notebooks

*Y*ou've had enough sitting at your desk, and it's time to get out of the office, but how do you take your data with you when you go home? What if you need to make a presentation at a client's office out of town? Do you drag your entire network infrastructure with you? Imagine the airline luggage fees.

In this chapter, you determine the best method for managing client computers that aren't tied down. Most frequently, these devices are notebook computers. Instead of having user home folders stored only on a server volume or only on the client computer, mobility settings offer a combination of these two choices. Mountain Lion Server lets you create mobile home folders for Mac, Windows, and Linux clients.

With a mobile account, domain information such as mobile preferences and user account data, as well as user data, is all updated when the user connects to the network. Mobile accounts can also have a portable home folder synchronized between a server volume and the internal hard drive. I examine the options in this chapter, and you see how to create a mobile account and a server-based home folder, which you then turn into a portable home folder.

Later in this chapter, I describe how to create and manage mobile accounts and home-folder synchronization in Workgroup Manager.

Connecting Workgroup Manager to a Shared Domain

As with several topics in this book, you need to know the basics of Workgroup Manager. You can run Workgroup Manager from any network-connected system or directly on an Open Directory server. (Remember, you have to download Workgroup Manager as part of the Server Admin Tools package, available at `www.apple.com/support/downloads`.) Follow these steps to launch and connect to the directory in Workgroup Manager:

1. **Launch the Workgroup Manager application from `/Applications/ Server` on your client system.**

2. **Choose Server⇨Connect.**

3. **In the Address field of the dialog that appears, enter the IP address or host name of the directory server.**

4. **Authenticate as the server's local administrator by typing in the Username and Password fields.**

5. **Click the Connect button.**

6. **Choose the shared directory domain from the pop-up menu just above the list of users in Workgroup Manager.**

   If this is strictly an Open Directory domain and you're working directly on the Open Directory server, choose `/LDAPv3/127.0.0.1`. If you're working on a connected system, choose `/LDAPv3/your hostname or IP address`. If you're using Active Directory, choose `/Active Directory/Your Domain` from the list. Other choices are possible, depending on your directory configuration.

7. **Click the lock icon to the right of the Shared Directory pop-up menu and authenticate as the directory administrator that you created as part of the directory configuration.**

You're now ready to manage the users, groups, and computers in the directory domain. Figure 17-1 shows Workgroup Manager logged in to an Open Directory master server and shared domain, with a user account selected.

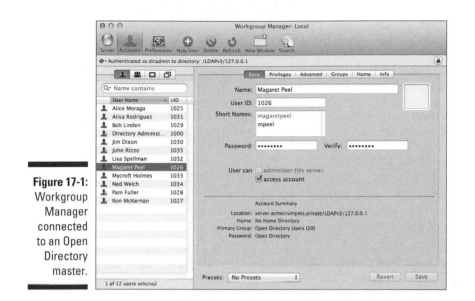

Figure 17-1:
Workgroup
Manager
connected
to an Open
Directory
master.

The Nightmare of Networked Notebooks

When notebook users take their notebook to another location, in or out of the office, what happens to the users' authentication information and data when they disconnect from the network? How can the users continue to log in to their notebook and access their documents and other data away from the network directory and file sharing? The answer is the mobile account.

Unlike other accounts, a *mobile account* caches the user's account credentials on the local hard drive. User data could be stored on the local hard drive or a network volume, but the local hard drive makes the most logical sense in this configuration.

To go even further, you can configure a mobile account to have a portable home folder. Building on the mobile account, a user's home folder is synchronized between a server volume and the local drive. Synchronization occurs at login and at predetermined intervals. The directory administrator configures the intervals.

This choice gives notebook users freedom of movement while maintaining their data on the server and local drive.

Here are some other options for accounts and home folders that can be used for notebook clients:

✔ **External account:** Like a mobile account, but the user's account data can be stored on any volume connected to the client, including an external USB or FireWire hard drive or a USB flash drive. That volume can be removed and connected to another Mac OS X system. The user can log in with the account credentials stored on the external volume.

✔ **External account with portable home folder:** The combination of an external account and portable home folder, both stored on an external volume attached to the client.

One of the most flexible choices, this option allows users to synchronize a home folder to a portable drive and take it to another computer and have full access to their data. It's also the most unsecured option because the portable drive can be easily lost or stolen.

Other users besides notebook users can benefit from external and mobile accounts and portable home folders. Regular network accounts can be used interchangeably with mobile accounts and portable home folders, with significantly less impact on network activity. Synchronizing users' home folders provides redundancy in the event of a hardware failure.

Creating portable home folders sets up a two-way mirror of files between the server and the local hard drive. Never combine regular network home folders with portable home folders: Data loss is a likely outcome. The portable home folder client tracks changes and performs the sync operation by comparing the files between the server and the local drive. If a file has previously changed on the server and the portable home folder process wasn't aware of the change, the local file will be overwritten back to the server.

Set a master password on each computer in the Security pane of System Preferences. You can also require a master password be set when a mobile account logs in to a managed computer.

Planning and Deploying Mobile Accounts

Just as you've seen with other services in OS X Server, planning before you decide on deploying mobile accounts and portable home folders saves you from wasting time and energy.

Here's the basic planning and deployment process: First, decide the type of account you'll use to manage mobility settings. Then examine the options for mobile accounts and portable home folders that I describe in the preceding section. Next, configure directory and file-sharing services on your servers. Finalize connections by binding clients to the directory and log in to mobile accounts, creating portable home folders as necessary.

Simplifying mobile management with computer and group accounts

As I discuss in Chapter 16, accounts come in different types: user, group, computer (or machine), and computer groups. Managing mobility options is possible for any of the account types or combinations thereof. But for simplicity, with multiple accounts needing mobility and portability settings, group and computer group accounts are the best choices.

Manage your notebook systems with computer groups. When users of multiple systems always need a particular setting, such as mobility, creating a group of those systems makes your job easier.

When managing desktop systems with mobile accounts and portable homes, unless you're managing only a few user accounts, also use groups and computer groups. You probably will separate your notebook and desktop systems into separate computer groups.

To create a computer group, you need one or more clients bound to a shared directory, as described in Chapter 5. After the clients are bound, use Workgroup Manager to create a computer group by following the directions in Chapter 16.

If you decide to manage settings based on a group of users instead of a group of computers, create a user group instead. You can use either the Server app or Workgroup Manager to create a user group, as I describe in Chapter 16.

You can designate a group to be a member of another group. Adding groups to groups creates *nested groups.* This technique can save you time when managing large numbers of user accounts. It also facilitates the inheritance of permissions and managed settings, which I discuss in Chapters 8 and 16, respectively.

You can manage a group or computer group by clicking Workgroup Manager's Preferences icon in the toolbar, which I describe in Chapter 16, and the mobility settings, which I examine through the rest of this chapter.

Configuring mobility settings

To get started with mobility, the user needs an account in a shared directory. Directory information, including the Lightweight Directory Access Protocol (LDAP) account and password data, is cached from the shared directory to the local system. By itself, a mobile account doesn't include any documents or data from the user's home folder.

When a mobile account is enabled, the user can log out and log in again without being attached to the network where the account data resides. After returning to the network and reconnecting to the directory, the local cached authentication data is resynchronized, and any updates to the LDAP or password data are cached again on the local system. You can also have a mobile account expire if it goes unused.

Any standard Open Directory network account can become a mobile account. Mobility settings can be configured for the account itself, a group of which the account is a member, a computer where a user can log in, or a group of computers where users can log in.

If, as the directory administrator, you set mobility in more than one of these locations, rules of inheritance and precedence for client preferences take effect.

Here's an example of how to configure the mobility settings for a computer group. To set up the mobile account, do the following:

1. **Open Workgroup Manager and connect to the shared directory.**

2. **In Workgroup Manager, click the Accounts icon in the toolbar and then click the Computer Groups tab above the list of accounts.**

   The Computer Groups tab is the icon represented by two overlapping squares (the fourth tab, sitting to the right of the Users, Groups, and Computers tabs.).

   If your planning leads you to manage individual user accounts, groups of users, or individual computers, select that account instead of the computer group in Workgroup Manager.

3. **Click the Preferences icon in the toolbar.**

   The right side of Workgroup Manager displays the icons for the various managed preferences.

   In Figure 17-2, note the small, dark gray circle enclosing a mouse pointer next to the Mobility icon. This circle indicates that the preferences are being managed for the selected account.

Figure 17-2: Managed preferences of a computer group in Workgroup Manager.

4. **Click the Mobility icon.**

5. **Select the Account Creation tab, and then click the Creation subtab.**

6. **By default, Manage is set to Never; select Always.**

   Preferences can be managed never, once, or always in Workgroup Manager. Once isn't an available option for some mobility settings. Figure 17-3 shows the mobile Account Creation settings for a computer group.

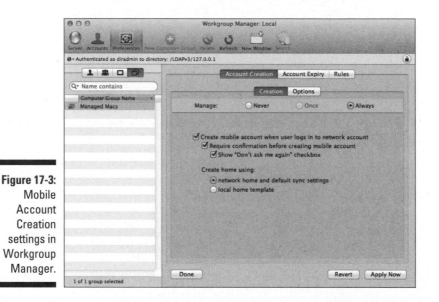

Figure 17-3:
Mobile
Account
Creation
settings in
Workgroup
Manager.

7. **Select the Create Mobile Account When User Logs in to Network Account check box.**

   Selecting this option creates the mobile account on the local hard drive of an OS X system.

8. **(Optional) Deselect the Require Confirmation before Creating Mobile Account check box to keep the user from having to confirm mobile account creation.**

   (Optional) Deselect the Show "Don't Ask Me Again" check box to prevent the user from having to confirm again when he or she logs in to a managed computer.

9. **(Optional) Choose how a new home folder is created by selecting Network Home and Default Sync Settings or Local Home Template.**

   The first option uses a network volume and creates either a network home or a portable home, depending on the sync settings in the Rules tab. The second choice (Local Home Template) uses the default home folder settings on the local hard drive.

10. **Click the Apply Now button to save the settings.**

11. **(Optional) Click the Options subtab under the Account Creation tab.**

    Here, you have choices for creating a FileVault-encrypted home folder and deciding where the users' home folders will be created. Click Always to manage these settings. Enable FileVault by selecting the Encrypt Contents with FileVault check box.

12. **(Optional) If using FileVault, under the Options subtab, select either the Use Computer Master Password, If Available or the Require Computer Master Password check box.**

    You select the second choice if you want to require and verify a valid master password on the local system.

    A master password is the critical fail-safe for encrypted FileVault home folders. It provides the capability to restore access to an encrypted account if the user forgets a password.

    The remaining choices under the Options subtab set where the home folder is stored. By default, On Startup Volume is selected. The other choices are At Path, with a field to enter the specific location in the file system where the home folder will be stored; and User Chooses, with a pop-up menu. The pop-up menu choices are Any Volume, Any Internal Volume, and Any External Volume. By choosing Any Volume or Any External Volume, the user can create an external account.

13. **After making any changes, click the Apply Now button to save your settings.**

Two more tabs are in the mobility settings after Account Creation. The second tab is Account Expiry. The settings on this tab control when mobile accounts will expire on the mobile computer, as shown in Figure 17-4 for a computer group. In other words, the cached account on the local hard drive will be deleted when it expires.

Your security policies may require accounts to be deleted if users don't connect periodically to the shared directory. But be careful with this setting. If an account goes unused for the period set by the expiry settings, the mobile account's home folder is deleted, and the user can't log in while away from the network.

Select the Delete Mobile Accounts check box and set the time frame for when the account will be deleted to have a mobile account deleted after that time frame. Select the Delete Only After Successful Sync check box if you want to be certain that a mobile account is synchronized to the server before deletion occurs.

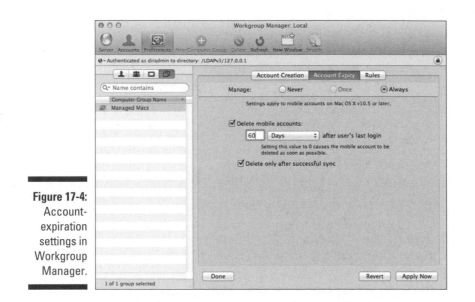

Figure 17-4:
Account-
expiration
settings in
Workgroup
Manager.

The third tab of mobility preferences is the Rules tab, where you configure the settings for portable home folders, as described in the next section.

Creating Server-Based Home Folders and Deploying Mobile Home Folders

Of course the account itself isn't terribly useful without the user's data. The solution is to use compatible file-sharing services on the network to create a portable home folder. To do so, you need an automountable share point configured in the directory for user home folders so that it appears to the user without intervention by the user. An automountable share point must have a network mount record in the directory domain.

Although synchronization of the user's home folder provides hardware redundancy — the user's account is easily synchronized with another system if a hard drive fails or another problem develops — synchronization isn't a replacement for a good backup strategy. Changes in files on the local system — for example, files that are modified, deleted, or corrupted on the local system — are synchronized to the server's volume. Similarly, if a problem exists on the server, the file changes get synchronized back to the local hard drive.

The next section describes creating a home folder that is located on the network. After that, I describe configuring the mobile home folder.

Creating server-based home folders

Any Open Directory user can have a home folder on the server. On a Mac, the *home* folder is the directory that's named after the user. This folder contains all of the user's data, settings, bookmarks, and so on. When you locate users' home folders on the server, they log in to a Mac and authenticate to the server. Users then can log in to different computers and still get the same access to their home folders.

When you create home folders for your users, take care to select the correct file-sharing protocol. For Mac clients, the home folder must be shared with the AFP protocol. (Don't use SMB for a Mac home folder.) Home folders for Windows clients must use SMB. Linux clients use SMB.

Server-based home folders can put a heavy burden on the server and take a lot of storage, but you can assign a limit to the size of the folder. Follow these steps to create a home folder on the server:

1. **In the Server app, share the `/Users` directory, select Make Available for Home Directories, and click Done.**

2. **In Workgroup Manager, click the Accounts button, select a user, and then click the Home tab.**

3. **In the list of share points, select the folder in which you would like to store the user's home folder.**

   The default is the Users folder, located on the startup drive. If you don't see the Users folder, click the Refresh icon in the toolbar.

4. **Click the Create Home Now button.**

5. **Click the Save button.**

   Workgroup Manager creates a home folder with the user's short name (for example, `/Users/ronmckernan`).

If you go to the Finder and look inside the new home folder, you'll see that Workgroup Manager has created the hierarchy of folders that a home folder contains to store a user's files and settings, including Documents, Library (which includes Preferences), Desktop, Downloads, and Pictures and Music.

(In Lion and Mountain Lion, the Library folder in a user's home folder is invisible, so you'll have to go to the Finder's Go menu, choose Connect to Folder, and type ~/**Library**.)

Configuring the mobile home folder

Your server should already be bound to the shared directory or configured as an Open Directory master or replica, as I describe in Chapter 5.

After the binding and the share point are ready, use Workgroup Manager to set the network home folder and enable portable home synchronization. Here's how:

1. **Open Workgroup Manager and connect to the shared directory.**

2. **In Workgroup Manager, click the Accounts icon and then click the Users tab above the list of accounts.**

   The Users tab is the icon represented by the single silhouetted figure — the leftmost tab.

3. **In the list of accounts under the tabs, click a user's name and then click the Home tab on the right side of the Workgroup Manager window.**

4. **Click the share point you previously created for user home folders and then click the Save button.**

   You've set the location where the home folder will be stored on the network, as shown in Figure 17-5.

5. **Select the Computer Groups tab, and then click the name of a group you want to use.**

   See the section "Simplifying mobile management with computer and group accounts," earlier in this chapter.

6. **Click the Preferences icon, and then click the Mobility icon.**

   If you haven't set up account creation yet, do so by following the directions in the section "Configuring mobility settings," earlier in this chapter.

Figure 17-5:
Setting a user's network home folder in Workgroup Manager.

7. **Click the Rules tab.**

   The Rules tab contains a multitude of options for the portable home folders. The second subtab, Preferences Sync, controls synchronization of preference files from the user's home folder. You come back to this subtab in just a minute.

8. **Click the Home Sync subtab.**

9. **Select Once or Always to set sync settings for each login or always, respectively, and then decide the intervals for sync by selecting one or more of the check boxes:**

   • *At Login:* Sync occurs when the user logs in to an account. The user sees a progress bar while the sync is in progress.

   • *At Logout:* Sync occurs when the user logs out of an account. The user sees the same progress bar.

   • *In the Background:* An automatic sync occurs without any user notification.

   • *Manually:* Sync is triggered by the user from the user's account in the Accounts (or Users & Groups) pane of System Preferences or by the user's selecting Sync Now from the Home Sync status menu when she is logged in.

Figure 17-6 shows the options for home-folder synchronization.

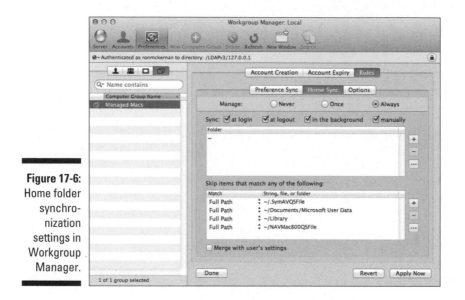

Figure 17-6:
Home folder
synchro-
nization
settings in
Workgroup
Manager.

10. **(Optional) Set the list of sync locations.**

    Below the four options for when sync occurs are the locations that will sync. By default, these include the user's home folder, indicated by the tilde (~). Add locations to sync by clicking the plus (+) button and then typing the path in the new field. Select any location, and click the minus (–) button to remove that sync path. Click the ellipsis (. . .) button to open a new window, and select a location in the file system to sync.

11. **(Optional) Set the list of locations that won't synchronize in the Skip Items That Match Any of the Following area.**

    By default, several locations in the user's home folder are skipped when sync occurs. Generally, these locations are unnecessary because they contain inconsequential files. The same plus, minus, and ellipsis buttons apply to this list.

12. **(Optional) Select the Merge with User's Settings check box to combine the synchronization settings a user can set in the System Preferences Users & Groups pane (called the Accounts pane in versions of Mac OS X before Lion).**

13. **Click the Preferences Sync subtab.**

   The settings in Preferences Sync are similar to those in Home Sync but affect only preferences files. This tab is configured the same way as Home Sync (refer to Steps 9–11).

14. **(Optional) Click the Options subtab.**

   To modify the background sync interval from its 20-minute default or to change the default for the Home Sync status menu, select Once or Always. Then modify the background interval and, if desired, deselect the Show Status in Menu Bar check box. See Figure 17-7 to view the additional options available when you're using a computer group.

15. **Click the Apply Now button to save the settings.**

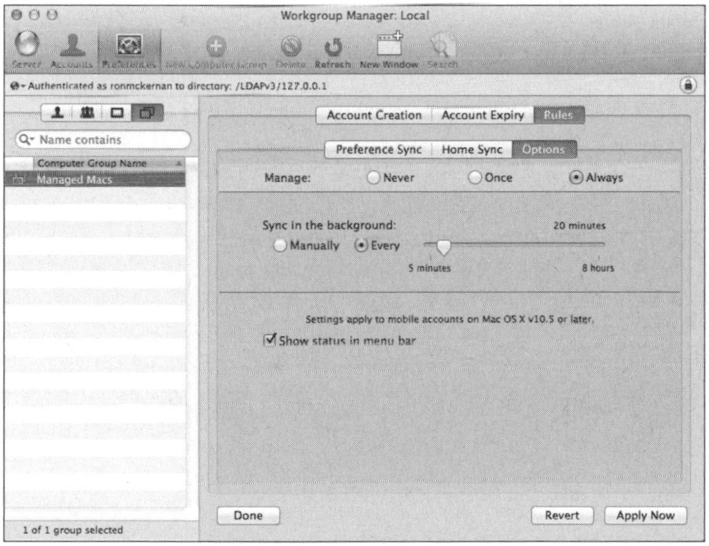

Figure 17-7:
Additional options for home-folder sync in Workgroup Manager.

Maintaining regular backups of the server volume and the local hard drive remains a critical part of your network deployment. Easier backup of just the server volume, if the portable home folders regularly and reliably sync to the server, is a side benefit of synchronizing home folders. An always-on backup system for laptops should still be part of your backup strategy, especially for road warriors whose systems are more susceptible to a bad fall or to evildoers looking to steal a fancy Mac laptop.

Putting sync to work on the client

After the services have been configured and managed preferences set, the client needs to connect to the directory and file sharing, and a user will log in to his account. During login and logout, if sync has been enabled at this time, the user sees a window with a scrolling bar indicating the synchronization status. In Figure 17-8, you see an example of this window on a Mac. This window is also displayed if a user triggers a manual sync.

If you selected the options to have the user confirm the creation of the mobile account in the section "Configuring mobility settings," earlier in this chapter, the user confirms the mobile account. From then on, the account is much the same as a local account. The following are the two differences a user sees:

✔ **The addition of the Home Sync status menu (shown in Figure 17-9) is indicated by an icon depicting two overlapping houses to the left of the clock and other menu extras in the menu bar.**

This menu displays the current status of home synchronization with the network home-folder server. The user sees the date and time of the last sync and can choose Sync Home Now to manually sync her home folder with the server.

The two house icons in the menu bar icon alternate between the normal black outline and a gray version of each house when the background sync process is running.

✔ **In the Users & Groups pane of System Preferences, a mobile tag is added under the user's name in the list of accounts.** A mobile account in System Preferences is shown in Figure 17-10. The user also sees an additional button under the Password tab: Mobile Account Settings. This user is running Mac OS X 10.6, which is supported along with OS X 10.7, 10.8, and even the older 10.5.

Figure 17-10:
A mobile
Mac user's
account
settings
in System
Preferences.

Clicking the Mobile Account Settings button displays choices for the background sync interval, the folders that are synced, and whether the Home Sync status menu is displayed. These settings, however, may be overridden by the managed preferences in the Mobility settings of Workgroup Manager.

Chapter 18

Keeping Your Server Healthy and Secure

*O*nc aspect of managing client computers and devices is using server security to keep clients from compromising the network. Mountain Lion Server comes with tools to prevent snooping, malware, and malicious attacks. In other chapters, I describe password encryption with authentication, Secure Sockets Layer (SSL) data encryption, the use of secure certificates, and spam and virus blockers for individual services, including file sharing, e-mail, and the web.

This chapter looks at overall issues, including using the firewall to guard access to the network and using and creating secure certificates for encryption. It ends with configuring a virtual private network to give offsite users secure access to the local network.

In case something does happen to your server, Mountain Lion Server comes with four tools for monitoring different aspects of the status of the server. Alerts notify you of problems that need attention now, and Stats monitors long-term trends. Experts use the Logs tool for troubleshooting. These three tools are part of the Server app.

Another tool, Activity Monitor, is a separate app and provides a view of what's happening at this instant. This chapter also describes these monitoring tools and explains how you might use and respond to them.

Configuring a Firewall

A *firewall* blocks certain types of incoming traffic from the Internet while allowing outgoing traffic to the Internet. If you're running a firewall, your job is to configure it to allow incoming traffic in response to outgoing traffic from your users. For example, if your users try to access a website, you want traffic from web servers to reach the users.

If your network already has a firewall on another server or a router or other security gateway appliance, you may not need to run OS X's firewall. You do need to run a firewall on your Mac server if it's acting as an Internet gateway, with the Mac between the Internet connection and the local network. You also need to run a firewall on the server if your Internet connection goes directly into a wireless router, and the router doesn't have a firewall built in or running on it. In this case, the server needs to be connected to the router via Ethernet.

Regardless of whether you're running a firewall on your Mac server or somewhere else, the next few sections provide useful information.

Setting up a firewall in Mountain Lion Server

Mountain Lion Server comes with Packet Filter (also known as *pf*), which is open source firewall software. Although you can access the pf firewall by using the command line, Mountain Lion Server's graphic interface does not give you many options in configuring it, as did previous versions of OS X Server. For that reason, you may want to use a third-party front end to the pf firewall.

A good front end for Mountain Lion's pf firewall is the free, open source Ice Floor (`www.hanynet.com/icefloor/`). Before I get to Ice Floor, let's look at what is provided with Apple's included tools.

Mountain Lion Server uses the System Preferences utility for configuring the firewall. This is the same interface used in every copy of Mountain Lion, server or client. Here's what you do:

1. **In the Server app, turn on any services you want to use.**

2. **In the Apple menu, choose System Preferences.**

3. **Click the Security & Privacy icon, as shown in Figure 18-1.**

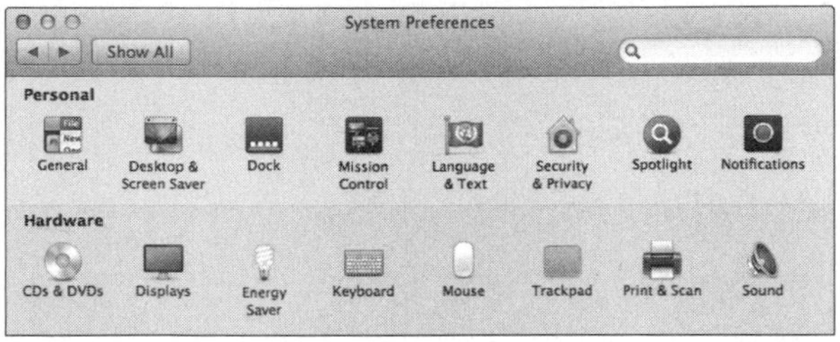

Figure 18-1:
Click
Security
& Privacy
in System
Preferences
to access
the firewall
settings.

4. **Click the Firewall tab.**

5. **Click the lock icon (in the lower-left corner), type your administrator password, and then click the Unlock button.**

6. **Click the Turn On Firewall button.**

7. **Click the Firewall Options button, as shown in Figure 18-2.**

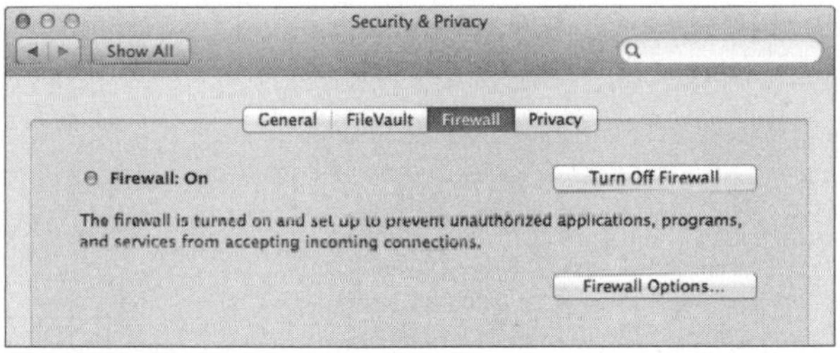

Figure 18-2:
The Firewall
tab of the
Security
& Privacy
pane.

8. **In the dialog that slides down, click the Add (+) button.**

9. **Browse to the Applications folder, select the Server app, and then click Add.**

   The Server app is added to the list of allowed connections, as shown in Figure 18-3.

10. **Click the OK button.**

The System Preferences interface for Mountain Lion Server's firewall does not give you a lot of options, such as changing port numbers or selecting individual services to allow or block. Here's where a third-party front end such as Ice Floor comes in. Ice Floor provides a simple, intuitive interface that even a beginner can use, but it also provides advanced configuration options for the pros.

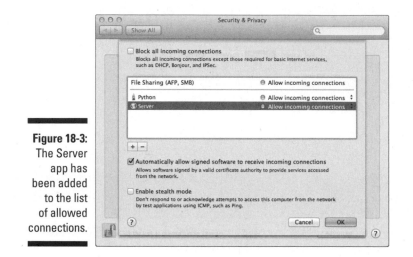

Figure 18-3:
The Server app has been added to the list of allowed connections.

Follow these steps to use Ice Floor for a basic firewall setup:

1. **Download Ice Floor from** www.hanynet.com/icefloor/ **and launch it.**

2. **In the top half of the Ice Floor window, shown in Figure 18-4, select the check boxes next to services for which you want to allow traffic.**

   You can select Mac or Windows file sharing, web service, printer sharing, screen sharing, and remote VPN access, as well as other services you have running. The firewall will block communications from services not selected.

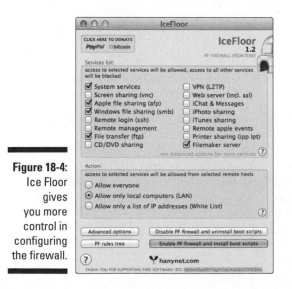

Figure 18-4:
Ice Floor gives you more control in configuring the firewall.

3. **In the Action area of the window, select the type of user who will be able to get access to the server through the firewall.**

   The default is Allow Only Local Computers (LAN). If you enable access by people from the Internet, select Allow Everyone.

4. **Click the Enable Firewall and Install Boot Scripts button.**

   The firewall is now running.

If you want to change port numbers (as described in the next section), click the Advanced Options button. In the window that appears, you can create a black list of IP addresses that you want to block. Many other advanced options are available as well, though you need to know what you are doing. These options are built into Mountain Lion Server's pf firewall, but Ice Floor enables you to access them with a graphics interface.

Port numbers used by Mountain Lion Server services

If you're using a firewall on another device (such as a wireless router), you'll likely have the option to designate port numbers for each service. A firewall blocks incoming traffic through software ports (settings identified by port numbers) and by port type: TCP (Transmission Control Protocol) and UDP (User Datagram Protocol). A port can be *open,* which allows traffic to come through, or *closed,* which blocks traffic. Each service is associated with a standard port. For example, the default port for IMAP e-mail is TCP port 143. When used with SSL encryption, the default IMAP port is TCP 993. Some services have a range of ports. Web service defaults to TCP 8080, but has a range of TCP 8000–8999 that you can use.

If you're configuring a firewall that's not on Mountain Lion Server, take a look at Table 18-1, which lists the default port numbers used by the services of Mountain Lion Server. You use these port numbers also if you're doing port forwarding for an Internet router. Of course, a firewall on Mountain Lion Server also uses port numbers, but the only way to view or change them is from the command line.

Apple has a more extensive list of ports that Apple networking software uses. To see this list, visit http://support.apple.com/kb/TS1629.

Table 18-1 TCP and UDP Port Numbers for Lion Server Services

Service	Port Number	Port Type
Contacts Server	8008	TCP
Contacts Server with SSL	8443	TCP
File-sharing AFP	548	TCP
File-sharing SMB	139	TCP
Calendar Server	8008	TCP
Calendar Server with SSL	8443	TCP
Messages Server	5222	TCP
Messages Server with SSL	5223	TCP
Messages server-to-server	5269	TCP
Messages Server file transfer	7777	TCP
Messages local	5678	UDP
Messages audio/video RTP and RTCP	16384–16403	UDP
Mail, SMTP standard	25	TCP
Mail service SMTP submission	587	TCP
Mail service IMAP	143	TCP
Mail clients IMAP with SSL	993	TCP
Mail service POP3	110	TCP
Mail clients POP3 with SSL	995	TCP
Profile Manager services	Same as web HTTP, HTTPS	TCP
Remote login SSH (Secure Shell)	22	TCP
Screen sharing (VNC)	5900	TCP
VPN L2TP	1701	UDP
VPN L2TP IKE NAT Traversal	4500	UDP
VPN L2TP ISAKMP/IKE	500	UDP
VPN L2TP ESP (firewall only)	IP protocol 50	n/a
VPN PPTP	1723	TCP
Web service HTTP	80	TCP
Web service HTTPS	433	TCP
Web service custom website	8080	TCP
Wiki, web calendar, web mail	Same as web HTTP, HTTPS	TCP

Firewalls, network routers, and NAT

Another security feature is network address translation (NAT), which provides private IP addresses to the users' computers on your network. The private IP addresses are not directly visible to the Internet. Although earlier versions of OS X Server let you run NAT on the Mac server, Apple removed this feature in Mountain Lion Server. Most network routers, such as DSL or cable routers, or wireless access points, do include the capability to provide NAT.

If you're using a network router that provides the Internet connection, network address translation, and a firewall, you have two options for configuring the router. (You use the router's software, often accessed through a web browser.) Your options follow:

- **Run the firewall on the server.** You must make the server the router's default host. This setting, which you make on the router, tells the router to send all incoming connect requests to the server.

- **Run the firewall on the router.** You must configure port forwarding on the router. *Port forwarding* (or *port mapping*) means that you set the router to forward traffic from the service port numbers to your server's IP address (shown in the Server Preferences Information pane).

Using an AirPort Extreme or Time Capsule firewall

Mountain Lion Server has some special features for Apple's wireless Internet routers: Apple's AirPort Extreme Base Station and Time Capsule. If you're going to run the firewall on the AirPort device, the Server app will display it in the sidebar, listed under Hardware. You can use the Server app to configure the firewall on the server or on the Apple router. You can also add another layer of security for users accessing your AirPort wireless network.

To use the Server app to configure AirPort devices running firewalls, you first need to configure a few items with AirPort Utility (in the /Applications/ Utilities folder of any Mac):

- Connection Sharing must be set to Share a Public IP Address.

- IPv6 Mode (an advanced option) must be set to Tunnel.

- Default Host must be set to Off.

By default, the firewall is turned on in AirPort Extreme and Time Capsule. To keep the firewall running on the device, you need to enable port mapping on the device with the AirPort Utility or the Server app, which I describe in the next section. To instead have the firewall run on the server, use AirPort Utility to enable a default host on the device.

Configuring firewalls on AirPort devices with the Server app

To use the Server app to configure port forwarding on an AirPort Extreme Base Station or Time Capsule, launch the Server app and follow these steps:

1. **In the sidebar under Hardware, select the Airport device.**

2. **Click the Add (+) button and choose a service (Messages, Mail, and so on) from the pop-up menu.**

   For services not listed, choose Other and enter the service name and port. (Refer to Table 18-1 for port numbers.)

   This setting tells the AirPort device to let traffic for these services through.

3. **To block traffic from listed services, select a service and click the Delete (–) button.**

4. **When you finish, click the Restart AirPort button and enter a password for the device if prompted.**

   This step interrupts services that the AirPort device may be providing, such as DHCP, access to a Time Machine hard drive, or Internet access.

RADIUS for extra AirPort security

Mountain Lion Server comes with another feature for Apple wireless routers: the Remote Authentication Dial In User Service (RADIUS). It provides an extra layer of security for users accessing your network wirelessly via an AirPort Extreme Base Station or Time Capsule. With RADIUS running, instead of logging in to the network with the wireless password, users log in with their server account usernames and passwords. You can also prevent users from accessing the Wi-Fi network and allow their accounts access only from Ethernet.

When an AirPort base station is running, you can turn RADIUS on in the Server app. Select the AirPort device under Hardware and then choose Allow User Name and Password login over Wi-Fi. RADIUS will be turned on, and all server user accounts will have access to the wireless network.

Working with Secure SSL Certificates

A *Secure Sockets Layer (SSL) certificate* is a small file that enables the server to prove its identity to client computers and other networks and enables encrypted communications. A certificate contains your server's domain name and organization information; it also has a cryptographic key associated with it (a *public key*). You have the option to use SSL certificates with contacts, web, e-mail, calendar, and messaging services to encrypt data sent between clients and the server.

When you installed OS X Server, a self-signed certificate was created that will work with the built-in services. This certificate includes the computer name that you designated. You can also create additional self-signed certificates on Mountain Lion Server, as described in the following sections. You need to do this if you change the host name of the Mac. With self-signed certificates, the user's software asks the user whether the certificate should be trusted.

For a higher level of security, you can use a certificate from a third party. For instance, when you set up the Apple push notification service, the Server app guides you through obtaining a certificate from Apple specifically for push notifications, as used by Profile Manager. For other services, you can purchase a signed SSL certificate from a trusted certificate authority such as VeriSign (www.verisign.com), Thawte (www.thawte.com), and GlobalSign (www.globalsign.com).

Using SSL certificates

In Mountain Lion Server, you enable SSL for a service simply by assigning an SSL certificate. With the Server app, you can select a certificate to use, create a self-signed certificate, and import a certificate. You can also add and delete certificates and renew a certificate with an updated or signed version.

Assigning an SSL certificate to a service

Follow these steps to specify a certificate for a service:

1. **In the Server app, select your server in the sidebar under Hardware.**

2. **Click the Settings tab.**

The SSL Certificate item will have one of these descriptions next to it:

- The name of the certificate selected for all running services
- Not Configured, if none of the running services has a certificate
- Custom, if different services use different certificates

3. **Click the Edit button next to SSL Certificate.**

4. **Choose a certificate from the pop-up menu or select Custom to change the certificate for specific services.**

   At least one certificate is listed: the self-signed certificate created by the server, named after the server.

5. **If you chose Custom in Step 4, click the double arrows next to the service and select a certificate (or select None), as shown in Figure 18-5.**

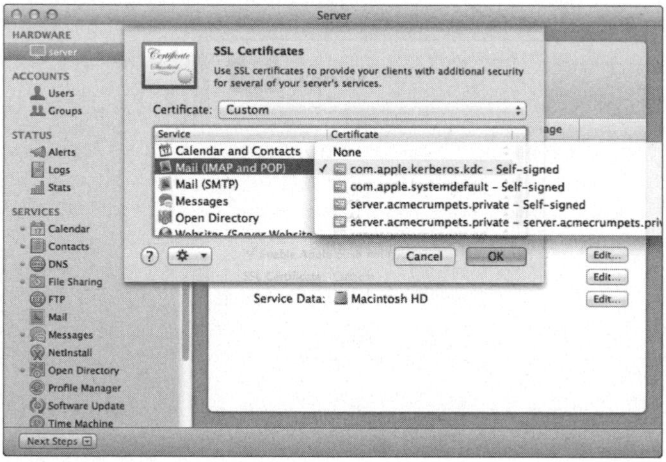

Figure 18-5: Selecting different certificates for individual services.

6. **Click the OK button when you're finished selecting certificates.**

Creating a self-signed certificate

If you don't see any certificates or want to create another, you can create a self-signed certificate:

1. **In the Server app, select your server in the sidebar under Hardware.**

2. **Click the Settings tab.**

3. **Click the Edit button next to SSL Certificate.**

4. **Click the gear icon and then select Manage Certificate from the pop-up menu.**

   The Manage Certificates dialog appears.

5. **Click the Add (+) button and select Create a Certificate Identity, as shown in Figure 18-6.**

   The Certificate Assistant appears.

Figure 18-6: Use the Manage Certificates dialog to create a self-signed certificate.

6. **Type a fully qualified DNS name for the server, shown in Figure 18-7, and then click Create.**

   Don't change the other default settings, which are shown in Figure 18-7.

Figure 18-7: The Certificate Assistant.

7. **Click the Create Button.**

8. **In the warning dialog that appears, click the Continue button.**

9. **In the Conclusion dialog, click the Done button.**

Creating a request to a certificate authority

You can use the Server app to create a certificate signing request (CSR) to send to a certificate authority. The authority *signs,* or authorizes, a certificate you created and supplies a public key. Follow these steps in the Server app:

1. **Select the server in the left column under Hardware and click the Settings tab.**

2. **Click the Edit button next to SSL Certificate.**

3. **Click the gear icon below the list of services and choose Manage Certificates.**

   A new dialog slides down (refer to Figure 18-6).

4. **Click the gear icon in the Manage Certificates dialog and choose Generate Certificate Signing Request (CSR).**

   A signing request is generated and displayed in a new dialog.

5. **Click the Save button.**

   A Save As dialog asks you to choose a location on the hard drive.

You can send this file (which ends in `.csr`) to a certificate authority, such as Comodo Group, Inc. (`www.comodo.com`), Thawte, Inc. (`www.thawte.com`), or VeriSign, Inc. (`www.verisign.com`). Just upload the file or copy and paste it in the authority's website. The certificate authority sends you a signed certificate. To use it, replace the certificate you used to generate the CSR, as I describe in the following section.

Importing a certificate

To import a certificate, such as one purchased from a certificate authority or created by another server, do the following:

1. **Locate the files containing the certificate and the matching private key in the Finder and then position the folder's window in a place where you can get to it.**

2. **In the Server app, select your server in the left column, select the Settings tab, and click the Edit button next to SSL Certificate.**

3. **Click the gear icon and choose Manage Certificates.**

   A new dialog slides down (refer to Figure 18-6).

4. **Click the Add (+) button and select Import a Certificate Identity from the Action menu (gear icon).**

5. **Drag the certificate and private-key files from the Finder to the dialog and then click the Import button.**

6. **Choose your imported certificate from the pop-up menu.**

Renewing or replacing an existing certificate

The process for renewing an expired certificate and replacing a self-signed certificate with a signed version is the same. Here's how to do it:

1. **In the Server app, select your server in the left column, select the Settings tab, and click the Edit button next to SSL Certificate.**

2. **Click the Certificates pop-up menu and then select the certificate that you want to replace.**

   If you're using different certificates for individual services, select Manage Certificates from the gear icon menu and then perform Step 2.

3. **Click the gear icon below the list of certificates and choose Replace Certificate with Signed or Renewed Certificate.**

4. **Drag the certificate file you received from the certificate authority and the private-key file to the dialog that slides down.**

5. **Click the Replace Certificate button.**

You must also replace certificates if you change the DNS name of the server or virtual hosts.

Becoming a certificate authority

You may want to act as a certificate authority, with the ability to sign certificates created elsewhere in the organization. You can use the Keychain Access utility to create a certificate authority and to sign certificates.

To create a certificate authority, do the following:

1. **Launch Keychain Access (in `/Applications/Utilities`).**

2. **In the Keychain Access menu, choose Certificate Assistant⇨Create a Certificate Authority.**

   The Certificate Assistant launches.

3. **Choose Self Signed Root CA from the Identity Type pop-up menu.**

4. **In the Email From field, type an e-mail address.**

5. **Click the Create button.**

You can use Keychain Access also to create a signed certificate for someone who's sent you a certificate signing request file. Here's how:

1. **Launch Keychain Access.**

2. **In the Keychain Access menu, choose Certificate Assistant⇨Create a Certificate for Someone Else as a Certificate Authority.**

   The Certificate Assistant launches.

3. **When asked, drag the CSR file you received from the Finder to Certificate Assistant.**

4. **Click through the screens, following the directions.**

At the end of the process, the Mail application launches and creates a new e-mail message with the new signed certificate file attached.

Using Virtual Private Networks

A *virtual private network (VPN)* is a secure encrypted connection to a local network from outside it, typically made over the Internet. Remote users connected through a VPN see the local network, including servers and printers, as though they're connected directly to it. You can also connect two remote local networks through a virtual private network.

If you set up Mountain Lion Server as a private server (with a .private domain name), not serving to the Internet, users outside the building can privately connect to your hosted websites, wikis, and other services through a VPN.

In Mountain Lion Server, you create virtual private network connections with the Server app's VPN pane, as shown in Figure 18-8.

Setting up VPN service is simple:

1. **In the Server app, click the VPN icon.**

2. **If necessary, edit the settings in the VPN pane, as described in the following sections.**

3. **Click the big switch to the On position.**

4. **Click the Save Configuration Profile button.**

   The vpn.mobileconfig file is created. You can use this file to configure Mac and iOS clients. The information in the file is automatically added to Profile Manager (see Chapter 16), if it is running before you save the configuration profile.

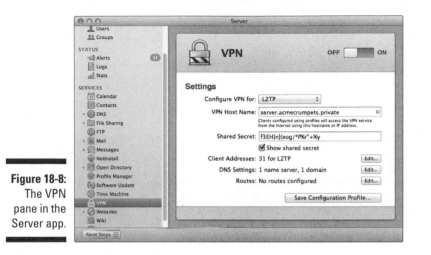

Figure 18-8:
The VPN
pane in the
Server app.

The next few sections describe the VPN settings options.

VPN protocols: L2TP/IPSec and PPTP

The VPN pane's Configure VPN For menu gives you two choices for protocols for transporting encrypted data: L2TP (*Layer Two Tunneling Protocol*) and PPTP (*Point-to-Point Tunneling Protocol*).

L2TP is the preferred VPN protocol in Mountain Lion Server for various reasons, including the fact that it supports Kerberos authentication. PPTP is a Microsoft technology that's long been used in Windows networks. If you have older clients, before Windows XP and before Mac OS X 10.3, use the L2TP and PPTP settings. L2TP/IPSec is a variation newer than L2TP, with bits coming from Cisco and Microsoft.

The shared secret

Virtual private networks use a *shared secret,* a password stored on the server and clients. The shared secret is *not* used for authentication or login, and it doesn't play a role in encryption. The shared secret is a token that's exchanged between computers to establish trust. If a client doesn't have the shared secret, it can't connect. Users don't type a shared secret; it's stored on the computers.

The shared secret must be at least 8 characters, but 12 or more is better, and it can include letters, numbers, and punctuation but no spaces. The shared secret shouldn't be easy to remember; it should be a random string of characters.

The Server app's VPN pane generates a shared secret for you. If you want to use your own, select the Show Shared Secret check box and type a new shared secret (refer to Figure 18-8).

Client addresses: IP address range

When you configure VPN service, you set a range of IP addresses that are assigned to the remote VPN users. These addresses are on the server's network. This range must not contain static IP addresses used on the network and must not overlap ranges provided by a DHCP server, an Internet router, or an AirPort Base Station. Make sure that these devices aren't assigning IP addresses from ranges that overlap with those that the VPN service is providing to remote users.

To edit the default range, click the Edit button next to Client Addresses (refer to Figure 18-14). The dialog that appears describes the first IP addresses used for VPN and the number of addresses that will follow it. So, if the Starting At address is 192.168.206.224, and the Address for VPN is set at 31, the range will be 192.168.206.224 to 192.168.206.255.

The IP address that the VPN service assigns to a remote computer for its VPN connection is in addition to the IP address that the remote computer is already using to connect to the Internet. The VPN IP address is released back to the server when the VPN session concludes.

Network considerations for VPN

Your network may require the following for VPN service:

- **Port forwarding:** If you have an Internet router, including a DSL or cable router, you need to set it up to use port forwarding (also known as port mapping) to forward traffic to your server's IP address.

- **Firewall VPN ports:** If you have a firewall running on the server or on a separate device, the administrator needs to open ports on the firewall to allow VPN traffic. These ports are TCP port 1723; UDP ports 500, 1701, and 4500; and IP protocol 50. (For PPTP, use TCP port 1723.)

- **Firewall ports for services:** If the only way you're allowing access from remote users is through an encrypted VPN connection, you don't have a reason to open the firewall ports for specific services; all the traffic goes through the VPN rather than the firewall. This means that you could set the firewall to block those ports for increased security.

You could also have a mixture: Keep open web and e-mail ports on the firewall, but close file sharing and calendar service to restrict those types of access to a VPN connection. If you have a firewall between your workgroup and the rest of your organization, you may also want to keep ports open for people in your organization who are outside the workgroup. You can do this easily by using a third-party front such as Ice Floor (described earlier in the chapter) if your firewall is on Mountain Lion Server.

Configuring VPN clients

Mac, Windows, Linux, and iOS devices can all remotely connect to your network through Mountain Lion Server's VPN. This section describes how to set them up.

Newer Mac clients and iOS devices

OS X clients and iOS devices can take advantage of Profile Manager for getting VPN configuration information; the Server app automatically includes the VPN setup file in Profile Manager (described in Chapter 16).

If you're not running Profile Manager, you can use the VPN setup file to configure Lion and Mountain Lion clients, as well as iOS devices. For Lion and Mountain Lion, copy the file to the desktop and double-click to install the settings. For an iOS device, e-mail the VPN.mobilconfig file to the device and then tap the file to run the installation process.

Older Macs running Snow Leopard or earlier

For Macs running Mac OS 10.6 and earlier, which aren't supported by Profile Manager, the Server app creates a VPN configuration file that you can use to make client configuration easier.

In the Server app's VPN pane, click the Save Configuration Profile button to create and save a file that you can distribute to Macs. The default name of this file is VPN.mobileconfig. On the OS X client, open System Preferences and click the Network icon. Now add a VPN interface by clicking the Add (+) button and selecting VPN.

With the VPN interface selected, choose Import Configurations from the gear icon's pop-up menu and then select the VPN configuration file you created.

Windows and Linux

For Windows and Linux clients, you need to manually configure VPN configuration the old-fashioned way, by typing information. You need the following information:

- **Account name:** The user account's short name on the Mac server.

- **User password:** The user's account password on the Mac server.

- **VPN server or host:** Your server's DNS name or IP address.

- **VPN type:** L2TP over IPSec or PPTP.

- **Shared secret:** Visible in the VPN pane of the Server app (click the Edit button and select the Show Shared Secret check box).

- **Firewall ports:** If users are running firewalls on their computers or on a remote network, that firewall must be configured to allow VPN traffic on TCP port 1723; UDP ports 500, 1701, and 4500; and on IP protocol 50. For PPTP, use TCP port 1723. These firewall-port settings apply also to Mac clients running their own firewalls.

Attention: The Alerts Pane

Mountain Lion Server monitors several dozen items and can send you an alert for certain events, such as software update, SSL certificates that are about to expire, low disk space, the presence of an e-mail virus, and changes to the server network settings. Each alert will tell you when the event occurred and give you options on how to react. You can view the alerts by clicking Alerts under the Status section in the Server app's sidebar. The default view is the Alerts pane, which is shown in Figure 18-9.

If you double-click an alert, the Server app displays information about the alert and Server's recommendations in an Actions section, as shown in Figure 18-10. In the case of a software update, the Actions section will include a button to install the update.

Responding to alerts

This section describes what some of the more common alert messages mean and how you might respond to them:

- **Your host name or IP address has changed.** This alert probably means that you don't have your server Mac configured with a static IP address, and that it is getting its IP address from a DHCP server, such as a wireless router (for example, an Apple AirPort device). This condition will cause problems with DNS service. Ignore this alert only if you're not running DNS service or not using a service that requires DNS.

✓ **A certificate is about to expire.** This alert tells you when an SSL certificate is about to expire. If the certificate is an Apple push notification certificate, not renewing it can interrupt push notification service, which is required for Profile Manager and is used by Calendar, Messages, and Mail Servers to push data to iOS devices. The alert will provide a button you can click to renew an Apple push notification certificate.

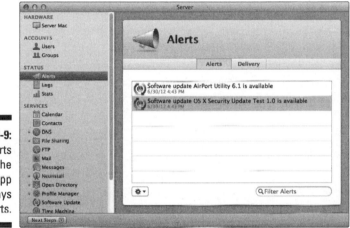

Figure 18-9:
The Alerts pane of the Server app displays alerts.

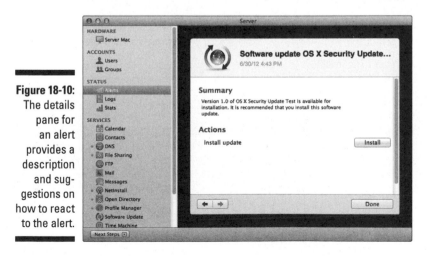

Figure 18-10:
The details pane for an alert provides a description and suggestions on how to react to the alert.

✔ **You are running low on disk space.** If you get this message, you may still be storing your user data on your startup disk. If this is the case, you may be slowing down your entire server. Disk drives with 20 percent or less free disk space slow down.

Fortunately, Mountain Lion Server provides an easy way to move user data to another location. In the Server app, select your server in the sidebar and click the Settings tab. Click the Edit button next to Services Data. Select a partition or drive in the dialog that appears and then click Choose. The server will shut off all running services and copy the user data to the new drive or partition, leaving the old data intact. You can delete it by going to the folder /Library/Server, which you can access from the Finder's Go menu.)

✔ **You have a software update.** This message refers to updates for the server Mac, not the clients. When you go to a details page for a software update alert (refer Figure 18-2), a click of a button will install the update.

✔ **There's been a change to the SMART status.** This alert message means trouble: Your hard drive may be about to fail. Run, don't walk, to your nearest hard drive vendor, do a backup of the server, and replace the hard drive.

Mountain Lion Server enables you to specify which alerts you want to be notified about. This process is described next.

Getting alerts delivered to you

Mountain Lion Server can get alerts to you in the following three ways:

✔ **Alerts are listed in the alerts pages in the Server app.** In the sidebar, a number next to the word *Alerts* tells you how many new alerts you have.

✔ **Alerts can be e-mailed to you or your team.** You can specify one or more e-mail addresses for receiving alerts.

✔ **Notifications can be sent via push notifications.** These pushed notifications appear in Mountain Lion's Notifications Center, on the right side of the screen. Push notification service must be turned on. To check the status of push notification service, go to the Delivery tab of the Alerts pane (shown in Figure 18-11). The check boxes in the Push column appear dimmed if push notification is disabled.

To turn on push notification service, select your server under Hardware in the sidebar of the Server App. Then click the Settings tab, and select the Enable Push Notifications check box.

Figure 18-11:
The Delivery tab of the Alerts pane lets you specify who gets which alerts.

With e-mail and notifications of alerts, you have complete control over which types of alerts get to you and who gets them. You can decide not to get them delivered at all. To change the settings, click the Delivery tab of the Alerts pane in the Server app.

At the top under Recipients, you (the administrator) are the default person to receive alerts by e-mail and push notification. For alerts sent by e-mail, you can delete yourself or add others by clicking the Edit button next to Email Addresses. In the dialog that appears, click the Add (+) button to add additional e-mail addresses, and click the Delete (-) button to remove addresses.

The Edit button next to Push Notifications is a little different. You can only select or deselect administrators for the server.

In the Settings box, you can enable or disable which types of alerts you want to receive. To do so, simply select or deselect the check box in the Email or Push columns next to each alert.

Seeing the Long View with the Stats Pane

The Stats pane of the Server app displays information useful when considering long-term trends. As Figure 18-12 shows, the Stats pane displays one of three graphs: processor usage, memory usage, and incoming and outgoing network traffic. You change which one to view with the pop-up menu at the lower left of the pane. The pop-up menu at the lower right lets you change the time period displayed, with choices ranging from the past hour to the past 7 days.

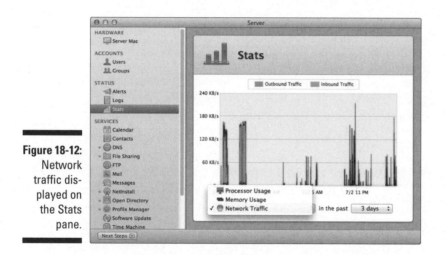

Figure 18-12: Network traffic displayed on the Stats pane.

All three graphs measure things that can affect server performance, which can slow if the processor, memory, or network usage get too high. Viewing these indicators over different time periods lets you see if the heavy usage is an anomaly, periodic, or constant. Heavy usage might be an indicator that your server is doing more than it can handle and that you might need to offload some its tasks to another server.

Even if the usage levels are not at a critical point, the graphs are useful. You can find the times of least usage to determine when to do maintenance, for instance.

Troubleshooting by Using the Logs Pane

The Logs pane of the Server app gives you access to several dozen log files kept by the services in OS X Server. Log files act like a black box, recording what is going on all the time. Log files list software events and the time and date they occurred. Log files can catalog events, or list requests. Some log files list only errors, while others record all events.

Figure 18-13 shows the Logs pane of the Server app displaying a DNS service log. You choose which log to view in the pop-up menu in the lower left, which displays almost three dozen log files, arranged by service (such as calendar, contacts, and DNS). Some services have several log files. For example, Mail Server has seven logs for the various protocols it uses and security monitoring it performs. The system also has its own log.

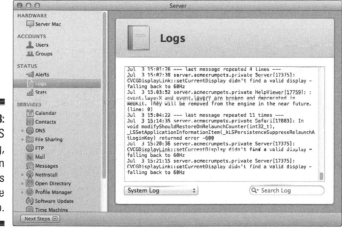

Figure 18-13:
The DNS service log, viewed in the Logs pane of the Server app.

If you're looking for something in a log file, the search field in the lower right actually has two functions. Click the small triangle on the left side inside the field, and a pop-up menu gives you a choice between Search Log and Filter Log. If you choose Search Log, the Server app will highlight in yellow text strings that match your search. Choose Filter Log, and the Server app displays only the log entries (lines) that contain your text string.

Server logs can be useful in troubleshooting problems such as mysterious slowdowns in server performance or services that aren't functioning correctly. Server logs are not user friendly: You need to know what you're looking for, and what you're looking at. Often when you have someone troubleshoot your system, they will ask you for the log files. Some may have computer programs that perform log file analysis to spot the cause behind a symptom.

If you need to send someone the entire file, click inside the log display and press the ⌘+A to select all the text. Then copy it and paste it into a word processing or text program.

Another place to view logs is the Console application in the /Applications/Utilities folder. In addition to server logs, Console shows logs that have to do with Mac processes and applications.

Monitoring Activity

Whenever my Mac or server starts to slow down or act in an odd way, I reach for Activity Monitor in the /Applications/Utilities folder to see what's going on. Every Mac comes with Activity Monitory.

As Figure 18-14 shows, the bottom part of the Activity Monitor screen lets you view memory, CPU, and disk usage, as well as how much network traffic is going into and out of the server. Although the Server app is good for identifying trends, Activity Monitor is good for telling you what's going on right now.

Figure 18-14:
Activity
Monitor.

Activity Monitor window showing a list of processes with columns PID, Process Name, User, % CPU, Threads, Real Mem, Kind:

PID	Process Name	User	% CPU	Threads	Real Mem	Kind
434	mdworker	johnrizzo	59.0	3	24.6 MB	Intel (64 bit)
51	mds	root	35.9	8	113.2 MB	Intel (64 bit)
411	vmware-vmx	root	26.5	29	2.13 GB	Intel (64 bit)
200	WindowServer	_windowsen	4.3	5	93.8 MB	Intel (64 bit)
0	kernel_task	root	2.2	71	546.3 MB	Intel
2297	iTunes	johnrizzo	2.0	13	48.6 MB	Intel
8314	Grab	johnrizzo	1.4	4	53.2 MB	Intel (64 bit)
13782	Camino	johnrizzo	0.8	12	79.4 MB	Intel
693	Kindle	johnrizzo	0.7	11	100.0 MB	Intel
57	fseventsd	root	0.7	16	2.4 MB	Intel (64 bit)
14779	activitymonitord	root	0.7	1	1.4 MB	Intel (64 bit)

CPU | System Memory | Disk Activity | Disk Usage | Network

% User: 38.60
% System: 29.57
% Idle: 31.83

Threads: 373
Processes: 75

CPU Usage

Most of the Activity Monitor window is taken up by a list of currently running software processes. You can list these processes in order of the amount of processor or memory they're using by clicking the corresponding column head. Activity Monitor can help you find processes that you didn't know were running and might not need.

You will see processes with unfamiliar names, such as mdworker or kernel_ task, using significant amounts of system resources for short periods of time. This is normal.

One handy feature of Activity Monitor is that you can turn its Dock icon into a live status icon. The icon can turn into a pie chart of memory usage, a CPU usage monitor, or a moving graph of network usage or disk drive activity. To turn this feature on, choose View➪Dock Icon, and select one of the choices from the submenu.

Part VI
The Part of Tens

In this part . . .

Steve Jobs's keynote addresses at Macworld Expo and Apple's developers' conferences often ended with a simple statement: "There's just one more thing."

He'd then go on to make another product announcement, often something big. Things like the MacBook Pro, the iPod touch, and the AirPort Base Station.

Well, here I am at the end of this book, and I have more to tell you. Nothing as big as the MacBook Pro, but I make up for it in quantity.

I have just 20 more things.

In Chapter 19, I present ten things you can add to Mountain Lion Server. These are mostly products from developers other than Apple, from free widgets to enterprise-level servers that add new capabilities.

Chapter 20 is my desperate attempt to get more information into this book — ten more, to be exact. Here you find condensed sections describing additional cool things to do with Mountain Lion Server, as well as some handy tips and some references to other information.

Chapter 19

Ten Things You Can Add to Mountain Lion Server

In This Chapter

▶ Protecting your Mac server

▶ Adding more enterprise services to Mountain Lion Server

▶ Monitoring and managing your entire network

▶ Using iPads and iPhones to help with your server

Mountain Lion Server comes with so many different services and features for your users and your administrators that it's hard to imagine that you need to add anything extra. Although you may not *need* to run additional server software, you can enhance Mountain Lion Server with new functionality. And if you want to manage your server from your iPad, iPhone, or iPod touch, you can find an app for that.

This chapter describes some of the things you can add to OS X Server for home, small, and mid-size networks, as well as enterprise environments.

Antivirus for Your Server

Mac viruses and malware are fairly uncommon. Virus programmers tend to focus mostly on the several hundred million Windows PCs in the world. This situation, however, doesn't let OS X off the hook.

In the previous edition of this book, *Lion Server For Dummies* (Wiley), I warned, "Mac malware has been appearing during the past few years, and one of these days, a big Mac-focused virus wave may hit." In April of 2012, it did indeed hit. Newspaper and tech trade headlines screamed, "Over 600,000 Macs infected with malware." The age of innocence was over.

Servers in particular are important computers to protect because an infected server can infect the other computers through your network. You can always load a generic Mac virus protection package on your Mac, but a malware product designed for Mountain Lion Server offers additional benefits.

Intego's VirusBarrier Server (www.intego.com) automatically checks files located on and launched from a Mac server. VirusBarrier Server quarantines infected files it finds and sends an e-mail message to an administrator. It can also repair files that have been quarantined. Like all good virus packages, VirusBarrier Server automatically checks for and downloads updates of the latest virus definitions.

Mountain Lion Server's e-mail server already comes with well-respected open source antivirus software, ClamAV. But if you want another layer of protection, use VirusBarrier Mail Gateway (included with VirusBarrier Server), which automatically checks all incoming and outgoing e-mail messages when running Mountain Lion Server's built-in mail server.

VirusBarrier Server can detect a variety of malware, including *scareware,* which is software that tells users that their Mac is infected, often to trick them into downloading more malware or buying something. VirusBarrier Server also detects spyware that monitors keystrokes, dialer viruses that dial your modem access number, and other sneaky invaders.

Kerio Connect

If you want a cross-platform groupware server with even more features, you can add Kerio Connect to Mountain Lion Server. Kerio Connect (www.kerio.com) is considered by some to be an alternative to Microsoft Exchange for small to mid-size businesses, and it syncs with Active Directory and Open Directory. The big advantage over the built-in groupware of Mountain Lion Server is that Kerio Connect supplies e-mail, calendar, contacts, notes, and tasks to just about any client: Outlook for Windows and Mac, Entourage, Apple Mail, Calendar and iCal, and Contacts and Address Book.

Like Mountain Lion Server, Kerio supports iPhone, but it also supports BlackBerry, Android, Windows Mobile, Symbian, and Palm Treo. The remote console is cross-platform, too: You can manage Kerio Connect from Windows, Linux, and Mac OS X. The server is also available for Windows and Linux.

Kerio MailServer has some expanded features, too. Although Mountain Lion Server lets users delegate calendars to other Calendar and iCal users, Kerio Connect lets users delegate calendars to Outlook and Entourage, as well as to Calendar and iCal users. Another thing that Kerio has that OS X Server doesn't is integrated, automatic server backup.

Network Backup of Clients

With Time Machine, Mountain Lion Server does some great backup for all your clients at home — as long as they're running Mac OS X 10.5 or later.

For backing up Windows or Linux clients and servers, or for larger networks, you can add third-party software to Mountain Lion Server. Time Machine can't back up to tape, which is used in some enterprise environments. The following three backup servers run on Mountain Lion Server, can back up Windows as well as Mac clients, and can back up to tape libraries:

- **Retrospect, Inc, Retrospect Single-Server or Multi-Server** (www.retrospect.com) is for small to medium-sized shops. Retrospect Server comes in several configurations, from a single server to multiple servers. Modules are used for your Mac, Windows, and Linux clients.

- **Tolis Group's BRU Server for Mac OS X** (www.tolisgroup.com) comes in packages from workgroup to enterprise levels. BRU Server can run concurrently with other services and includes error recovery for restoring from damaged media.

- **Quest NetVault: Backup for Mac** (www.quest.com/netvault-backup) is a full-blown enterprise-level backup system for big, complex networks. Quest NetVault: Backup for Mac supports Apple's Xsan, features modular scalability, and is optimized for virtual machine backup. You can apply policy management tools to individuals and groups.

Media Asset Management and Workflow

Asset managers organize the thousands of photo, image, video, and audio files sitting in a pile on your server. They keep track of the assets that are part of a workflow and what final projects they're used in. Asset managers tell you which version of a project is the current version, and they let you return to older versions. They also automate workflow, performing routine tasks such as assembling pieces into a whole and converting files to different file formats. Lots of server-based asset manager products are available. The following list provides just a sampling of different types:

- **Adobe InDesign Server** (www.adobe.com/products/indesignserver) is aimed at automating InDesign-based print publishing, design, typography, and page layout. Because InDesign Server is highly customizable with an InDesign markup language, third parties sell premade workflow systems based on your type of publishing.

✔ **Canto Cumulus** (www.canto.com) is a data asset manager designed for photo, graphic, audio, video, layout files, and any other type of file. Because Cumulus is a sophisticated workflow product, you can send the Cumulus server an e-mail to have it place an attached file in a catalog. Cumulus tracks users' actions and lets you see what's being used. It also has a built-in photo editor. Users can be your workers or outside people such as clients. Users automatically receive the latest version of a file when they search.

Database Servers for Home or Office

For home or office, multiuser databases can give users access to shared data from their Macs, Windows PCs, and even iOS devices. Although Mountain Lion Server has the built-in PostgreSQL database software, you have to be a database programmer to use it. If you want to create or install a multiuser database with a graphics user interface, you have several choices. Here are two:

✔ **FileMaker Server** (www.filemaker.com) can invoice, label, track inventory, and manage contacts with maps and video. Users of Mac, Windows, and iPads can access the database server with some nice-looking interfaces. For the user, you can create simple data entry forms or use sophisticated graphical interfaces. FileMaker is also a software development platform, so lots of prebuilt FileMaker-based applications are available. FileMaker also comes with several prebuilt databases that might meet your needs out of the box. For iPads and iPhone clients, just download the free FileMaker Go app from the Apple App Store.

✔ **Panorama Enterprise Server** (www.provue.com) is a RAM-based database that focuses on speed. Data fetchers are thousands of times faster than disk-based data retrieval. This server can also distribute the database to clients, automatically syncing changes with all users, which reduces the server load. And the software comes with powerful data analysis tools, as well as tools for building HTML and CSS forms for websites. As the name suggests, Panorama Enterprise Server is appropriate for mid-to-large networks.

Apple Remote Desktop to Manage Macs

Apple Remote Desktop (www.apple.com/remotedesktop) is a remote administration tool for Mac clients and servers. You can use this tool to manage any Mac running Mac OS X 10.4.11 or Mac OS X 10.5.7 and later, including Mountain Lion Server.

Apple Remote Desktop is, at heart, a remote control program — it lets you operate and control a Mac from another Mac on the network. Because you can see the desktop of the remote Mac, you can use the remote control feature to give tech support to a user or fix a problem remotely.

But Apple Remote Desktop can do much more than that. For one, you can use this tool to distribute, install, and upgrade software on hundreds of Macs at the same time.

You can also use Apple Remote Desktop for asset management. It can read what's installed on users' Macs and generate reports about what applications are being used, what versions of OS X are installed, and who is logging into the computers.

Apple Remote Desktop can also perform remote Spotlight searches on the Mac clients. You can even copy any files you find to your Mac or delete them.

You have to set up each Mac that you're going to administer with Apple Remote Desktop, but you can partly automate that procedure with Apple Remote Desktop itself.

InterMapper, a Network Monitor

Dartware's InterMapper (www.intermapper.com) is a tool for your entire network; at its base, it provides maps of your network. You can create a map to show the location of servers, clients, switches, and routers, as well as notebook computers. You can create schematic maps and maps superimposed on a building floor plan or on city or school district maps. InterMapper even interacts with Google Earth for long-distance mapping. Other maps get you back into a building.

InterMapper is also a problem-solving tool: It can point out problems before they manifest themselves in downtime or slowdowns. You can check router utilization and traffic at various points on the network. InterMapper can perform tests that target an area or a device. A traffic analyzer can show you exactly who (or what) is generating a large amount of network traffic. InterMapper stores its data in an SQL database, which lets you generate various types of reports.

You can receive alerts by e-mail and other methods. You can use InterMapper from a web browser or from an iPhone. InterMapper runs on OS X, Windows, and several flavors of Linux and Unix.

TechTool Pro

If something goes wrong with your server hardware, MicroMat's TechTool Pro (www.micromat.com) is good to have on hand for its hardware checking, troubleshooting, and repair and data recovery functions. TechTool Pro can check your Mac's system memory, which can cause all sorts of mysterious problems if it goes bad; it also checks the memory on your graphics card. TechTool Pro scans disks for bad blocks and directory corruption, scans files for problems, and performs a number of other tests.

The tests are also useful to run before you have problems. You can run individual tests or the entire suite. TechTool Pro can detect a potential problem with a piece of hardware and recommend a way to proceed. You can run tests while your server does its thing because the software doesn't require a lot of resources.

The eDrive feature creates a bootable drive partition with every TechTool Pro tool installed. You don't have to erase the drive to create this partition, which you can use when your Mac refuses to boot.

TechTool Pro can also fix drive problems. The Volume Rebuild feature re-creates disk directories, even on damaged drives, to bring a drive back to life or to improve performance with optimization. TechTool Pro includes several types of data recovery to pull important files off damaged drives; it can even recover deleted files.

iOS Apps to Manage Servers

Who needs a notebook when you have an iPad, iPhone or iPod touch? Well, I do, but a growing number of apps let you manage and monitor Mountain Lion Server from an iPad or iPhone. Here's just a sampling, which you can buy at the App Store in iTunes and from your iOS device:

- **Server Admin Remote** (www.harlekins.org) is not from Apple, but it can be more convenient to use than the Server app on a Mac for certain tasks. You can start and stop services, monitor the running status of services, and view server logs. You can also check on server CPU usage and network traffic. It works over EDGE, Wi-Fi, and 3G/4G connections.

- **Workgroup Manager Remote**, also from Harlekins, lets you view and edit OS X Server Open Directory accounts.

- ✔ **iTeleport** (`www.iteleportmobile.com`), from the company of the same name, lets you remotely view and control Mac, Windows, and Linux PCs, including Mountain Lion Server; just enable sharing on the computer. iTeleport lets you use Apple's server tools running on a Mac. iTeleport has great use of iOS gestures and a smooth typing implementation. The zoom also works well.

- ✔ **iNag Nagios Viewer** (`http://idevelop.fullnet.com/iapps`) is an iOS interface to the open source Nagios network monitoring system, described in the next section. iNag lets you monitor multiple servers through Nagious and issue commands to Nagios. You can't do everything that you can from a computer, but some prefer iNag to Nagio's native web interface. If you're using Nagios, John Fullington's iNag is a must.

Nagios for Network Monitoring

Keeping tabs of multiple servers and services on a larger network can be a challenge, especially with mixed operating systems. Nagios (`www.nagios.org`), from Nagios Enterprises, is a set of open source network monitoring software that runs on OS X Server as well as Windows and Linux servers. Via e-mail or SMS, Nagios can tell you about software problems with services and hardware, enabling you to attend to issues before they become major mishaps. Nagios can also automatically fix certain software problems, such as restarting services or applications that have crashed.

Nagios uses a plug-in architecture that lets you add features from the Nagios project or from third parties. Your IT group can write its own plug-ins and scripts. Nagios is serious enterprise software and requires technical expertise, but help is available through conferences and a large online library that includes videos and tutorials.

Chapter 20

Ten Cool Things That Didn't Make It into the Rest of the Book

*O*ne of the difficult things about writing this book was deciding which of Mountain Lion Server's many aspects didn't fit in the 400-plus pages. Some features are cool but obscure; others just don't fit in with the other topics. So in this chapter, I want to squeeze in a few more useful bits, in no particular order. Some are simple things that anyone can use, and others are technical, but they're all pretty cool.

Big, Fast External Storage

A server can never have too much storage, and speed doesn't hurt either. So how about 6 terabytes (TB) connected to your Mac with a Thunderbolt cable?

Yes, I did talk about the need for storage in Chapter 2. But I didn't give specifics. Here are two storage devices that will make your mouth water:

✔ The LaCie 2big Thunderbolt Series from LaCie (www.lacie.com) is a case that holds two hot-swappable drives. If one fails, pull it out without shutting off the unit. Drives get bigger every year, but as of this writing the 2big comes in 4TB and 6TB sizes. You can use the two drives separately as drives or together as a RAID for redundancy. These are 7200 rpm drives with promised transfer rates up to 327MB/s, according to LaCie. Storage costs are also changing all the time, but at publishing time, the big 2big cost less than a Mac mini server.

✔ If you want to spend as much as a Mac Pro, there's the 12TB, 6-disk Pegasus R6 RAID System, also with the Thunderbolt interface, from Promise (www.promise.com). The promise of Promise is that the enclosure will deliver 800MB/s of speed. By the way, 12TB would hold 1300 full length movies, 3 million songs, or 2.6 trillion pages of text.

Xsan

Speaking of big, fast storage, you may have noticed an item called Xsan, all the way at the bottom of the Server app's sidebar. Xsan is Apple's storage area network (SAN) file system that provides massive amounts of data over high-speed Fibre Channel. Xsan supports up to 2 petabytes of data. Promise, whose desktop storage I mention in the preceding section, has rack-mounted, Fibre Channel RAID systems that work with Xsan.

Xsan has features such as quick Spotlight searches through these petabytes of data. Apple says it's great for film and video editing with Final Cut Pro.

But back to the Server app. The Xsan pane is where you turn on access to Xsan if the Mac must be connected to a Fibre Channel SAN. In addition, the Xsan Admin item in the Server app's Tools menu is an assistant that helps you set up a new SAN system or connect to an existing one.

Running Mountain Lion from the Command Line

One of the things that I try to do in this book is spare you from typing commands. But the fact remains that you can do just about everything in this book — and much more — with commands in a Unix shell, Terminal, which you can find in /Applications/Utilities.

Apple offers a 300-page *Command-Line Administration* PDF reference at www.apple.com/server/macosx/resources/documentation.html. If you know your way around a Unix shell, you'll find it all in Apple's PDF.

Speeding Up Networks with VLANS

A virtual local area network (VLAN) is a way to get computers on different network segments to communicate as if they were on the same local area network. This can be useful on networks with high network traffic. VLANs can reduce use of network bandwidth and increases security.

OS X Mountain Lion provides supports VLANs on Mac Pro machines, specifically supporting built-in Ethernet ports and secondary PCI gigabit Ethernet cards.

You set up and manage VLANs in the VLAN area of the Network pane of System Preferences. You must be logged in to the Mac as an administrator:

1. **Open the Network pane of System Preferences.**

2. **From the Action menu (gear icon), choose Manage Virtual Interfaces.**

   This choice appears only if you have a Mac that supports VLANs, mainly a Mac Pro.

3. **Click the Add (+) button and then select New VLAN.**

4. **In the VLAN Name field, enter a name for the new VLAN.**

5. **In the Tag field, enter a tag (a number between 1 and 4094).**

   This VLAN tag designates the VLAN ID (VID). Each logical network has a unique VID. Interfaces configured with the same VID are on the same virtual network.

6. **Select the interface.**

7. **Click Create.**

8. **Click Done.**

Researching Ruby on Rails

If mail clusters aren't geeky enough for you (see the preceding section), try this tip: Mountain Lion Server comes with built-in support for Ruby on Rails (www.rubyonrails.org), an open source language and framework for creating web-based applications. OS X Server comes with several Ruby on Rails component packages (called *gems* in Ruby-speak), one of which is the Mongrel web server.

Apple has information about developing Ruby on Rails applications here:

```
http://developer.apple.com/tools/developonrailsleopard.
        html
```

Apple also has some information about deploying Ruby on Rails and the Mongrel web server in the *Web Technologies Administration* PDF document, available here:

```
www.apple.com/server/macosx/resources/documentation.html
```

Setting the Server to Autorestart

If you want your server to get back up and running after a power failure or a system freeze, you can tell Mac OS X Server to start up automatically:

1. **While logged in to the server Mac as an administrator, open System Preferences.**

2. **Click the Energy Saver icon.**

3. **Select the Restart Automatically After a Power Failure check box, or the Restart Automatically If the Computer Freezes check box, or both.**

   For the second setting, the power management hardware restarts five minutes after a kernel panic or a freeze.

Finding Help at Apple.com

Apple has quite a bit of information about OS X Server on its website. Unfortunately, finding what you want can take some time. Here's a list of several ways you can enter Apple.com that might provide a quicker route to what you need regarding Mac OS X Server:

- **Recently updated tech-support articles:** This page lists the newest and most recently modified troubleshooting and how-to articles. This page is a good one to check a few days after Apple releases a software update.

  ```
  http://support.apple.com/kb/index?page=articles
  ```

- **OS X Server support:** Here, you can find links to support pages for individual OS X Server services, such as file sharing, Calendar Server, and the rest. It also has links to popular how-to and troubleshooting articles and to recent software updates related to OS X Server.

  ```
  www.apple.com/support/mac
  ```

- **Apple Discussions pages:** Here, you can post a question or search the forum for an answer to a question that someone else may have asked. This first page lists forums for everything Apple, but the Server Product category has areas for OS X Server, Xserve, and other IT topics. To post a question, log in with an Apple ID, such as your iTunes account.

  ```
  http://discussions.apple.com
  ```

Server in a Virtual Machine

Running Mountain Lion Server on a Mac is a powerful addition to a network. Running two Servers can be even more powerful. You can run multiple operating systems on one Mac by using virtual machine software.

When running in a virtual machine, each operating system thinks and acts like it's running in a real machine. It can network, communicate with other computers, and use peripherals, all of which makes virtual machines a great way to test server configurations. Instead of having them running on drive partitions, virtual machines exist as sets of files. To uninstall the OS, just throw away the file. And with one or more copies of Mountain Lion Server running in virtual machines, you can keep them separate from your user files and applications.

Two worthy virtualization products for the Mac are Parallels Desktop (www.parallels.com) and VMware Fusion (www.vmware.com). Both products are less than $100 and can import virtual machines from each other, so if you decide to switch, you can move over your virtual machines.

For running OS X Server in a virtual machine, I think VMware Fusion has the edge. The installation is easy: Just drag the OS X Installer file into a new virtual machine window, and the installation process begins by itself. Parallels Desktop, however, runs Windows a bit faster.

Macs are the only computers that allow you to run OS X along with Windows at the same time. Apple doesn't allow running copies of OS X in virtual machines on non-Apple hardware.

PostgreSQL Database

PostgreSQL is the back-end database for Wiki Server, Contacts and Calendar Servers, and Profile Manager. This open source software is powerful in the hands of database programmers.

PostgreSQL is sometimes called the "open source Oracle," in that it is compatible with SQL, can be easily upgraded to Oracle, and is reliable for enterprise uses.

Although many people feel that real database programmers use the command line, don't discount the graphical front ends that are available for the Mac. One is RazorSQL (www.razorsql.com) from Richardson Software. You can use it to browse and administrate the database, do SQL queries, and edit code.

Ethernet Link Aggregation

For a heavily used Mac Pro server, network bandwidth can be a bottleneck. Fortunately, the operating system gives you an inexpensive way to more than double your Ethernet bandwidth.

Link aggregation combines two or more Ethernet ports to enable them to work as one port. The bandwidth of the aggregated port is the sum of all the ports, so aggregating two 1-gigabit Ethernet ports gives you a 2-gigabit port. Before you aggregate the Mac ports, you need to set up link aggregation on your Ethernet switch. How you do this depends on the switch you are using.

But on the Mac, OS X lets you aggregate ports in the Network pane of System Preferences. Click the Action (gear) icon at the bottom of the pane and then select Manage Virtual Interfaces to display a screen of the same name. Click the Add (+) button and then select New Link Aggregate. In the dialog that appears, enter a name for the aggregated link and select the check boxes for the Ethernet ports that you want to include in the aggregate. Finally, click the Create button. Your new aggregate appears in the dialog.

Index

Notes

Notes

Notes

Notes

Math & Science

Algebra I For Dummies,
2nd Edition
978-0-470-55964-2

Biology For Dummies,
2nd Edition
978-0-470-59875-7

Chemistry For Dummies,
2nd Edition
978-1-1180-0730-3

Geometry For Dummies,
2nd Edition
978-0-470-08946-0

Pre-Algebra Essentials
For Dummies
978-0-470-61838-7

Microsoft Office

Excel 2010 For Dummies
978-0-470-48953-6

Office 2010 All-in-One
For Dummies
978-0-470-49748-7

Office 2011 for Mac
For Dummies
978-0-470-87869-9

Word 2010
For Dummies
978-0-470-48772-3

Music

Guitar For Dummies,
2nd Edition
978-0-7645-9904-0

Clarinet For Dummies
978-0-470-58477-4

iPod & iTunes
For Dummies,
9th Edition
978-1-118-13060-5

Pets

Cats For Dummies,
2nd Edition
978-0-7645-5275-5

Dogs All-in One
For Dummies
978-0470-52978-2

Saltwater Aquariums
For Dummies
978-0-470-06805-2

Religion & Inspiration

The Bible For Dummies
978-0-7645-5296-0

Catholicism For Dummies,
2nd Edition
978-1-118-07778-8

Spirituality For Dummies,
2nd Edition
978-0-470-19142-2

Self-Help & Relationships

Happiness For Dummies
978-0-470-28171-0

Overcoming Anxiety
For Dummies,
2nd Edition
978-0-470-57441-6

Seniors

Crosswords For Seniors
For Dummies
978-0-470-49157-7

iPad 2 For Seniors
For Dummies, 3rd Edition
978-1-118-17678-8

Laptops & Tablets
For Seniors For Dummies,
2nd Edition
978-1-118-09596-6

Smartphones & Tablets

BlackBerry For Dummies,
5th Edition
978-1-118-10035-6

Droid X2 For Dummies
978-1-118-14864-8

HTC ThunderBolt
For Dummies
978-1-118-07601-9

MOTOROLA XOOM
For Dummies
978-1-118-08835-7

Sports

Basketball For Dummies,
3rd Edition
978-1-118-07374-2

Football For Dummies,
2nd Edition
978-1-118-01261-1

Golf For Dummies,
4th Edition
978-0-470-88279-5

Test Prep

ACT For Dummies,
5th Edition
978-1-118-01259-8

ASVAB For Dummies,
3rd Edition
978-0-470-63760-9

The GRE Test For
Dummies, 7th Edition
978-0-470-00919-2

Police Officer Exam
For Dummies
978-0-470-88724-0

Series 7 Exam
For Dummies
978-0-470-09932-2

Web Development

HTML, CSS, & XHTML
For Dummies, 7th Edition
978-0-470-91659-9

Drupal For Dummies,
2nd Edition
978-1-118-08348-2

Windows 7

Windows 7
For Dummies
978-0-470-49743-2

Windows 7
For Dummies,
Book + DVD Bundle
978-0-470-52398-8

Windows 7 All-in-One
For Dummies
978-0-470-48763-1